Qualitative Marketing Research

Qualitative Marketing Research

David Carson, Audrey Gilmore,
Chad Perry and Kjell Gronhaug

SAGE Publications
London • Thousand Oaks • New Delhi

First published 2001

SAGE Publications Ltd
6 Bonhill Street
London EC2A 4PU

SAGE Publications Inc
2455 Teller Road
Thousand Oaks, California 91320

SAGE Publications India Pvt Ltd
32, M-Block Market
Greater Kailash – I
New Delhi 110 048

British Library Cataloguing in Publication data

A catalogue record for this book is
available from the British Library

ISBN 0 7619 6365 0
ISBN 0 7619 6366 9 (pbk)

Library of Congress catalog card number available

Typeset by Keystroke, Jacaranda Lodge, Wolverhampton
Printed in Great Britain by Biddles Ltd, Guildford, Surrey

Contents

About the Authors

David Carson is Professor of Marketing at the University of Ulster, Northern Ireland, UK. His research interests lie in marketing of small-to-medium sized enterprises (SMEs) and quality of marketing in services industries. He has published widely in both of these areas. He has championed the development of qualitative research methodologies in marketing over many years. He instigated the Academy of Marketing Doctoral Colloquium in 1994.

Dr Audrey Gilmore is a Reader in Marketing at the University of Ulster. She has specialized in qualitative research in marketing services throughout her academic career. Her PhD research used a single case methodology focusing on management issues. She leads a qualitative research group at University of Ulster.

Chad Perry is Professor and Head of Department of Marketing and Management at Southern Cross University, Coolangatta, Australia. He is a specialist researcher in qualitative methodologies and has pioneered innovative research over many years. He has published widely in research methodologies and aspects of strategic management.

Kjell Gronhaug is Professor of Marketing at the Norwegian School of Economics and Business Administration in Bergen. He is one of the most widely published academics in marketing in the world, with a vast range of interests. He is highly respected for his work in research methodologies both in marketing and in the wider management domain.

Preface

There have been many books describing and extolling the virtues of qualitative research methods in social sciences. Indeed, some of the leading texts have been published by Sage, who can be considered as pioneers in disseminating social science research and methodologies, particularly in relation to qualitative research.

This book is one of the latest in this lineage, and it attempts to bring different perspectives to the descriptions of qualitative research methods. Whilst it acknowledges its origins in social science research, it purposefully focuses upon what may be called management studies and most specifically the marketing domain.

Many of the foundations of marketing decision making are based on findings from market research. Recognition that markets and consumers represent a complex variety of views and perspectives led to the development of market research as a business function. Marketing learned to cope with increased market complexity by researching it in order to identify key issues and to try to anticipate and satisfy market requirements.

Early marketers, most notably those working in the advertising industry, used a simple format for researching consumers, through friendly/informal questioning and trials combined with some observation. As the perceived value of researching the market to aid marketing related decisions grew so too did the need for more formal techniques of research. The information requirement moved from intuitive trial and testing to seeking findings with a foundation of accuracy, dependability and reliability. Marketing is an *applied* social science and as such attracted many trained social scientists as market researchers. Coupled with the growth in the importance and contribution of marketing to business success was the growth of the 'science' of market research.

For many years market research was dominated by scientific approaches. Examples of this can be found in consumer opinion surveys employed for a wide range of reasons from assessing voter opinions and attitudes to monitoring consumer and economic trends in society. Research training for industry graduates was constructed around a curriculum displaying the best traditions of social science research, that of the 'one best method' which provided validity and reliability and demonstrated clear cause and effect. Indeed, any self-respecting researcher would naturally emphasize the dependability of their research by providing comprehensive descriptions of the methods used to gather the findings.

The place of qualitative research in this process was in the context of traditional social science research. Traditionally social scientists, when faced with a new phenomenon employed qualitative research methods such as in-depth interviews with key informants (people who know about or work within the domain of the phenomenon in question), and/or focus groups with people likely to be affected by the phenomenon. In this way the research issues and parameters were determined. Out of such findings, social science researchers would construct appropriate questions for surveying a wider audience. The expected outcomes would provide statements of generalization about a population as a whole. Thus the market research industry has developed 'tried and trusted' methods and tools for performing tasks with accuracy and reliability.

A significant characteristic of marketing is its peculiar and sometimes unique requirements. Marketing as a concept and function is unique in that it 'faces-out' from a business. Its purpose is to take things to the market and bring information and ideas back from the market. Because of the dynamics of any market, marketing activities and ideas are continuously changing and revising. Marketing for enterprises today will be different to yesterday's marketing and will change to something different again in the future. Because of this dynamic, marketing and marketers must constantly seek and gather information. Most enterprises have established information flows, whereby statistics on sales and fluctuations in these will be continuously monitored. However, such statistical information flows are not enough: marketers gather information and market intelligence intuitively and continuously as an everyday occurrence in doing business. This in turn contributes to and sometimes shapes the constant marketing flux. As the value of marketing to business grows and as new concepts and applications of marketing emerge and evolve, so to does the need for up to date market intelligence. Thus marketers' need for deep and detailed qualitative research becomes more crucial. Its importance lies in the need to *understand* phenomena and to gain meaningful insights into circumstances and changes. The contribution that qualitative research can make to this understanding and insight is immense, hence the rationale for this book.

The book is organized into three parts. Part I focuses on social science research and marketing. Chapter 1 outlines a philosophy of marketing in the context of science or art (activity). The chapter also considers the methodological implications of the choice of a philosophy. In addressing some of the social science research terminology we have been conscious of the danger of confusing the uninitiated reader by the use of this 'language'. To social science research scholars our discussions on types of research position, and the descriptive terms used in this position, would appear simplistic in many ways. We make no apology for this; instead we hope that scholars will recognize that we are trying to explain with brevity some quite complex terminology so that the new social science researcher might gain an appreciation of it. Also in regard to brevity, we have used the terms that we believe fit most appropriately with aspects of our discussion, and in this context we state our own research position and philosophy.

Chapter 2 outlines the scope of research in marketing by addressing some perspectives of marketing, principally in two broad aspects, marketing management research and consumer research. The marketing management domain is viewed as an area that offers significant potential for new understanding and insights. Chapter 3 considers aspects of designing a research problem, specifically in terms of justification of the problem and the value of a research topic in marketing. We also consider the merits of using prior research dissemination in the literature both in formulating the research problem and in refining the topic. A brief mention is made of appropriate research methodologies. Chapter 4 considers the purpose of research in marketing from the perspectives of academic researchers, business researchers and somewhat unconventionally marketing *practitioner* (or DIY) researchers who require information for marketing.

Part II centres on the qualitative research methods best suited to marketing. We set the scene in Chapter 5 by justifying qualitative research methodologies, explaining their range and scope in the full spectrum of social science research. We also emphasize the value of *interpretive* research for qualitative research methodologies in marketing. Chapter 6 is about in-depth interviewing. We chose to address this method first because we consider it to be the bedrock for meaningful insights and understanding. Within the chapter we argue the value of *convergent* interviews as a means of gaining greater insights. Chapter 7, on case-based research, follows naturally from the previous chapter and in it we describe quite a rigorous case method approach in order to give a solid framework from which to build research cases. In addition though, we suggest that more interpretive approaches are possible and sometimes desirable. In Chapter 8, on focus group interviewing, we give a step by step framework for applying this method. Chapter 9 is about observation studies and the variety of types. Here we provide guidance on how to prepare for observation studies and an example in the context of marketing management in practice. Chapter 10 combines ethnography and grounded theory methodologies on the basis of their strong overlapping foundations. Finally in Part II, Chapter 11 addresses the various elements of action research and its relation to action learning.

Part III is about the applications and outcomes of qualitative research. In Chapter 12 we describe how to organize fieldwork and process qualitative data. We give some emphasis here to the value and use of *pictorial models* for visualizing data. Chapter 13 describes the writing process in the context of different reports for examiners, reviewers, practitioners and policy makers. Chapter 14 presents the notion of integrative multiple mixes of methodologies, which we argue enables the researcher to achieve the greatest insights and understanding of phenomena. Chapter 15, on future evolution of qualitative research, is a speculative look at the potential future of methodologies in the marketing context. Rather than attempt to predict a *common* future we each make our own individual speculation, sight unseen of each other's contributions, in the hope that our personal creativity will not be stifled or overly influenced. The outcomes indicate both a unity and a diversity of views which is part of the richness of qualitative research methodology.

Acknowledgements

Special thank you to Darryl Cummins and Aodheen O'Donnell, research assistants in marketing at the University of Ulster, for their unstinting devotion to reference checking and library searching. Also to Marilyn Healy of Griffith University Australia for her contribution to the chapter on focus group interviewing.

Part I SOCIAL SCIENCE RESEARCH AND MARKETING

1 Philosophy of Research

What is the purpose of considering a philosophy of research? Simply, to understand the philosophy that underpins the choices and decisions to be made in staking a research position. A research position will have implications for what, how and why research is carried out. Consideration of the philosophy of research helps to contribute a deeper and wider perspective of research so that our own specific research projects can have a clearer purpose within the wider context.

For most of its history the big question in social science has been: is social science scientific? This chapter addresses the question at a number of levels: philosophical, epistemological and methodological. Social science research in marketing, based on rigour, validity, cause and effect, precision in measurement and the pursuit of theory testing and building has led to the wide acceptance of the use of a variety of scientific approaches. Social science research in marketing has been concerned with accuracy of research outcomes, with the emphasis on gathering reliable data. Further, the scientific approaches of social science research have enabled and encouraged theory testing and development, which has contributed to enhancing the scope and perspectives of the marketing discipline.

The term *scientific* is drawn from the presupposition that natural science is the benchmark against which all cognitive endeavours should be measured; thus scientific language and words, such as *purposeful* and *systematic*, are often used to describe the nature of research. Similarly, by choosing a methodology, a researcher implies the use of certain 'rules and procedures' with different connotations and purposes, such as the logic used for arriving at insights and as a means of communication, so that other people can inspect and evaluate the research.

In this chapter we discuss the wide parameters of scientific research in order to take a position within these parameters. That is to say, this text does not belong to the full range and scope of the social science research paradigms, but is firmly positioned within a defined context of qualitative research. The justification for this positional context is the overriding driver that social science research in marketing must have a clear *purpose* and, most importantly, must be relevant to the particular purpose of carrying out research in marketing.

The Philosophy of Marketing: Science or Art (Activity)?

There have been many debates about the nature of marketing. These have focused on whether marketing can be deemed to have genuine scientific foundations and approaches to research, or whether marketing is more akin to an art where aspects of marketing are created out of the imagination and vision of the marketer. In pursuit of the notion of *marketing science* or *scientific marketing*, much scholarly thought and energy has been devoted to searching for an all-encompassing theory of marketing or a cohesive collection of theories that will determine the objective rigour of the discipline.

The scope and range of the social science research paradigms is illustrated by the long running debate on whether marketing is a science or an art/activity. This issue has been raised over many years by both academics and practitioners of marketing (Brown 1996; Hunt 1976, 1990, 1994; McKenna 1986; Sheth et al. 1988). There have been many interpretations of the definition and purpose of marketing research. Two examples serve to highlight this point. The first represents the academic perspective:

AN ACADEMIC DEFINITION OF MARKETING

Marketing is a 'university discipline which aspires to be a professional discipline' . . . Its responsibilities are:

- To society, for providing objective knowledge and technically competent, socially responsible, liberally educated graduates;
- To students, for providing an education which will enable them to get on the socio-economic career ladder and prepare them for roles as competent, responsible marketers and citizens;
- To marketing practice, for providing a continuing supply of competent, responsible entrants to the marketing profession and for providing new knowledge about both the micro and macro dimensions of marketing;
- To the academy, for upholding not only its mission of retailing, warehousing and producing knowledge, but also its contract with society of objective knowledge for academic freedom and its core values of reason, evidence, openness and civility. (Hunt 1994: 21–22)

This academic view of marketing is clearly positioned in the scientific perspective of marketing research paradigms. The perspective of Hunt is that of a scientific researcher and marketing academic emphasizing knowledge, not a business person. An alternative is offered by McKenna (1986), who may best be described as a consultant marketer whose view is from the perspective of business rather than academe:

A PRACTITIONER DEFINITION OF MARKETING

- Focus on 'understanding the market, moving with it, and forming relationships';
- 'Companies (must) view marketing as an educational process. The complexity and diversity of today's products confuses and intimidates many customers. When customers are confused, companies must find ways to educate them. When customers are intimidated, companies must find ways to reassure them';
- Marketing managers must 'be creative, smart, aggressive and open to change';
- Marketing is positioning between the product, market and company. (McKenna 1986: 8–9)

Comparison of these two perspectives highlights the professional position of both contributors. One is an academic and the other a practitioner. A superficial examination of the perspectives will suggest that Hunt (the academic) views marketing as a scientific discipline, while McKenna (the practitioner), views marketing as an *activity* more aligned to the dimensions of *art*. These two perspectives highlight variances when asking some fundamental questions. For example, is marketing a discipline? 'Yes', believe most academics; 'perhaps' say some practitioners with a high awareness of the wider aspects of marketing. Similarly, is marketing a science or is it merely science related? Again most academics will believe it to be a science or science related, whereas practitioners may not know or, more likely, will ask why such a question is deemed to be important. Consider, is marketing an activity? Only some academics will agree that it can be an activity (driven by knowledge: see Hunt's second point above), whereas almost all practitioners believe that it is.

These summary examples illustrate that, if marketing is positioned as a continuum with science/discipline at one end and applied/activity/art at the other end, most academics believe that marketing is a discipline which has scientific foundations whereas practitioners view marketing simply as an applied activity which may have creative (and artistic) foundations. The academic (scientific/ objective) approach is predicated on explaining and predicting phenomena, while the practitioner (artistic/ subjective) approach emphasizes describing and understanding phenomena. In such a continuum, academics and practitioners would seldom converge in their perspectives. Thus it is easy to detect a gulf between the two views outlined above. This need not be so, particularly in relation to research in marketing. Research in marketing may take a number of *positions*. Firstly, it is possible to be positioned firmly within the scientific marketing domain. Indeed, much of the academic research carried out and published in academic journals can be said to hold such a position. Secondly, it is possible, indeed appropriate in certain circumstances, to be positioned in the practitioner/artistic domain where research will seek to solve practical problems and provide potential solutions to practical problems rather than seek to break new ground or establish new theories.

It can also be entirely appropriate to adopt a dual position, whereby a variety of research philosophies and positions can be adopted depending upon the circumstances prevailing and the nature of the topic or research problem. This book advocates that such a multiple approach and position is suitable for research in marketing management decision making and business problems/issues. Indeed, Borch and Arthur (1995: 423) claim that *both* approaches should be used, arguing that mixed methodologies would 'contribute to the richness' of the research. Their bipolar approach to research is common: for example, Easterby-Smith et al. (1991) in their book, *Management Research*, share it. In brief, a researcher's methodology may 'aim to blend the rigour of the scientific validity of objectivist research with the contextual elements and insights of subjectivist research' (Borch and Arthur 1995: 425).

A cornerstone of the present book's positional context is to suggest that instead of taking an extreme position of either a scientific or artistic approach, the blend of two approaches could be taken within the one large domain of interpretivism/relativism for marketing management contexts. We discuss this domain in our notes to this chapter.

The elements and characteristics of the dominant philosophies of research and how they impact upon research decisions, values and appropriateness for purpose are addressed in the following section.

Some Research Philosophies

Ontology and epistemology

We briefly discuss the meaning and perception of ontology and episte-mology here. Essentially, ontology is *reality*, epistemology is the relationship between that reality and the researcher; and methodology is the technique(s) used by the researcher to discover that reality (Perry et al. 1999).

An ontology assuming that individuals have direct, unmediated access to the real world subscribes to the theory that it is possible to obtain hard, secure, objective knowledge about this single external reality (the basis of positivism, described in the following section). Conversely, an ontology which holds that individuals do not have direct access to the real world but that their knowledge of this perceived world (or worlds) is meaningful in its own terms and can be understood through careful use of appropriate interpretivist and relativist procedures is described in the following section.

Positivism or interpretivism

The positivist ontology holds that the world is external and objective, therefore its epistemology is based on the belief that observers are independent and that science is value-free. The positivist or natural science school relates to the facts or causes of social phenomena and attempts to explain causal relationships by means of objective facts. Positivist research concentrates on description and explanation, where thought is governed by explicitly stated theories and hypotheses. A research topic is identified through the discovery of an external object of research rather than by creating the actual object of study. Researchers remain detached by maintaining a distance between themselves and the object of research; they try to be emotionally neutral and make a clear distinction between reason and feeling, science and personal experience. Positivists seek to maintain a clear distinction between facts and value judgements, search for objectivity and strive to use a consistently rational, verbal and logical approach to their object of research. Statistics and mathematical techniques for quantitative processing of data are central to the research methods adopted by researchers from the positivist school of research. Hence positivists use a set of specific *formalized* techniques for trying to discover and measure independent facts about a single reality which is assumed to exist, driven by natural laws and mechanisms.

Table 1.1 illustrates the broad definition of the positivist and interpretivist ontologies and epistemologies, and the characteristics of relevant methodologies for both philosophies.

Interpretivism (derived from the Greek *hermeneuein*, to interpret) is inspired by a series of other qualitative concepts and approaches. Tesch (1990) lists a total of 46 such possibilities, Patton (1990) lists 10 theoretical traditions, and Helenius (1990) makes a synthesis of seven traditions into the concept of hermeneutics. However the broad term *interpretivism* takes account of the most important characteristics of the research paradigm on the opposite side of the continuum from positivism. To summarize, the interpretivist approach allows the focus of research to be on *understanding* what is happening in a given context. It includes consideration of multiple realities, different *actors'* perspectives, researcher involvement, taking account of the contexts of the phenomena under study, and the contextual understanding and interpretation of data.

Positivism has been considered by many scientific researchers in the past to be the *correct* scientific paradigm. However, interpretivism avoids the rigidities of positivism in relation to certain types of problems in the social field. Instead of trying to explain causal relationships by means of objective 'facts' and statistical analysis, interpretivism uses a more personal process in order to *understand reality*. Thus the term *interpret* is important in this approach to research. The term *relativism* is often used also; this recognizes that in the social field (marketing) phenomena are relative to each other in some way as opposed to seeking to isolate variables as in

Table 1.1 *Broad definitions/explanations of positivism, interpretivism, ontology, epistemology and methodology*

	Positivism	Interpretivism
Ontology		
Nature of 'being'/nature of the world	have direct access to real world	no direct access to real world
Reality	single external reality	no single external reality
Epistemology		
'Grounds' of knowledge/ relationship between reality and research	possible to obtain hard, secure objective knowledge	understood through 'perceived' knowledge
	research focuses on generalization and abstraction	research focuses on the specific and concrete
	thought governed by hypotheses and stated theories	seeking to understand specific context
Methodology		
Focus of research	concentrates on description and explanation	concentrates on understanding and interpretation
Role of researcher	detached, external observer	researchers want to experience what they are studying
	clear distinction between reason and feeling	allow feelings and reason to govern actions
	aim to discover external reality rather than creating the object of study	partially create what is studied, the meaning of the phenomena
	strive to use rational, consistent, verbal, logical approach	use of pre-understanding is important
	seek to maintain clear distinction between facts and value judgements	distinction between facts and value judgements less clear
	distinction between science and personal experience	accept influence from both science and personal experience
Techniques used by researcher	formalized statistical and mathematical methods predominant	primarily non-quantitative

positivist studies adhering to scientific rules. Our preference is for the term *interpretivism* because it accentuates the involvement and personal interpretive processes involved in understanding and making sense of phenomena in specific contexts in marketing.

Traditionally, positivism was based on empirical testing as the sole means of theory justification. After much antagonistic debate on the relevance of scientific theories for marketing phenomena (see for example *Journal of Marketing*, 47, Fall 1983 and *European Journal of Marketing*, 28 (3) 1994), there is now more general agreement that such a polarized position is not warranted, and indeed unnecessary. The idea of a 'sole means of theory justification cannot be maintained as a viable description of the scientific process or as a normative prescription for the conduct of scientific activities' (Anderson 1983: 25). In addition, no consensus exists as to the nature or the very existence of a unique scientific method. The search for research approaches other than those guided by pure positivism has led to a number of competing perspectives in the philosophy and sociology of science. However, wherever these perspectives have been derived from, they also need to be assessed to establish their value to research in marketing and marketing management domains.

There is no one best method and it is not appropriate to seek a single best method for the evaluation of marketing phenomena (Anderson 1983: 25). It will be more useful to look at the value and validity of a number of theories.

The position of this book in relation to ontology and epistemology is that we believe reality is socially constructed rather than objectively determined. Much of the focus of research in marketing is on understanding why things are happening. Therefore the task of the researcher in marketing should not only be to gather facts and measure how often certain patterns occur, but to appreciate the different constructions and meanings that people place upon their experience. The aim is to understand and explain why people (actors) have different experiences, rather than search for external causes and fundamental laws to explain their behaviour. Human action (especially in a marketing context) arises from the sense people make of different situations, rather than as a direct response to external stimuli (Easterby-Smith et al. 1991).

Let us take a moment to define and explain interpretive techniques as we perceive them (our *reality*) and their value in the context of research in marketing. The philosophies under the interpretivist umbrella incorporate a wide range of philosophical and sociological ideas such as hermeneutics, relativism, humanism, phenomenology and naturalism. These are primarily concerned with understanding human behaviour from the researcher's frame of reference. Figure 1.1 illustrates the range of philosophies in the context of positivist/scientific and interpretivist/relativist philosophies. The philosophies on the right side are positioned within the interpretivism domain of the continuum because we view them as being predominantly interpretivist. However, we also recognize that some of the philosophies draw on the positivism domain in their origin and structure. Hence their position within a continuum between positivism and interpretivism, but with a positional *direction* stemming from interpretivism. The fundamental aspects of each of these philosophies as we have 'interpreted' them from a composite of many authors' work are described in our notes to this chapter.

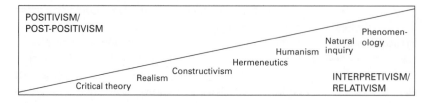

Figure 1.1 *Continuum of research philosophies*

Our interpretivist/relativistic stance appears to give a viable solution to the 'which philosophy' question in relation to understanding and evaluating marketing phenomena. Interpretivism/relativism implies that there are few truly universal standards of scientific adequacy (Anderson 1983). Different research studies will require different ontological, epistemological and methodological commitments. Research in the marketing/marketing management domain may be context, industry or company specific, and *knowledge* will be generated through communication and interaction with a number of sources. Theories can be justified to the extent that they fit or are appropriate to specific research problems and contexts. Indeed research areas tend to evolve as changes take place in methods, concepts, values, beliefs and theories.

Although some effort will be made to differentiate between types of interpretivism/relativism philosophies (see the notes) this book will use the broad label of *interpretivism* to cover all non-positivistic research approaches that commonly use qualitative methods. This encapsulates methods that do not adhere to scientific or positivist principles but instead allow research designs, approaches and methodologies to be adapted and related to specific research contexts and problems or issues in marketing.

The broad umbrella term 'interpretivism' has many different research perspectives. It is enough to say that all of the interpretivist theories outlined in Figure 1.1 and described in our notes have a different emphasis, for example

- their basic beliefs, that is the chosen ontology and epistemology;
- the researcher's focus, either searching for facts or looking for meanings and understanding; and
- the preferred methods for collecting data, either measuring concepts and taking large samples or using multiple methods in depth or over time (Easterby-Smith et al. 1991: 27).

The key criteria differentiating the two paradigms are that

- in positivism the researcher is independent but in interpretivist research the researcher is involved;
- in positivism large samples may be used whereas interpretivist research uses small numbers;
- in positivism, testing theories pervade whereas interpretivist-type research focuses on generating theories or 'theory building'.

Although the distinction between the two broad paradigms (positivism and interpretivism) may be clear at the philosophical level, when it comes to the use of quantitative or qualitative methods and to the issues of research design the distinction breaks down (Burrell and Morgan 1979). Indeed, some researchers have attempted to 'classify' and in so doing 'simplify' different types of research methods using criteria drawn from positivism. For example, Guba and Lincoln's (1994) framework (also adapted by Healy and Perry 2000; and Jacob 1988) classifies qualitative research into a number of paradigms: positivism, realism, critical theory and constructivism. On one level this approach is useful in that it attempts to list the characteristics of each domain under the headings of ontology, epistemology and methodology. However, other researchers have found the use of traditions and paradigms which are firm and fixed unhelpful, too rigid and often too positivist in stance (Atkinson 1995; Atkinson et al. 1988). This type of classification often stems from concepts and definitions of 'realism' that recognize only one reality viewed from different directions and perspectives (for more on the critical realist perspective see Archer et al. 1998; Bhaskar 1978, 1979; Fleetwood 1999).

Acceptance of such an argument makes it difficult to recognize or accept the *multiple realities* of interpretivism as viewed by authors such as Brown (1995); Habermas (1970); Hirschman (1986); Odman (1985); Peter and Olson (1989); Taylor and Bogdan (1984). Such multiple realities exist in the domain of management and marketing, where the view is that there is often not one superior reality out there to be found. Both these perspectives – that there is one reality viewed from different directions, as in realism, or that multiple realities may exist according to the researcher's perspective, as in interpretivism/relativism – have strong foundations and justifications. However, this book prefers to use the loosest framework and recognize that there are many different approaches to carrying out research under the broad interpretivist or relativist umbrella which can be adapted to suit the context of research in marketing and management (that is, non-physical sciences).

Traditionally some authors have advocated the use of both quantitative and qualitative methods (Fielding and Fielding 1986). This has been a common combination whereby qualitative research methods may be used to generate key research phenomena that can then be quantitatively researched for general perspectives. Using multiple methods allows more perspectives on the phenomena to be investigated. This book will argue later that researchers involved in the study of marketing and marketing management will find it beneficial to use more than one method, and that these may belong to either domain.

This book is positioned firmly within the interpretive paradigm. The research it advocates emphasizes the importance of understanding and interpreting the phenomenon under study in the context of its occurrence in marketing. It also recognizes the importance of the involvement of the researcher in the phenomenon under study, the existence of researcher pre-understanding and experiential learning which influences the focus and progression of the research and the development of interpretive analysis.

The choice of research philosophy will also have implications for research methodologies, and for how phenomena can be accessed, described and evaluated.

Methodological Implications of Choice of Philosophy

The philosophical stance impacts upon the perspective and approach to how research is actually carried out, how the problem is conceptualized, and how data is gathered and analysed. These methodological emphases and choices are considered in relation to the following questions:

- What is the role of prior theory?
- Is the focus on theory building or theory testing?
- Will research be inductive or deductive?
- Will the research be structured or unstructured?
- What is the role of the researcher?

The role of prior theory

There is often a debate about which should come first: theory or data? Again this is linked to whether the guiding philosophy is predominantly positivist or interpretivist; and also on the prior knowledge of the researcher. Most philosophies would agree with Fetterman that the researcher usually brings some prior theory to his or her research:

> (T)heory is a guide to practice; no study, qualitative or otherwise, can be conducted without an underlying theory or model. (Fetterman 1989: 17)

Positivist researchers and interpretivist researchers tend to use theory in different ways. Traditionally positivist researchers consult prior theories in the literature in order to arrive at hypotheses or research questions at the early stages of the research study and are unlikely to add to that prior theory during later stages. In contrast, theory can be used at various stages in research using an interpretivist approach. A researcher's prior theory can help to define the problem and how to tackle it. However, setting even very loose parameters at the start of qualitative research can pose some early problems for the researcher. Research studies in the interpretivist paradigm are generally *inductive* (see below); they make few explicit assumptions about sets of relationships. The drawbacks of this approach are that it may impose a self-blinding framework and may result in the accumulation of incoherent, bulky, maybe irrelevant and meaningless observations which could prove impossible to interpret. Therefore for practical purposes it is often beneficial to recognize that some preliminary frameworks can be developed quite early on in a research study but 'these will be revisited repeatedly over the life of the project' (Miles 1979: 591).

There are many benefits of considering and setting some tentative, loose guidelines and parameters of the research study early on, being open to what the site has to tell researchers and taking the time and effort to slowly evolve a coherent framework rather than imposing one from the start (Glaser and Strauss 1967; Miles 1979). Hence the interpretivist approach allows for a compromise or balance between these two extremes that incorporates the strategy of developing preliminary frameworks early on (Miles 1979) or allowing the researcher to figuratively put brackets around a temporal and spatial domain of the social world (Van Maanen 1979). These brackets or frameworks will tentatively define the territory about which descriptions will be fashioned.

Theory building or theory testing

The main focus of research can be either theory building or theory testing. Theory testing occurs where an existing theory or hypothesis is taken as the guide to a piece of research and is then tested using methods that will allow it to be measured and evaluated. Thus, theory testing would most likely be positioned under positivism/post-positivism in our continuum in Figure 1.1 (see also Figure 5.1, p. 62). In contrast, where the emphasis of research is on theory building then the purpose of a study is to seek out meaning and understanding of the phenomena. So theory building is positioned under interpretivism/relativism at the other end of the continuum in Figure 1.1. The distinction between theory testing and theory building is intrinsically linked to the issue of using either a deductive or an inductive approach to research.

Deduction or induction

Deduction entails the development of a conceptual and theoretical structure prior to its *testing* through empirical research methods. It begins with some kind of abstract conceptualization and moves on to testing through the application of theory in order to create new experiences or observations. The researcher decides which concepts represent important aspects of the theory or problem under investigation. Given that these concepts are drawn from theory, they will be quite abstract: 'concepts are abstractions that allow us to select and order our impressions of the world by enabling us to identify similarities and differences' (Gill and Johnson 1991: 28). The theory or hypothesis may link two or more concepts together in a causal chain which consists of untested assertions about the relationships between the concepts. These asserted relationships based upon the theory will not be suitable for empirical testing until these abstractions are translated into *observables* or indicators: that is, they need to be operationalized. A concept is operationalized when it is defined in such a way that rules are laid down for making observations and determining when an instance of the concept has empirically occurred (Gill and Johnson 1991: 29).

Induction, on the other hand, is allowing the data to guide the research and theory building. It involves using the observations of the empirical world to allow the construction of explanations and theories about what has been observed. Induction is based on reflections of particular past experiences, through the formulation of abstract concepts, theories and generalizations that explain the past, and predict future experience.

Through deductive research's use of conceptual and theoretical structures, theory is used as a basis and guide. In contrast theory is the outcome of inductive research. Induction might prevent the researcher benefiting from existing theory, while deduction might prevent the development of new and useful theory. A balance of inductive and deductive approaches will be most appropriate for interpretive philosophies/approaches to research. For example, a deductive framework/conceptualization may be derived from a literature analysis and this may be evaluated empirically and inductively to allow new insights to emerge.

Relatively 'structured' or relatively 'unstructured'

Research in marketing often requires a balance between a structured approach (where research is a logical, sequential, step-by-step process following a clear plan and protocol), and an unstructured approach (where research may evolve, emerge and develop as it progresses). Research can have an unstructured approach initially, until the researcher has some understanding of the situation and issues to be researched. The balance between a structured and unstructured approach can be managed and directed through careful use of literature as a foundation to the research study; a literature review might be used to construct a conceptual model or framework which will form the background of subsequent inductive empirical research. Similarly, the use of experiential knowledge gained by the researcher during different stages of the research can contribute to the development of a conceptual model or framework.

Role of the researcher

To a large extent, the role of the researcher will be dictated by whether a positivist approach or an interpretivist approach is guiding the research. It is dictated by the epistemological position of the research where the researcher will be required to be either a *detached observer* or part of the *research instrument*.

Positivist researchers believe that the researcher should remain distanced from the material being researched. The traditionalist assumption in science is that the researcher must maintain complete independence if there is to be any validity in the results produced. However, interpretivist researchers require the researcher to get involved with the material being researched. The *objectivity* and the emotionally neutral stance of the researcher is emphasized in positivist research designs. More recently it has been recognized that this is not always possible. For example, the very act of asking respondents questions will affect their perceptions, and researchers as human beings cannot avoid becoming less than *neutral* to the research process and outcomes.

Interpretivists place considerable emphasis on the researcher and his/her role in the research process and progression. In fact the researcher is often referred to as 'the human instrument' (Fetterman 1989; Hammersley and Atkinson 1983). Being a subject in the research process demands that the background and previous experience of the researcher be explained (Storbacka 1994). The experience forms the individual's approach or the experiential knowledge of the researcher in relation to the research area and this will have an impact upon how the researcher structures an understanding and may simultaneously prevent him/her from seeing a certain aspect of the problem. The researcher's pre-understanding of the research area is largely a result of his/her own experience (Gummesson 1991). Pre-understanding, knowledge and experiential learning are essential in order to fully understand processes in a marketing or managerial context. For example, specialization in a particular industry contributes considerable institutional knowledge which will be useful when doing research in such a context.

We conclude this discussion by outlining our research position in relation to using and adapting these research philosophies and methodologies for doing research in a marketing context.

Authors' Research Position

The book considers qualitative research methodologies from a marketing perspective. Whilst recognizing that research in marketing can broadly cover managerial and consumer aspects, it is considered that the book will have greater focus and purpose by being written from a primarily **managerial marketing perspective.** However, sufficient material and description will be provided to allow qualitative researchers from a consumer perspective to shape their methodology.

Our philosophical position is demonstrated in Figure 1.2. We are positioned somewhere between positivism at one extreme and inter-pretative relativism at the other extreme of the spectrum. **Our position is skewed towards the interpretive/relativism end of the spectrum.** This position is defined further by acknowledging that we enter the spectrum from the interpretive/relativism end. The foundations of our own research come from this perspective rather than the more established, traditional perspective of our early research training.

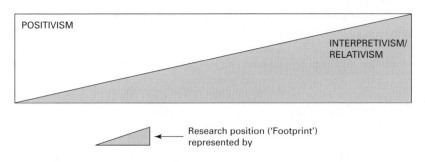

Figure 1.2 *Authors' research position*

It can be seen from the figure that most of the 'accepted' qualitative methodologies can be approached from an interpretivist/relative direction and is comparable with our research 'footprint'. **This 'Authors' Research Position' imposes upon us the requirement to acknowledge the dominance of this position in our worldview and approach to doing research, perhaps requiring some significant repositioning of methodology descriptions, many of which stem from the positivistic perspective.** Even though traditionally some of these research methodologies were approached from a positivistic perspective, for example in the work of Yin (1994) on case study methodologies, this work is deemed to be of considerable significance to qualitative methodology research. However, much of Yin's (1994) work is positioned towards the positivistic end of our continuum, whereas much of the description in our text will place qualitative research in a 'contextual' setting, and emphasize analysing data in a manner which takes account of its *holistic* research context and completeness.

Summary

The purpose of this chapter has been to position the book within the context of the broad philosophical, ontological, epistemological and methodological issues in social science research. The emergent rationale behind discussing these issues is to argue that much of the research in marketing that employs qualitative methodologies is interpretive in nature. Much of the discussion attempts to *position* this research within the wider scope of scientific/academic research in social science.

This chapter has provided a brief overview of social science research and arrives at a research position that dictates the focus and position of the rest of the book. Some aspects of this research position are further examined in Chapter 2 in the specific context of research in marketing.

LEARNING QUESTIONS

Explain the characteristics of ontology, epistemology, positivism and interpretivism; and determine how they are positioned in relation to each other.

Research can be deductive or inductive, structured or unstructured. Outline how these would differ in the context of methodological issues.

Describe the importance of the role of the researcher in interpretive, qualitative research.

Describe the *intrinsic* value of interpretive qualitative research.

Notes: Different Research Perspectives under the Umbrella term of 'Interpretivism'

Post-positive perspectives. This is a broad term to denote philosophies other than positivism used in research. Here researchers use a variety of interpretive approaches, seek to understand the deeply set beliefs, emotions and meanings that are embedded in the activities, rituals and behaviour of individuals in different contexts. However, there are some differences in emphasis and focus in these different interpretive approaches, as illustrated by the brief summaries below.

Realism theory assumes that reality is 'out there' and 'real' but is only imperfectly and probabilistically apprehensible. In other words, perception is not reality; instead a perception for realists is a window onto reality through which a picture of reality can be triangulated with other perceptions. Realists acknowledge the difference between the world and particular perceptions of it, and the pre-eminent importance of that world. In marketing, a piece of research using a realist approach might examine phenomena such as 'typical' marketing practices within an industry, with perceptions triangulated from managers in different parts of the distribution channel, for example manufacturers, intermediaries and retailers.

Critical theory assumes discoverable social, political, cultural or economic realities incorporating a number of virtual or historical structures of these realities that are taken as real. In critical theory the researcher is a transformative intellectual who 'liberates' the participants from their mental chains. Its principles are that

- research should comprise a critique of society (marketing) or of its processes;
- this criticism should be interdisciplinary;
- theory and practice are inseparable;
- facts and values are interdependent;
- genuine knowledge is a potential instrument of emancipation. (Brown 1995)

Critical theory researchers and their investigated subject (marketing) are interactively linked: the belief system of the researcher influences the inquiry, which requires a dialogue between the researcher and the participants. Therefore no objective knowledge exists, as all claims are relative to the values of the researcher (Anderson 1986; Gabriel 1990; Guba and Lincoln 1994). An example of marketing research using critical theory might be in a 'cause' marketing situation such as the evaluation of anti-smoking attitudes or instigating change in other social behaviour.

Constructivism is based upon the acceptance of multiple discoverable realities which are socially and empirically based, intangible mental constructions of individuals (in contrast to critical theory's focus on a society or a group). Thus the created knowledge depends on the interaction of researcher and respondent. From a constructivist's perspective, truth is a construction that refers to a particular belief system held in a particular context, for example within an industry or a specific organization.

The aim of constructivists is to achieve an understanding of the similarities and differences of constructions that both the researcher and respondent held initially; so that the researcher becomes more aware of the context and meaning of these constructions (Anderson 1986; Guba and Lincoln 1994; Peter 1992; Peter and Olson 1989). Marketing research here might involve a longitudinal evaluation of a reorganization of management infrastructures and its impact upon a marketing organization and its processes as perceived by both the researcher and key managers in the organization.

Phenomenology is described by Husserl (1960) as the 'science of the subjective'. It assumes that even though we cannot be certain about the independent existence of objects in the external world, we can be certain about how they appear to us in consciousness (Brown 1995). Phenomenology seems to be the prevailing approach to qualitative research in the social sciences literature. There are variants such as interpretive sociology (Habermas 1970); naturalistic inquiry (Lincoln and Guba 1985); social constructionism (Berger and Luckmann 1966); qualitative methodology (Taylor and Bogdan 1984); 'new paradigm' inquiry (Reason and Rowan 1981); and 'alternative inquiry' paradigms (Guba and Lincoln 1994). Each of these takes a slightly different stance in the application of phenomenology and in the features of positivism that it finds more inappropriate.

Overall, Taylor and Bogdan (1984) contend that the 'phenomenologist is committed to understanding social phenomena from the actor's own perspective. He or she examines how the world is experienced'. Therefore objects are not regarded as things in themselves but as things intended by consciousness. The act of thinking and the object of the thought are interdependent. Thus the external world is reduced to the contents of consciousness alone. The exploration of individual consciousness, either through introspection or third-person accounts of others' experiences, enables genuine, meaningful knowledge to be attained (Kearney 1986, Macann 1993 in Brown 1995). In a marketing context a phenomenological approach could be used to research how managers perceive their marketing decision making roles within their work environment.

Hermeneutics. Odman (1985: 2162) clarifies the differences between phenomenology and hermeneutics as follows:

> Whereas phenomenology is primarily oriented toward the immediate phenomena of human experience, such as thinking and feeling, hermeneutics is more context directed. In interpreting human traces, hermeneutics often tries to go beyond the observable in order to 'read between the lines'. It can therefore be characterized as more transphenomenonal.

If we refer back to the marketing context example in the last paragraph: using a hermeneutic approach would entail collecting other data such as observing managers' behaviour in relation to marketing decisions, in addition to collecting data on how managers perceive their marketing decision making roles in an effort to reach a more contextual understanding of the phenomena.

Naturalistic inquiry. A naturalistic perspective holds that there are multiple constructed realities that can be studied only holistically. Inquiry into these multiple realities will inevitably diverge because each inquiry raises more questions than it answers. Therefore prediction and control are unlikely outcomes although some level of understanding can be achieved (Lincoln and Guba 1985).

The inquirer and the 'object' of inquiry interact to influence one another; knower and known are inseparable rather than being independent of each other. The aim of inquiry is to develop an idiographic body of knowledge in the form of 'working hypotheses' that describe the individual case rather than being concerned about finding 'generalizations' which hold anywhere and at any time. All entities are in a state of mutual simultaneous shaping so that it is impossible to distinguish causes from effects.

According to Lincoln and Guba (1985) naturalistic inquiry is value bound in the following ways:

- Inquiries are influenced by inquirer values as expressed in the choice of a research problem, and in the framing, bounding and focusing of that problem.
- Inquiry is influenced by the choice of the paradigm (positivist or interpretivist variance) that guides the investigation into the problem.
- Inquiry is influenced by the choice of substantive theory used to guide the collection and analysis of data and in the interpretation of findings.
- Inquiry is influenced by the values that are inherent in the context.

Humanism. Humanism emphasizes a point already raised as it explicitly advocates that 'rather than standing apart from the system being studied, the researcher immerses the self within it' (Hirschman 1986: 238). Researcher understanding arises from direct personal experience, rather than by the manipulation of experimental variables. A humanistic perspective is made up of the following assumptions:

– that human beings construct multiple realities
– that the researcher and the phenomenon under study are mutually interactive
– that research inquiry is directed towards the development of idiographic knowledge
– that causes and effects cannot be separated
– that research is inherently value-laden
– the outcome of research, knowledge, is socially constructed and not discovered (Brown 1995).

Therefore such an approach will take account of the values of the researcher and context of the research.

References

Anderson, P.F. (1983) 'Marketing, Scientific Progress, and Scientific Method', *Journal of Marketing*, 47(4), 18–31.

Anderson, P.F. (1986) 'On Method in Consumer Research: A Critical Relativist Perspective', *Journal of Consumer Research*, 13(2), 155–173.

Archer, M., Bhaskar, R., Collier, S., Lawson, T. and Norrie, A. (eds) (1998) *Critical Realism: Essential Readings*, Routledge, London.

Atkinson, P. (1995) 'Some Perils of Paradigms', *Qualitative Health Research*, 5(1), 117–124.

Atkinson, P., Hammersley, M. and Delamont, S. (1988) 'Qualitative Research Traditions: A British Response to Jacob', *Review of Educational Research*, 58(2), 231–250.

Berger, P. L. and Luckmann, T. (1966) *The Social Construction of Reality: A Treatise in the Sociology of Knowledge*, Doubleday, New York.

Bhaskar, R. (1978) *A Realist Theory of Science*, Harvester Press, Hassocks, England.

Bhaskar, R. (1979) *The Possibility of Naturalism*, Harvester Press, Hassocks, England.

Borch, O.J. and Arthur, M.B. (1995) 'Strategic Networks among Small Firms: Implications for Strategy Research Methodology', *Journal of Management Studies*, 32(4), 419–441.

Brown, S. (1995) *Postmodern Marketing*, Routledge, London.

Brown, S. (1996) 'Art or Science? Fifty Years of Marketing Debate', *Journal of Marketing Management,* 12(4), 243–267.

Burrell, G. and Morgan, G. (1979) *Sociological Paradigms and Organisational Analysis: Elements of the Sociology of Corporate Life*, Heinemann Educational, London.

Easterby-Smith, M., Thorpe, R. and Lowe, A. (1991) *Management Research: An Introduction*, Sage Publications, London.

Fetterman, D.M. (1989) *Ethnography: Step by Step*, Sage, Newbury Park, CA.

Fielding, N.G. and Fielding, J.L. (1986) *Linking Data*, Sage, Beverly Hills, CA.

Fleetwood, S. (1999) *Critical Realism in Economics: Development and Debate*, Routledge, London.

Gabriel, C. (1990) 'The Validity of Qualitative Market Research', *Journal of the Market Research Society*, 32(4), 507–519.

Gill, J. and Johnson, P. (1991) *Research Methods for Managers*, Paul Chapman, London.

Glaser, B.G. and Strauss, A.L. (1967) *The Discovery of Grounded Theory: Strategies for Qualitative Research*, Aldine De Gruyter, New York.

Guba, E.G. and Lincoln, Y.S. (1994) 'Competing Paradigms in Qualitative Research', in N.K. Denzin and Y.S. Lincoln, *Handbook of Qualitative Research*, Sage Publications, Thousand Oaks, CA, pp. 105–117.

Gummesson, E. (1991) *Qualitative Methods in Management Research*, Sage Publications, Newbury Park, CA.

Habermas, J. (1970) 'Knowledge and Interest', in D. Emmet and A. MacIntyre (eds), *Sociological Theory and Philosophical Analysis*, Macmillan, London.

Hammersley, M. and Atkinson, P. (1983) *Ethnography: Principles and Practice*, Tavistock Publications, London.

Healy, M. and Perry, C. (2000) 'Comprehensive Criteria to Judge Validity and Reliability of Qualitative Research within the Realism Paradigm', *Qualitative Marketing Research: An International Journal*, 3(3), 118–126.

Helenius, R. (1990) *Forsta och Battre Vets*, Carlssons, Stockholm cited in E. Gummesson (1991), *Qualitative Methods in Management Research*, Sage Publications, Newbury Park, CA.

Hirschman, E.C. (1986) 'Humanistic Inquiry in Marketing Research: Philosophy, Method and Criteria', *Journal of Marketing Research*, 23(3), 237–249.

Hunt, S.D. (1976) *Marketing Theory: Conceptual Foundations of Research in Marketing*, Grid Inc, Columbus, OH.

Hunt, S.D. (1990) 'Truth in Marketing Theory and Research', *Journal of Marketing*, 54(3), 1–15.

Hunt, S.D. (1994) 'On Rethinking Marketing: Our Discipline, Our Practice, Our Methods', *European Journal of Marketing*, 28(3), 13–25.

Husserl, E. (1960) *Cartesian Meditations: An Introduction to Phenomenology*, Humanities Press, Atlantic Highlands, NJ.

Jacob, E. (1988) 'Clarifying Qualitative Research: A Focus on Traditions', *Educational Researcher*, 17(1), 16–24.

Kearney, R. (1986) *Modern Movements in European Philosophy*, Manchester University Press, Manchester.

Lincoln, Y.S. and Guba, E.G. (1985) *Naturalistic Inquiry*, Sage Publications, Beverly Hills, CA.

Macann, C. (1993) *Four Phenomenological Philosophers: Husserl, Heidegger, Sartre, Merleau-Ponty*, Routledge, London.

McKenna, R. (1986) *The Regis Touch: New Marketing Strategies for Uncertain Times*, Addison-Wesley, Reading, MA.

Miles, M.B. (1979) 'Qualitative Data as an Attractive Nuisance: The Problem of Analysis', *Administrative Science Quarterly*, 24(4), 590–601.

Odman, O.J. (1985) 'Hermeneutics', in T. Husen and N. Postlewaite (eds), *The International Encyclopedia of Education*, Pergamon, Oxford.

Patton, M.Q. (1990) *Qualitative Evaluation and Research Methods*, Sage Publications, Newbury Park, CA.

Perry, C., Reige, A. and Brown, L. (1999) 'Realism's Role among Scientific Paradigms in Marketing Research', *Irish Marketing Review*, 12(2), 16–23.

Peter, J.P. (1992) 'Realism or Relativism for Marketing Theory and Research: A Comment on Hunt's "Scientific Realism"', *Journal of Marketing*, 56(2), 72–79.

Peter, J.P. and Olson, J.C. (1989) 'The Relativistic/Constructionist Perspective on Scientific Knowledge and Consumer Research', in E.C. Hirschman (ed.), *Interpretive Consumer Research*, Association for Consumer Research, Provo, UT, pp. 24–29.

Reason, P. and Rowan, J. (1981) *Human Inquiry: A Sourcebook of New Paradigm Research*, Wiley, Chichester.

Sheth, J.N., Gardner, D.M. and Garrett, D.E. (1988) *Marketing Theory: Evolution and Evaluation*, Wiley, New York.

Storbacka, K. (1994) 'Research Design', in *The Nature of Customer Relationship Profitability: Analysis of Relationships and Customer Bases in Retail Banking*, Publications of the Swedish School of Economics and Business Administration, Helsingfor, pp. 25–53.

Taylor, S. J. and Bogdan, R. (1984) *Introduction to Qualitative Research Methods: The Search for Meanings*, 2nd edition. Wiley, New York.

Tesch, R. (1990) *Qualitative Research: Analysis Types and Software Tools*, Falmer, London.

Van Maanen, J. (1979) 'Reclaiming Qualitative Methods for Organisational Research: A Preface', *Administrative Science Quarterly*, 24(4), 520–526.

Yin, R.K. (1994) *Case Study Research: Design and Methods*, 2nd edition. Sage Publications, London.

2   Scope of Research in Marketing

The purpose of this chapter is to offer a 'concept of research for marketing' which is relevant to the way managers think and do business in the context of marketing management decision making and business problems and issues. There is some discussion of marketing concepts, theories and applications within the scope and range of marketing. The focus is to recognize a need to apply or develop the best ways of doing research for marketing management and business purposes. That is, our discussion aims to give some practical emphasis.

Social science methods used for research in the management domain are borrowed from other disciplines and at best, are merely adapted to suit a managerial circumstance; few have been specifically devised for management or by managers. Therefore before considering what are the most suitable methods for researching marketing phenomena, some aspects, characteristics, and component parts of marketing within the business context are considered in order to set in context research in marketing management.

A Perspective of Origins and Rationale

Marketing as a discipline, concept, activity, process, or any other manifestation of description covers a huge domain. A useful perspective in grasping this notion is that marketing can be drawn from the world of the *marketing professional*. There is a widely held perception that marketing is indeed a profession. This is reflected in the many Associations and Institutes of Marketing throughout the world. Almost every European country has its professional body of marketing, as indeed do most other countries east and west of Europe. The USA has the largest marketing professional body in the American Marketing Association (AMA). The UK is the home base of the Chartered Institute of Marketing (CIM), which claims to be the largest 'international' professional body in marketing with branches and influence in many of the old British colonial countries in South-East Asia and Africa. Regardless of the apparent size and representative nature of such bodies, their memberships add up to a minority of those employed in some form of marketing activity in industry, commerce and the wider aspects of society. One might ask why more *marketers* do not belong to their local professional body? An answer may be that these individuals do not primarily perceive themselves as marketers. How many times have you heard someone, anybody, describe themselves as a marketer? 'What do you do?' 'I'm a marketer', is unfamiliar dialogue in social introductions or interactions, in contrast to the way that people describe themselves as doctors, dentists, engineers, teachers or members of most other professions. The implication here is that marketing as a *profession* is a weakly held perspective. Why should this be so? An answer might be that a majority of marketers, or more correctly, people working in or at marketing, perceive themselves as *businesspeople* who merely happen to work in marketing and sales or some other related activity. Thus many of such people will perceive themselves in an industry- or profession-specific way, for example 'I work in advertising', or 'I work in banking . . . travel . . . shipping . . . aerospace . . . exporting'.

Such perspectives are reinforced when considering industry *get-togethers* at conferences and exhibitions. Marketers will naturally gather together at industry events where they know many other delegates whom they have met before or know of from other acquaintances or because of a prior profile of news and gossip. Just about everybody at a trade show could be described as belonging to some aspect of the marketing profession. They number many hundreds, and even thousands if the event is a world exhibition or convention. Take most of these people (marketers) out of their *industry context* and perhaps set them into another industry convention and they will feel like strangers who have little in common with other delegates and only a mild interest in another industry's products or services. This may be so, even though most or all of these other people are also working in marketing in some form. Furthermore, the number of delegates at a professional marketing event (perhaps one which is organized by the local chapter of a professional membership body), will be few in number compared to those at an industry-specific event. Indeed, most of these delegates will know each other from some prior network, such as that of college alumni, or perhaps because their other profession is one which requires proactive networking in order to do business, for example consulting.

This discussion paints a rather fragmented picture of the 'marketing profession'; but there may be a more plausible reason for an apparent lack of *collegiality*. Marketing covers a huge domain. The scope of this domain is illustrated by Hunt who, when addressing the issue of the scope of marketing, offered the following description of many, many topics:

> consumer behaviour; pricing; purchasing; sales management; product management; marketing communications; comparative marketing; social marketing; the efficiency/productivity of marketing systems; the role of

marketing in economic development; packaging; channels of distribution; marketing research; societal issues in marketing; retailing; wholesaling; the social responsibility of marketing; international marketing; commodity marketing; physical distribution; etc. (1976: 7)

Hunt's illustration is by no means fully descriptive of the scope of marketing. Some might argue that his list is rather selective, although his description does continue with the questions, 'What more to include? What to exclude?'

Marketing, when considered over time and history, presents various eras of dominance and research focus, including product orientation, sales orientation, customer orientation, consideration of wider 'macro' aspects of society, strategic issues, services, relationships, international and global, small firms, and so on. Inherent in this and Hunt's illustration are aspects of management, function, philosophy and style – all of which impact upon the scope of marketing.

Furthermore some authors (such as Brownlie et al. 1994 and Dholakia et al. 1987) have recognized the need to periodically rethink the underlying theory, concepts and scope of marketing in order to prevent the discipline becoming myopic, complacent and inward looking. Brownlie et al. (1994) present three suggestions to overcome such complacency and take a wider perspective:

- recognize the need to undertake more in-depth ethnographic studies of what marketers in different contexts actually do, relating the intention and understandings of those managers to the marketing actions that are subsequently taken;
- consider marketing in a more comparative perspective, that is, in relation to other disciplines and professions, other countries and other times; and
- encourage and develop forums for more reflexive, interdisciplinary and pluralistic work in marketing.

Perhaps the only realistic conclusion that can be arrived at in this discussion is that marketing is indeed a wide domain. So wide in fact that many marketing professionals have little in common outside the relatively specific or niche perspectives and indeed may perceive themselves to be different professionally from others working in another industry. How does such a wide domain come to terms with the term *research in marketing*, if at all? One aspect that does lend itself to commonality within marketing is that of marketing *management*. Marketing managers have a common requirement to take decisions with regard to aspects of marketing. Such decisions are founded upon a knowledge base gleaned through some form of accumulation process. This accumulation of knowledge occurs in a multiplicity of ways ranging from a semi- or subconscious cerebral awareness to formal research in gathering meaningful information that will aid marketing decision making.

A discussion on the origins of marketing research is a huge thesis in itself. It is not our purpose here to consider in detail such origins. Suffice to say that marketing research arises out of a want or need for information (Dibb et al. 1997; Jobber 1998; Malhotra 1996; Tull and Hawkins 1990). Such a want or need can be wide and varied depending on who desires the information and for what purpose. In a general sense, marketing research will be carried out because of a cognitive requirement that might range across a spectrum from simple interest or awareness to requiring knowledge and understanding. Generally, marketing research can be expected to provide insights that will achieve the desired level of cognitive perception (Baker 1991; Gordon and Langmaid 1988; Moutinho and Evans 1992; Zikmund 1991). In understanding all these research requirements it is useful to consider the nature of marketing management.

Nature of Marketing Management

Most textbook definitions of marketing extol the importance of knowing and satisfying customers' needs and wants. A typical example of a definition from a textbook is:

> The marketing concept holds that achieving organisational goals depends on determining the needs and wants of target markets and delivering the desired satisfactions more effectively and efficiently than competitors do. (Kotler et al. 1996: 15)

Whilst this definition clearly places the focus of marketing upon the customer it ignores, except perhaps implicitly, the aspect of *managing* marketing. Indeed, Hunt's description of marketing in our previous section talks about sales management but not explicitly of management of other parts of the marketing function. That is, it may be one thing to have a philosophy of customer focus but it is quite another thing to manage a range of activities that impact not only upon the market place but on the organization as a whole. An earlier definition of the marketing manage-ment *concept* by Felton serves to emphasize this purpose and nature:

> A corporate state of mind on the integration and co-ordination of all of the marketing functions which, in turn, are melded with other corporate functions, for the basic objective of producing maximum long range corporate profits. (1959: 55)

Most managers will relate more closely to this management version of the marketing concept than to the narrow textbook one. Indeed, most commercial organizations are headed by managers whose chief motivation and overwhelming need is for profit. These managers will recognize that acceptable profits cannot always be gained by blind adherence to the customer focus view of the marketing concept. However, such managers will be concerned that they have a comprehensive knowledge of their business and its industry and markets. Much of this knowledge will be derived from the accumulated experience of being in an industry and market. In addition, such managers will gather information in a variety of ways to enhance the accumulated knowledge. In some cases this information may be gathered by what can be termed research. However, this information gathering may not adhere to the rigours and requirements of scientific or academic research methodologies. The reasons for this may be multiple but are most likely to stem from the characteristic of the manager's job. This characteristic is that of *multiple diverse variety*. This diversity is intriguing. What makes a good manager? How do managers manage? What impacts and influences management? Indeed, what is the nature of marketing management? A host of like questions all serve to fuel the intrigue of management and hence the vast array of research in the domain.

Given that people undertake research in order to systematically increase their knowledge, it follows that marketing and management research focuses on gathering information to find out things about marketing and management. Finding out may include describing, explaining, understanding, criticizing and analysing (Ghauri et al. 1995). In summary, Easterby-Smith et al. (1991) argue that three things combine to make business and management a distinctive focus for research:

- the way in which managers (and researchers) draw on knowledge developed by other disciplines;
- the fact that managers tend to be powerful and busy people; and
- a requirement that the research has some practical consequence. This means it needs either to contain the potential for taking some form of action or to take account of the practical consequences of the findings.

Research for marketing and management needs to provide and involve procedures for solving managerial problems and addressing business issues in tandem with trying to advance knowledge (Gill and Johnson 1991). Research must be useful: it must have practical implications. In attempting to solve managerial problems and address business issues within the context of advancing knowledge there is potential for many variations in the nature and types of research studies. Some research studies may require the understanding and explanation of certain phenomena. Other research studies may focus on exploring the ways in which different organizations and managers do things; yet further research may combine an in-depth investigation of an organization with the context of a wider understanding of the processes that are operating. Taking account of such variety it may be helpful to visualize the scope of research in marketing and management. As we discussed in our Science versus Art debate in Chapter 1, academic research studies focusing on understanding the processes within marketing and management and their outcomes could be placed on one end of a research continuum. Research or information gathering at the other end of the continuum could represent research that has direct and immediate relevance to managers, addressing issues they see as important and is presented in ways they relate to and can act upon. These issues are further explored and developed in Chapter 4.

Perspectives of Marketing Management Research and Consumer Research

From a research perspective it is possible to hypothetically divide the marketing domain into that which is primarily concerned with aspects of management and that which is primarily concerned with consumers (see Figure 2.1). It is worth noting that business-to-business marketing accounts for approximately 80 per cent of business activities, therefore user or consumer marketing is only a part of a much bigger picture. However both business-to-business and consumer marketing are commonly concerned with the importance of the buyer/customer focus.

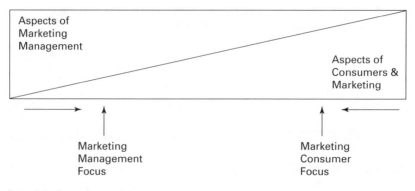

Figure 2.1 *Research in marketing*

Research into consumers and marketing

Research topics concerned with marketing to consumers cover a vast array of areas. Indeed, research into consumers and consumer studies is a huge domain in itself, as consumption is an integral part of life. This research domain is strong in its basic and underlying focus, but it is possible to consider broad categories of consumer studies research, for example:

• broad consumer perspectives within the overall context of society (societies);

- consumer perspectives within the context of a variety of marketing segmentation categories;
- specific consumer perspectives within the context of consumers of a product.

Of course, there are a host of specific research fields both within and beyond these broad categories, but for the purpose of our discussion it is enough here to focus briefly on these three categorizations. Marketing will utilize research outcomes from any and all of these broad categories, and also more specific categories as required. Let us take a moment and elaborate a little on each of these categories.

Broad consumer perspectives within the overall context of society (societies)

There is a large field of research which gathers statistics on society and its underlying changes and trends. Most governments seek data on societal structures both for the purpose of historical records or general records, and more importantly for monitoring changes and trends so as to plan and prepare appropriate societal and governmental infrastructures for the future. In many areas such statistics generate fascinating details of a society's (consumers') preferences, desires, changes, attitudes and perceptions. These statistics are often segmented into mainstream, peripheral and emerging categories. From a marketing perspective, all of this forms important general and non-specific data that may or may not impact upon industry or company specific marketing. Broad data such as this may indicate trends in car ownership, housing, consumer or household appliances for example; but little of it is industry, brand or type specific. So, for example, car ownership statistics may state the number and age of cars per household but not the type and style of preference. The significance of such research data lies in the categorization of the members of society as *consumers* in that, as consumers, they are making choices and demonstrating broad preferences for product categories in spending disposable income.

Consumer perspectives within the context of a variety of marketing segmentation categories

There is a field of research which examines aspects of consumer perspectives, attitudes and behaviours. Whilst the heterogeneity of consumer perspectives is both interesting and informative, much more penetrative knowledge is obtained by applying known and new aspects of homogeneity. To know how consumers behave as a homogeneous group enables meaningful insights into the range of stimuli, triggers, preferences, dislikes, mainstream opinions and extreme perspectives. Consumers have been segmented into a host of categories, some historical, current and future. So, socio-economic categories such as status, income, location, etc. are plentiful. A variety of *lifestyles* are common categories. Furthermore, by combining several elements such as age, income and profession sub-categories can be derived. The range is immense and varied. Such categorization allows marketing managers to identify product needs and preferences as well as broad trends and changes in perspectives.

Specific consumer perspectives within the context of consumers of a product

Another immense field of consumer research lies in researching customers or 'users' of products and services. This research tends to be much more specific in its desired outcomes. It seeks to go further than broad cate-gorizations of perspective to find detailed perspectives on needs and wants in relation to specific product or service categories. Research may examine the usage of products and services in terms of frequency and regularity of consumption, conformity or non-conformity, alignments with other users, etc. In much of this research, the aim of marketing managers will be to know the perspective of their own customers and at the same time to know the perspectives of key competitors and their customers, and to compare the variances and similarities of these consumers. It is this category of consumer research that is closest to, and perhaps part of, the marketing management research domain. Such research might focus upon consumer decision making with regard to the purchase of one or a variety of products or services. It would seek to quantify consumer purchasing in some way or perhaps seek to determine attitudes, percep-tions or behaviours. Similarly, consumer research may be concerned with consumers in relation to products, price/value, impact of marketing, competition and a host of other issues.

Whilst most of the issues in this book can be placed in either the consumer or the management domain, the main perspective of the book is that of the marketing management domain. The outcomes of the consumer research described above can be viewed as having significance for marketing management decision making, that is, it will enable market-ing managers to *do* marketing. Thus, the first two broad categories of consumer research may be of general interest to marketing management in that they offer general perspectives on a wider domain. Most marketing managers require situation-specific knowledge about their own sphere of decision making. This sphere can be described as *multiple* and *diverse*. In this complex sphere much decision making in marketing is not fully understood. Marketing theories may present specific frameworks, tools and techniques, but *how* these are *applied* and used is often a mystery, except in the most conceptual and general sense. Thus, just as consumer researchers seek to understand both the broad and the intimate perspectives of consumers' attitudes and behaviours, marketing management researchers seek to *understand* the intimate perspectives of managers operating in their own sphere of decision making.

Research into marketing management issues

Qualitative research methodologies and the interpretive philosophies emphasized in Chapter 1 are comfortably applied to consumer research studies. However, such research philosophies are still emerging in the marketing management field. To date, that which is known and understood about marketing management decision making is both limited and fragmented. Researching managers is often difficult as they are competitive and so may be secretive about their activities and do not see the benefits of participation in research into what they do. Add the increasingly dynamic market and marketing change, the resulting new circumstances in which marketing management decision making is set, and the need for meaningful interpretive research is underlined.

Within the marketing management research domain a number of variable and overlapping perspectives can be discerned, as illustrated in Figure 2.2.

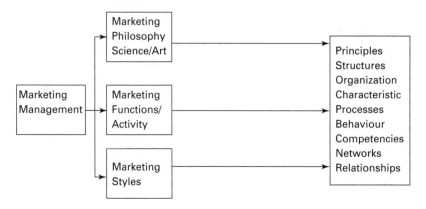

Figure 2.2 *Marketing management research framework*

The philosophy of marketing and the domains of science and art have been discussed in Chapter 1. In Figure 2.2, these domains are related to the managerial aspects of marketing, both in terms of structures and procedures represented by management principles, structures, processes and organization, and people oriented aspects involving behaviour, competencies, networks and relationships.

In addition, research in marketing management can focus on marketing as a function or activity, which will embrace techniques, approaches, processes of marketing which relate to *doing* marketing and marketing *being seen to be done*. In marketing management, research can also focus on the people dimensions and thus be concerned with management behaviours, skills and competencies, networks and relationships, styles and interactions. Of course, research can be done from either a firm's perspective or a researcher's perspective.

Many areas for researching aspects of marketing in the management domain can find a source among the headings listed in the third column of Figure 2.2. Thus, an examination of management principles may consider the broad guidelines and key aspects of management activities and perhaps the guiding values. Management structures may be viewed as the predetermined arrangements which managers set in motion and which may involve flows of information and communication and may be defined as regularly occurring procedures. Management organization can be deemed to be the tasks of breaking work up into component and manageable parts and co-ordinating activities on the lines of *what* to do and *how* to do it. Management processes are activities of communication and decision making. Management characteristics, competencies, skills can be likened to personal attributes and how they vary across all those participating. How marketers interact with others for the purpose of doing better marketing in terms of marketing decision making and managing activities can be considered in the context of networks and relationships. All of these areas of research can also be considered in relation to aspects of marketing perception and performance. These can be roughly encompassed under concepts, functions and activities. All of these areas are, in essence, concerned with management decision making. That is, a research topic could focus on the kind of decisions that are taken with regard to marketing issues, or the way in which managers take decisions about marketing and how these decisions influence marketing.

This last point warrants further clarification. It is relatively easy to identify marketing decisions by focusing the research topic on an aspect of marketing, for example obvious areas such as marketing strategy decisions, marketing planning, marketing tactics, or marketing decisions taken in response to competitive activity. Equally, it is relatively easy to identify decisions about aspects of marketing activities such as product decisions, communications, pricing, distribution and so on. However, not all management decisions are specifically concerned only with marketing aspects. Many will be taken with a different focus in mind, but such decisions may have a significant impact upon marketing issues. For example, management may decide to raise the cost base of the company by introducing new wage structures. This will need to be passed on to the customer, thus necessitating a change in price and so it becomes a marketing issue. Similarly, a decision to reduce stocks in the warehouse will impact, not only on price but also on promotional messages.

Following our earlier assertion of the need to understand the manager's perspective, a research focus upon marketing management will invariably be concerned with *how* or the way in which decisions are made. The research focus may also be concerned with the *processes* behind such decisions and the variation and style of the managers taking the decisions. Indeed, the scope and type of decisions in management is a research issue in itself. Decisions are made for a multiplicity of reasons, so the nature of these decisions varies. Even though it will be possible to categorize such decisions as marketing type decisions, they may still vary enormously within the domain of marketing. In recognition of this there is a large literature on management decision making, covering different styles from extremes of authoritarian to humanistic; timescales from short to medium and long term; scope in terms of strategic and tactical; and so on. The range and domain is vast and this is mirrored in the field of research. The focus of such research is largely on understanding the phenomena behind marketing management decision making, and such a search for understanding is continuous if for no other reason than the passing of cultural, social and economic eras and the emergence of new ones. Whatever the aspect, research in this domain is concerned with the management of marketing and is therefore not concerned, except perhaps implicitly, with consumers and marketing.

The two research domains of marketing management and consumers in marketing are not necessarily mutually exclusive (this is demonstrated in our third category of consumer research), so they should be viewed as existing on a continuum between two extremes. At the extremes a research focus will consist of only one of the domains or perspectives. The 'middle ground' will incorporate some combination of both domains and perspectives, with an emphasis on one or the other, as illustrated in Figure 2.1.

In both domains, interpretive research is relevant and useful. In consumer marketing research, interpretive approaches and research methods have an important role to play in determining consumer attitudes and extracting consumer opinions on issues relating to a broad range of marketing, both inside and outside an organization, and also in understanding broad aspects of consumers and markets. Similarly, in management research, interpretive research and the use of multiple qualitative methods are important for gathering attitudes and opinions of managers and also in understanding management and managerial processes. In either of these domains, the essence and value of qualitative marketing research is the understanding of phenomena rather than determining a general perspective on a marketing phenomenon. Indeed, whilst qualitative research will allow a statement on what occurs in a given context, a 'general' statement is better achieved by a more positivistic approach using quantitative methodologies, which may if required have derived its frameworks from qualitative research.

Summary

This chapter has outlined the nature and perspective of research in marketing and research in marketing management in particular. The discussion has built on the research position explained in Chapter 1 in the context of doing research in marketing, and in particular the sphere of marketing management decision making. Our research position is underlined by a focus here on research in marketing contexts. It is argued that because of the need to *understand* marketing management perspectives, qualitative research methodologies are most appropriate. The relevance and value of interpretive philosophies and the value of interpretive qualitative research methods for in-depth understanding of phenomena in the marketing domain, for managerial and consumer contexts is presented in Chapter 5. For now it is enough to recognize and appreciate the scope and parameters of research in marketing. It is easy to acknowledge that their range is immense, so it is important to identify meaningful marketing research targets if sound research is to be carried out. Chapter 3 attempts to do this by examining how to identify a marketing research problem and then considers how to go about building a rationale and justification for a sound piece of research.

LEARNING QUESTIONS

Describe the nature and scope of doing research in the marketing domain.

What are the fundamental differences between doing research with a management focus and research with a consumer focus?

What is the value of research in the context of marketing management and consumer marketing?

References

Baker, M.J. (1991) *Research for Marketing*, Macmillan Education, Basingstoke.
Brownlie, D., Saren, M., Whittington, R. and Wensley, R. (1994) 'The New Marketing Myopia: Critical Perspectives on Theory and Research in Marketing', *European Journal of Marketing*, Special Issues on Critical Perspectives on Theory and Research in Marketing, 28(3), 6–12.
Dholakia, N., Firat, F. and Bagozzi, R. (1987) 'Rethinking Marketing', in F. Firat, N. Dholakia and R. Bagozzi (eds), *Philosophical and Radical Thought in Marketing*, D.C. Heath, Lexington, MA, pp. 375–384.
Dibb, S., Simkin, L., Pride, W.M. and Ferrell, O.C. (1997) *Marketing: Concepts and Strategies*, 3rd European edition, Houghton Mifflin, Boston.
Easterby-Smith, M., Thorpe, R. and Lowe, A. (1991) *Management Research: An Introduction*, Sage Publications, London.

Felton, A.P. (1959) 'Making the Marketing Concept Work', *Harvard Business Review*, 37 (July–August), 55–65.

Ghauri, P.N., Gronhaug, K. and Kristianslund, I. (1995) *Research Methods in Business Studies: A Practical Guide*, Prentice-Hall International, London.

Gill, J. and Johnson, P. (1991) *Research Methods for Managers*, Paul Chapman, London.

Gordon, W. and Langmaid, R. (1988) *Qualitative Market Research: A Practitioner's and Buyer's Guide*, Gower, Aldershot.

Hunt, S.D. (1976) *Marketing Theory: Conceptual Foundations of Research in Marketing*, Grid Inc., Columbus, OH.

Jobber, D. (1998) *Principles and Practice of Marketing*, 2nd edition, McGraw-Hill, London.

Kotler, P., Armstrong, G., Saunders, J. and Wong, V. (1996) *Principles of Marketing: The European Edition*, Prentice-Hall International, London.

Malhotra, N.K. (1996) *Marketing Research: An Applied Orientation*, Prentice-Hall International, London.

Moutinho, L. and Evans, M. (1992) *Applied Marketing Research*, Addison-Wesley, Harlow.

Tull, D.S. and Hawkins, D.I. (1990) *Marketing Research: Measurement and Method: A Text with Cases*, Prentice-Hall, Englewood Cliffs, NJ.

Zikmund, W.G. (1991) *Exploring Marketing Research*, 4th edition, Dryden Press, Chicago.

3   Design of a Research Problem

This chapter is concerned with the process of identifying a research topic and problem in the domain of marketing using qualitative research within an interpretive philosophy. In the previous chapter we outlined the scope and parameters of marketing domains and the value of interpretive research using qualitative research methods. In turn, the aim of this chapter is to consider how to refine a topic idea until it becomes a clear statement of a research problem. In doing so the chapter explores and defines issues such as topic identification and problem justification, the background and origins of the research and acknowledges the role played by basic assumptions and hypotheses or propositions. It gives some description and framework to the early construction and process of a specific piece of research. Furthermore, it incorporates some fundamental issues to be considered by the researcher, encapsulated in the following questions:

'What am I going to do?' This is answered by consideration of the research problems and any assumptions and hypotheses as appropriate.

'Why am I going to do it?' This is addressed by a justification for all of the above.

'How is it going to happen?' The answer to this requires an outline of appropriate research methodologies.

'What will the results mean?' This is a useful speculation on the expected outcomes and conclusions of the research.

Justification for a Research Problem

Justification for a research problem stems from the broad area of the topic itself. A research topic area is often broad; working towards a research problem requires refinement and specific narrowing of the research topic in order to reach a manageable and appropriate research problem. In relation to the value of the topic the research should be in an area of marketing which interests not only the researcher (of course!), but also marketing academe and the profession as a whole (Jankowicz 1995). Within this context the research should have some value and purpose (Varadarajan 1996). Three ways of evaluating whether a topic has some value and purpose are:

- Typically, the research may be an *inquiry* into some aspect of marketing that has generated some doubts or questions over its validity.
- The research may be directed towards an issue of *query* in marketing about an aspect which hitherto had been accepted without question.
- Alternatively, the research may address an *unexplained* area of marketing that has previously received little attention.

Examples belonging to each of these areas will emerge as we focus upon the justification of the research problem a little more closely. Further explanation of how to justify a research problem in marketing can be achieved by considering the three aspects that contribute to the justification of a research problem:

- a topical aspect of marketing;
- an aspect of marketing deficiency;
- consideration of a research topic in a specific marketing context.

A topical aspect of marketing

A research topic starts off in a broad or general area that can be specified into multiple research problems. Whether a research topic is concerned with issues surrounding marketing management or consumers and marketing, the research can take a number of different perspectives. For example, the research may consider any aspect from an historical perspective in terms of what happened and in which context. Alternatively, a future perspective may be taken in terms of what is planned or expected to happen. A current perspective considers what is happening *now*. In all of these perspectives a researcher may be seeking to evaluate an existing phenomenon or perhaps some aspect of a new phenomenon.

Whatever perspective is chosen, it should be topical, that is, of interest now. Thus topicality of a research issue is a key consideration in assessing the purpose and value of a piece of research. This can be stimulated by themes within journal articles, local and national press stories, current debates, research reports, experiential knowledge and interest. In addition topics may be identified as a result of market and competitive pressures and events.

In all of the variety and scope of research topics in marketing it should be remembered that marketing is a highly interrelated and interactive domain. Thus, whilst a research topic may *belong* primarily to one aspect of marketing, it may and indeed will often encompass various other aspects or themes which in themselves will bear significant influence upon an area of research (Perry 1998). For example within the services domain a research topic might focus on any aspect of:

- service quality – development, delivery, failure and recovery;
- dimensions of service quality appropriate to a new or existing services situation;
- service delivery in a specific context such as financial services and the effect of technological advances on service quality perceptions.

While considering this width and scope of a topic, choices about their application need to be made. Each aspect of service quality could be studied either within a narrow framework or in the context of the wider dimensions of the topic. For example,

- within the context of the whole service industry, within one industry sector, or within company;
- all or a selected number of service quality variables across a range of different companies or industry sectors.

That is, the particular application of the study could involve one industry, one company, or a selected number of issues in relation to a specific number or type of companies. However it is worth emphasizing that if only one industry is chosen, there must be a commitment to a more *in-depth* investigation than if two or more industries are chosen. Trade-offs between depth and width of study need to be recognized.

These topical aspects of marketing will vary and change for many reasons. A *fashion* for particular products may create a topical marketing enthusiasm, long-term market trends may lead towards new marketing approaches that become topical as they grow, or significant happenings in an economy or in the wider world may stimulate new marketing activities that become topical as they develop. A few examples of 'topical' marketing serve to illustrate the above. Small firms have been viewed by most developing and growing economies as being the cornerstone of such development and growth (Hisrich 1986; Storey 1994). It is generally accepted that small firms can represent as much as 95 per cent of all enterprises in an economy, and so on this basis alone they are a topical area of marketing (Carson 1990; Pelham 1997). Since small firms are generally given support towards growth and this growth may be led by marketing activity, obviously marketing is important to small firms. Add this to the number of enterprises that are small and it becomes clear that marketing in small firms is of considerable significance.

Another area of marketing that may be perceived to be *topical* is services marketing (Curtis and Murthy 1999). Most developed economies now depend heavily on the service sector for economic wellbeing and growth. Furthermore the vast majority of transactions between firms are between service firms as intermediaries within a distribution channel. However, many service firms are small. As economies grow and service firms become more sophisticated in their marketing, the quality of such service is very much a topical area in marketing.

A third example of a *trend* in marketing that can represent a topical area is that of relationship marketing. This is an area that has seen significant growth in interest and is likely to continue to evolve for the foreseeable future (Coviello et al. 1997). Much of topical research in this area focuses on establishing, building and maintaining relationships within the context of relationship marketing.

However, there are research topics that have been *overdone*! For example, SERVQUAL (Parasuraman et al.'s (1988) service quality measurement tool) has been used in almost every service and quasi-service industry as a means of measuring service quality. Also research about *trust* and *relationships* is beginning to pervade the marketing literature and has been applied to many contexts of marketing. There are indications of areas that are becoming over-researched where it would be difficult to find a new context or new marketing issues to research.

An aspect of marketing deficiency

Some research studies may focus on an aspect of marketing that has previously not been researched in much depth. This can either be in the context of a relatively new marketing circumstance or an area that has been neglected. Given that it is often relatively difficult to identify *neglected* areas of research, finding them will involve some degree of rational thinking built upon a thorough search of the literature, consideration of current marketing practice, and identifying areas of potential. It is important to ensure that any identified areas of research deficiency have indeed been neglected, rather than illustrating a failure by the researcher to find appropriate previous studies in the area (Robson 1993).

Although it is often difficult to identify neglected areas of research, there are many areas of marketing deficiency. Some are long standing, others emerge as marketing is introduced into new areas, some are mainstream marketing, others at the periphery of marketing activity. Some examples of these areas of relative deficiency are considered here. It has long been recognized that there is a gap between academic marketing theories and the way in which marketing practitioners perform marketing (Carson 1990; Greenley and Bayus 1994). These deficiencies have been raised frequently in the media and trade press. However, some academics are recognizing the non-applicable nature of much of their theorizing on marketing issues. Much of this deficiency relates to textbook literature that is increasingly being questioned in relation to its suitability and appropriateness for marketing practitioners: for example, few textbooks cover relationship marketing and networks in depth. Similarly, the academic journal literature has been accused of being of interest only to academics and having little to offer to practitioners (Nataraajan et al. 1998). This may be indicative of a need to interpret theories more appropriately for specific contexts. Many theories relate to general explanations that apply over several contexts and so are built upon some assumptions. Given that they are *general* theories, deviations may be a result of some assumptions no longer being relevant and/or some contextual factors being overlooked.

For example, should the customer be the main focus of marketing strategy, when most other fields of academic inquiry such as strategic management acknowledge that a firm must find a balance between the claims of competing stakeholders? Indeed, there is a growing recognition of a dichotomy between company and customer objectives (Carson et al. 1998). In practice, whilst most companies will acknowledge the importance of satisfying customers there is increasing pressure on companies to prioritize the needs of direct stakeholders, and thus place customers at the periphery (Gronroos 1996). A contemporary example of this is the commercialization of clubs and societies that previously existed for the benefit of members. Examples of these can be found in the financial sector, from building societies to commercial banks; sports clubs to commercial businesses. Other areas of marketing deficiency can be found where some industries are changing their focus and direction. For example, in the rapidly expanding financial services sector, many new entrants are using marketing techniques in a cumbersome and crude fashion. Equally, many of the old established financial institutions are struggling with employing marketing techniques once deemed to be beyond their scope of business activity. Another area of marketing deficiency is the vast domain of not-for-profit marketing where no significant marketing theory exists that encompasses the vast array of organizations (Balabanis et al. 1997). Further, a sometimes developing, sometimes stalling area of marketing deficiency is *ethics* in marketing, which is largely led by academic champions and a few practitioners.

A specific context in marketing

So topicality is a first consideration in choosing a research topic; looking for areas of research deficiency is another. Further refinement towards determining the specifics of the research problem can be achieved by positioning the research in one of a range of contexts. The research topic may be *industry specific*, where consideration takes account of characteristics which prevail within that industry. A further specific can be added by positioning the research within a *single market* within an industry. In such research, characteristics peculiar to that specific market will be considered and further specificity can be added by positioning within an *existing* market circumstance or a *new* market situation. Even further refinement can be achieved by research that examines aspects of marketing within a *distribution channel*, whereby aspects of marketing between the various channel intermediaries may be examined. A research topic can also add specificity by considering markets that are *local, domestic or international*, or by an examination of *competitors' marketing activity*, directly, indirectly or both.

Another positioning feature is one where the research topic will concentrate on certain phenomena or characteristics pertaining to the marketing or influencing the marketing within a domain. So, *industrial and consumer* marketing will have inherently different phenomena and characteristics that distinguish them from each other. For example, industrial marketing may have fewer customers, while in most cases consumer marketing has many customers. Industrial marketing may be more personal and relationship focused whereas consumer marketing may be more impersonal in its interactions with customers. *Services marketing* offers other clearly distinctive characteristics which differentiate the domain. It is easy to find further ranges of factors that distinguish a variety of domains, for example *small firms* marketing, *electronic* marketing, *direct* marketing, *international* marketing and so on: the variety is infinite. Finally each of these can be considered in relation to specific regions or countries, such as Asia, Japan, Europe, Scandinavia or Australasia.

Industry specifics as outlined above can be viewed as part of marketing in a specific context. Furthermore, a researcher could consider an aspect of marketing within a specific market or industry. Some examples might be distribution logistics, promotional messages and vehicles, or technological advancements. Similarly, marketing issues which address aspects of marketing within a specified market domain are important topical areas, for example aspects of local or domestic marketing, regional marketing, international marketing, and so on.

Whatever the chosen specific context, nature of the phenomena and characteristics of a research topic, the research problem can be identified and refined further by the specific focus represented by the nature and type of research. Thus research may set out to *define* aspects of marketing and/or to redefine some issues. It may wish to examine the *scope and range* of a given domain. The research may seek to discover the *how or what* of a domain. An issue might be to consider the *impact of a new phenomenon* upon an existing marketing circumstance. The research can incorporate aspects of *conceptualization, measuring, comparing, analysing, assessing, evaluating, experimenting, adapting* or *adopting*, any aspect of marketing theory or techniques. Of course a refined and defined research dissertation may incorporate any combination of these aspects or may only consider one as its distinctive characteristic.

The Value of a Research Topic in Marketing

A research topic has value if it has the potential to be a *comprehensive* piece of research on an aspect of marketing. From an academic point of view this can mean contributing to research in a broader area of interest such as *consumer satisfaction* or *market orientation*. From a practitioner's point of view this can be research that leads to doing better marketing and having better results. This comprehensiveness is determined by a depth of study that may be founded on substantial and extensive consideration of prior research represented by appropriate literature or other prior event. Similarly, the research progression may be expected to lead to significant outcomes that go beyond describing a certain phenomenon by breaking new frontiers in understanding (Saunders et al. 1997).

All these *quality* assessments mean that some topics can be said to be insufficient for academic research even though many of the fundamental research procedures may be adhered to. Indeed, some topics such as writing a marketing plan or carrying out a feasibility study or examining a specific company problem, would benefit greatly from discipline and rigour, but would they introduce elements of *depth and discovery*? Another area for caution in research is where a researcher is committed to a *cause* that generates flag-carrying, banner-waving enthusiasm and passion. These attributes may be welcome motivators but caution must prevail if they are not to dominate the research and bias or twist the discipline and rigour of the research process. It is sometimes easy to be blinded by the enthusiasm and passion of a cause and to confuse or miss the true research issues and outcomes from rigorous academic research. It is recommended that research topics should be generated from a consideration of what the *marketing issues/problems* are in this context before the researcher becomes committed to a research topic. That is, the researcher should be able to anticipate some outcome in terms of a *production of knowledge*.

In summary, the value of a research topic in marketing is its *contribution* to knowledge (Varadarajan 1996) and the importance of that contribution. Such a contribution must demonstrate an intrinsic value both to the researcher and to subsequent readers of the researcher's report. This value must stem from the novelty and implications of research findings and be articulated and evaluated in the research report's outcomes and con-clusions. In contrast, a simple common question to emerge from a piece of research which has little significance or contribution is, 'So what?' A simple benchmark of *value and contribution* helps to avoid the 'so what?' response.

Using Literature for Initial Justification of a Research Problem

Justification of a research topic

A full justification of the overall research will occur as the research progresses from the early stages, but it is important to use appropriate literature to justify the research problem at an early stage (Francis 1998).

The use of literature referencing need not be extensive at this stage, but needs to be highly specific in purpose (Robson 1993). Its purpose is to serve as a foundation for the justification and to strengthen the importance of the research problem (Borg and Gall 1989). It should illustrate that the researcher knows the existing literature and is likely to be researching something new. In the development of a research foundation this helps to position the research problem and illustrate the unique aspects of the proposed research.

The selective reading of the literature here is best achieved by using *seminal* work combined with *state-of-the-art* articles which will help the researcher to get a head start into the research topic and begin to focus on possible research problem(s). Seminal articles are those which were written early in the conceptual development of a specific topic area and include detail of the early thinking and classification of the topic area. State-of-the-art publications are those which comprehensively review the literature and often point to new research directions, that is literature which not only serves the purpose of justifying the research problem by its argument, but also sends a signal to the reader that such seminal and state-of-the-art work is widely recognized as being an important contribution to a domain of research. The reader would expect to find some references from authors who are recognized as being leaders in the field of the research topic (Saunders et al. 1997). So seminal work and state-of-the-art articles are widely referenced and cited because they come from authors who have established a reputation as the leading conceptual thinkers in their field and who have contributed theories and concepts which are widely used in the area.

Some examples serve to underline the above. If a researcher is seeking to seminally justify a topic such as 'Small firms marketing is different to large company marketing', it might be expected that definitions of marketing would be founded on the textbook gurus such as Kotler and Levitt. Definitions of small firms would be drawn from the work of Storey and Gibb, for example; and 'Small firms marketing is different to large company marketing' might reference Hills, Carson and others. Similarly a topic which addresses 'Service quality as an important aspect of customer service' would expect seminal references in the services marketing literature to recognize the work of the Nordic School of Normann, Gronroos and Gummesson; and the work in the US of Parasuraman, Zeithaml and Berry on aspects of research in service quality.

References at this stage can be used sparingly but must be effective in supporting the justification discussion. The overall purpose is to indicate that the research topic has been chosen as a result of significant prior reading and considered research and a demonstration is being made as to how this prior knowledge justifies the chosen research problem.

Research assumptions and hypotheses or propositions

Rather than deliberating over *all* aspects of a research topic and the justification for a research problem, it is entirely appropriate and acceptable to make some assumptions and hypotheses or propositions about the research in order to position the research and give it a focus (Lindsay 1995). Assumptions are particularly useful in framing some broad issues that may be examined later, but to do so at an early stage of the research would distract or deflect the researcher from achieving a clear focus. That is, assumptions, defined as broad generalizations that have a probability of existence, can be used to set the research topic in context. An example would be to make a sweeping statement about the state of an economy, such as 'The economy can be expected to continue to grow over the period of the research'. Such an assumption signals that, whilst the economy has important influences upon research outcomes, it is an issue which is not being researched as part of the dissertation.

Assumptions can be made about more specific and direct aspects of a research topic. For example, 'Consumers wish for satisfaction' is a reasonable assumption that would allow a topic to address issues of consumer satisfaction in more specific ways. A more specific statement in this context would be to suggest that consumers *must* have satisfaction or that they *demand* satisfaction, both of which belong as part of a hypothesis or proposition (a point addressed later in this section). Similarly, an assumption which states that 'Market research will provide information' acknowledges generalizable common sense without asserting a judgement on the value or otherwise of such information. In the same way, 'Advertising has some impact' is a reasonable assumption in most circumstances of marketing without an assertion of the nature of that impact.

Assumptions are broad generalizations but hypotheses or propositions are more specific and definite. We are using the two terms 'hypothesis' and 'proposition' interchangeably here as they are both widely used to refer to the statements or questions that aim to refine the research problem. A hypothesis can be defined as a precise statement of effect, often stemming from theories of 'cause and effect', or an assumed relationship/association between two or more variables. The term 'proposition' is sometimes used instead of 'hypothesis' in order to signify a less precise or specific statement early on in a research study. Hypotheses or propositions imply some relationship between two constructs, for example amount of income can be related to degree of prosperity. Some examples of hypotheses or propositions in marketing are:

'An increase in advertising spend will lead to an increase in sales.'

'More marketing activity than competitors leads to increased market share.'

'New products stimulate demand.'

These are all perfectly acceptable statements to make. Whereas assumptions are the boundaries of a research study, hypotheses or propositions will be an integral part of a research study and can be seen as some specification of the research problem. Therefore if these hypotheses/propositions were included in a research framework it would be reasonable to expect the data collection and analysis stages of the research to provide some firm conclusions in relation to the hypotheses/propositions. A conclusion can be positive and thus confirm the hypothesis, or negative and thus assert that the hypothesis does not hold. To achieve either is satisfactory and important, since it shows that the research process can arrive at a logical and objective conclusion on an assertion based on empirical findings.

Hypotheses and propositions are widely used in many aspects of social science research and not least in marketing research. Whilst they provide a strong focus and direction for organizing and analysing empirical research findings, it is possible to carry out empirical research without hypotheses or propositions. Whether to use hypotheses or not is the decision of the researcher in conjunction with his/her supervisor.

Relationship between justification and research problem

Justification is the foundation of a research problem, as noted above. It is an indication of the degree of rigour and objective assessment of a research topic and serves to substantiate a research problem's significance. A justification will identify and track the core and established factors surrounding a research topic. It will indicate the significant factors of the research issue that appear to be unanswered, and that led to the research problem. The justification is a clear demonstration of prior knowledge, intuitive understanding and grasp of a topic, whereby the reader is given the clear impression that all aspects of history, origin and background to a research problem have been covered by way of logical and rational assessment. In addition, the justification must lead the reader in a precise direction toward the core issue of the research problem. In doing so, it must demonstrate the strong linkage between the overall research topic and through the justification to the research problem.

Referring to the earlier example of researching marketing in small firms, the topic may have an underlying assumption that, 'Small firms marketing is different from large company marketing'. In the justification for this assertion the researcher will explore prior literature which claims that indeed this is the case. As part of this justification it will become clear that whilst it can be claimed that small firms marketing is different it remains unclear exactly what small firms marketing entails. This allows the introduction of the research problem, often asked as a question, 'What is small firms marketing?' Such a research problem may be stated in a variety of ways, which will have the important implication of determining the type of research methodology that will be employed to solve the problem. So the problem may alternatively be stated as: 'To determine the characteristics of small firms marketing', or 'Defining the nature, scope and parameters of small firms marketing'.

Similarly, a justification that asserts: 'Service quality is an important aspect of customer service', may lead to a research problem of: 'What levels of service quality are needed in order to offer customer service in a given context, for example, an up-market restaurant?'

In turn, a justification based on the assumption that, 'Relationship marketing creates stability and more satisfied customers', may raise the research problem of, 'How is relationship marketing developed, maintained and terminated?'

Another assumption based on identifying similarities and differences in relation to a specific topic or context, could be: 'Marketing theories are different to marketing in practice'. This would lead to a research problem of: 'How do marketing practitioners adopt marketing theories?' And in the case of a justification based on a dichotomy such as, 'Companies must meet shareholder needs *and* customer needs', a research problem might be, 'How do companies *balance* shareholder and customer needs?'

In all of these examples, the linkage between the justification of the research topic and the defined research problem should be clear, acknowledging that a variety of research problems could stem from each and all of the examples used. In qualitative and interpretive research, the research problem is usually based upon a *how* and/or *why* statement or question. The emphasis on including *why* as part of the question prevents the research from becoming merely descriptive and encourages it to be explanatory.

In essence, the research problem is one or two sentences that cannot be answered with a simple *yes* or *no*. It is the broad problem that the researcher will examine more precisely in the hypotheses or propositions, and is the problem prompting and placing a boundary around the research without specifying what kind of research is to be done (Emory and Cooper 1991). As Leedy notes, 'the statement of the research problem must imply that, for the resolution of the problem, thinking on the part of the researcher will be required' (1989: 61).

Identifying the research problem will take some time. It is an exercise in 'gradually reducing uncertainty' (Phillips and Pugh 1994: 37), as it is narrowed and refined. Nevertheless, early identification of a preliminary research problem focuses research activity and literature searches and so should be a key part of the research.

What Method Will Be Used to Research a Problem?

There is a vast range of research methodologies in the social sciences. This text reviews and considers some interpretive approaches using qualitative methods that can be used in marketing research studies. We outline these approaches in Chapters 5–11. However, in defining the research problem it is useful to consider whether and indeed how the problem can be resolved through the research method (Francis 1998). Research problems will require outcomes and conclusions that fall into two broad categories of findings: firstly outcomes that identify *general* statements (*generalizations*); and secondly, those that identify *specific* understanding and findings of an in-depth nature.

In the first category, generalizations are statements about what prevails in the world *at large* in relation to a particular issue. That is, the research problem and the resultant methodology will produce outcomes that can be applied to or will belong to all other similar units within a domain. Thus a properly constructed representative sample in a survey produces results which will be reflected in all other units even though these have not been specifically part of the sample. Examples of research problems that address *generalisms* can be found in statements or questions such as:

- What are consumer attitudes (about/on/in relation to/etc.) . . . ?
- How many people (do/behave in/own/have done/etc.) . . . ?
- What are the differences (in/in relation to/opinions of/etc.) . . . ?
- Who did what in the past? How many?
- Who will do what in the future? How many?

Essentially, this kind of research problem/question will require a methodology which reaches a large number of respondents since much of the outcome is a quantification of the world in question (Daft and Weick 1983). Invariably the main research method will incorporate some kind of survey method in gleaning the data.

On the other hand, research problems concerned with seeking a specific understanding usually seek this understanding about a small number or a single phenomenon. Typical examples are issues concerned with marketing in a specific context or situation. Such circumstances require in-depth analysis of a single or specific case (group of people, company or industry) and the context in which that company operates. Similarly, if the research is concerned with understanding the way in which marketing happens, or the processes behind an aspect of marketing, it is likely that these can best be determined by focusing upon a single case or a small number of cases. Deep understanding will require methodologies such as in-depth interviews and analysis of a few sources, which will achieve the appropriate amount and type of data (Patton 1990).

Thus the nature of the research problem, founded upon a strong justification, requires an appropriate methodology for gathering the data. As such, it is useful to give consideration to possible methodologies at an early stage of the research since it is important to assess whether the data *can* be gathered as well as *how* it will be gathered.

Summary

This chapter considered how to identify and design a research problem. In discussing the early stages of research development, justification of a research problem was considered in terms of looking at topical areas of interest for research, searching for areas of marketing deficiency, and considering a research topic in a specific context.

We discussed the value and purpose of using the academic literature for the initial justification of a research problem, the use of research assumptions and hypotheses or propositions, and the relationship between justification and the research problem. Finally some broad directions were given in relation to how to choose an appropriate research method for different types of research problems.

The next chapter deals with the differences and similarities in research that is carried out for different constituents: academics, businesses and practitioners.

LEARNING QUESTIONS

What factors might be taken into account in justifying a research problem?

Outline, in brief, research which might consider:

- a topical aspect of marketing
- an aspect of marketing deficiency
- a specific context of marketing

In terms of value and purpose, what constitutes a research topic?
How can literature be used to justify a research problem?
Outline what you understand by research assumptions, hypotheses and propositions.
The research method should be appropriate for addressing the research problem. Discuss.

References

Balabanis, G., Stables, R.E. and Phillips, H.C. (1997) 'Market Orientation on the Top 200 British Charity Organizations and its Impact upon Performance', *European Journal of Marketing*, 31(7–8), 583–584.

Borg, W.R. and Gall, M.D. (1989) *Educational Research: An Introduction*, Longman, New York.

Carson, D. (1990) 'Some Exploratory Models for Assessing Small Firms' Marketing Performance (A Qualitative Approach)', *European Journal of Marketing*, 24(11), 1–51.

Carson, D., Gilmore, A. and Maclaran, P. (1998) 'Customer or Profit Focus: An Alternative Perspective', *Journal of Marketing: Applied Marketing Science*, 4(1), ISSN 1355–2538, internet journal.

Coviello, N.E., Brodie, R.J. and Munro, H.J. (1997) 'Understanding Contemporary Marketing: Development of a Classification Scheme', *Journal of Marketing Management*, 13, 501–522.

Curtis, D.C.A. and Murthy, K.S.R. (1999) 'Restructuring and Economic Growth in OECD Countries: 1964–1992', *Eastern Economic Journal*, 25(1), 17–30.

Daft, R. and Weick, K. (1983) 'Toward a Model of Organizations as Interpretation Systems', *Academy of Management Review*, 8, 284–295.

Emory, C.W. and Cooper, D.R. (1991) *Business Research Methods*, Homewood, Irwin.

Francis, H. (1998) 'The Research Process', in N. Graves and V. Varma (eds), *Working for a Doctorate: A Guide for the Humanities and Social Sciences*, 2nd edition, Routledge, London, pp. 18–34.

Greenley, G.E. and Bayus, B.L. (1994) 'Marketing Planning Processes in UK and US Companies', *Journal of Strategic Marketing*, 2, 140–154.

Gronroos, C. (1996) 'Relationship Marketing: Strategic and Tactical Implications', *Management Decision*, 34(3), 5–14.

Hisrich, R.D. (1986) *Entrepreneurship, Intrapreneurship and Venture Capital*, D.C. Heath, Lexington, MA.

Jankowicz, A.D. (1995) *Business Research Projects*, Chapman and Hall, London.

Leedy, P. (1989) *Practical Research*, Macmillan, New York.

Lindsay, D. (1995) *A Guide to Scientific Writing*, Longman, Melbourne.

Nataraajan, R., Henthorne, T.L. and LaTour, M.S. (1998) 'Reinforcing the Importance of the Marketing Practitioner–Marketing Academic Interface', *American Business Review*, 16(2), 109–112.

Parasuraman, A., Zeithaml, V. and Berry, L.L. (1988) 'SERVQUAL: A Multiple-item Scale for Measuring Consumer Perceptions of Service Quality', *Journal of Retailing*, 64(1), 12–35.

Patton, M.Q. (1990) *Qualitative Evaluation and Research Methods*, Sage Publications, Newbury Park, CA.

Pelham, A.M. (1997) 'Mediating Influences on the Relationship between Market Orientation and Profitability in Small Industrial Firms', *Journal of Marketing Theory and Practice*, 5(3), 55–76.

Perry, C. (1998) 'A Structured Approach for Presenting Theses', *Australasian Marketing Journal*, 6(1), 63–86.

Phillips, E.M. and Pugh, D.S. (1994) *How to Get a Ph.D.*, Open University Press, Milton Keynes.

Robson, C. (1993) *Real World Research*, Blackwell, Oxford.

Saunders, M., Lewis, P. and Thornhill, A. (1997) *Research Methods for Business Students*, Financial Times Management, London.

Storey, D. J. (1994) *Understanding the Small Business Sector*, Routledge, London.

Varadarajan, P.R. (1996) 'From the Editor: Reflections on Research and Publishing', *Journal of Marketing*, 60, October, 3–6.

4   Academic, Business and Practitioner Research

This chapter considers the scope of research in marketing (as opposed to research *per se*), from the perspective of *who* does marketing research; who or what is it done for; and what is its chief purpose. In discussing these issues three constituencies of research in marketing are examined:

- *academic* research in marketing, that is, research carried out by academe;
- *business* research in marketing: research carried out by and for the business profession (either marketing research commissioned by business managers or that carried out by the marketing department in an organization); and
- *practitioner* research in marketing, more correctly termed *information gathering*, which is carried out by marketing practitioners, managers and marketing business people, that is, *individual* market managers.

A key aspect about research in marketing is who actually requires information, the desired cognitive perception, and for what purpose. In the broad sense, it is argued here that most research in marketing (using this term in its widest sense with regard to its purpose) is carried out by all three constituencies.

Different Perspectives of Research in Marketing

It could be argued that the three constituencies of marketing research cover many of the same issues in terms of scope and focus. Whilst this may be true at the general, conceptual and definitional level, there is a strong difference in perspective and emphasis. We can draw on some analogies to clarify this assertion and to emphasize the different positions of the three constituencies:

- *Science or art* – Without returning to the quagmire of this debate beyond our positional comments in Chapter 1, it is enough to say that a scientific approach will carry rigour, discipline, validity, and so on. An artistic approach may not, but instead may be creative, spontaneous, and free of strictures. It is not unreasonable to argue that much academic and business research in marketing must attain some form of scientific rigour. By implication, it may be that practitioner information gathering in marketing does not.

- *Fingerprints and people* – Fingerprints are unique, but fingers are essentially the same the world over. Human beings are human beings but they are different in a myriad of ways, physically and culturally. In the same way research in marketing is both one and diverse.
- *General and specific* – As we have alluded to above, all marketing research is 'one' at the general, conceptual, definitional level but it can also be uniquely specific to the particular situation and as such, may appear to be very different in scope and content.

The point of outlining these analogies is this: research in marketing is recognizable as marketing research regardless of who does it and for what purpose it is carried out. However, although it can be argued that each piece of research is unique it is contended that there are several strong and different perspectives on research in marketing. This difference is recognized by Brindberg and Hirshman (1986), and Saunders et al. (1997), who identify the different emphases of academic research and business research. This chapter goes further and argues that there is also a difference in perspective and emphasis in relation to marketing practitioners. The academic constituency is strong and well documented along the lines discussed above. This constituency is *positioned* in relation to business marketing research and practitioner marketing information gathering in Figure 4.1 (refer also to the note at the end of this chapter).

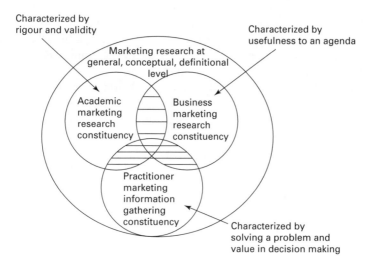

Figure 4.1 *Scope of marketing research*

It is worth emphasizing that before carrying out any research the research problem must be defined clearly. In doing this, the research approach will be influenced by the person who has defined the research problem. Thus, the belief, perception and understanding of a managerial research problem would be different from the perspectives of an owner-manager, a business practitioner and an academic researcher.

Whilst research in marketing is one domain, the perspective and emphasis of each of the three constituencies are different in terms of the style and type of marketing research required. The dimensions, characteristics, style and emphasis of academic research, business marketing research and practitioner marketing research are reviewed briefly below.

Academic Research in Marketing

Academic research is scholarly research carried out by academics. The belief, perspectives and perceptions of academic researchers will be different from those of business researchers and practitioner information gathering.

In the field of marketing, academic research could be called 'research in marketing' as well as 'marketing research': these terms are considered here as meaning the same and are used interchangeably throughout. Generally, the purpose of academic marketing research is to expand knowledge about marketing both in terms of theory and practice. Thus, such research outcomes might hope to provide some general principles and/or findings destined for publication, teaching and wider dissemination. Such research is carried out by qualified academics or students of marketing and is characterized by *rigour and validity*. Indeed much traditional academic research seeks not only to be objective but to be neutral; it is non-interventionist and non-partisan. Gibb (1992) in a broad review of the academic literature and a similar review of the approaches taken by academic grant-giving bodies, revealed a number of assumptions about what constitutes quality academic research. Amongst these assumptions was that research is best carried out by someone with deep traditional disciplinary strengths; and that research undertaken as consultancy has less value than that undertaken with a research grant from an independent foundation. Indeed in marketing academic circles *pure* or *basic* research still tends to draw more public or quasi-public funding than research of an 'applied' or specific nature.

Considering marketing specifically, it is possible in academic research to choose from a range of topics that come into the broad domain of marketing. The refinement of a research topic will be based on reviewing appropriate foundation literatures that serve to highlight the research problem. This will create the foundation for determining the research aims and objectives. The scope and range of potential topics is immense, and such topics can be interlinked in a multiplicity of ways. Readers will recall we have discussed these issues more fully in Chapters 2 and 3.

In brief, it is reasonable to define academic research as having rigour and validity. Further, it is clear that academic research can choose from a wide variety of research methodologies depending on its purpose. So academic research in the broad sense may utilize either quantitative and/or qualitative methodologies and still seek, indeed require, rigour and validity. In so doing it is likely to be *positioned* differently to either business or practitioner research. Figure 4.2, showing the positional sense of academic research, illustrates this point by presenting two continua.

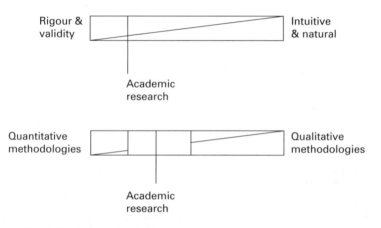

Figure 4.2 *'Positional' sense of academic research*

Thus *most* academic research, in the general sense, will be predominantly quantitative in displaying rigour and validity; and academic research that uses qualitative methodologies will still give strong credence to rigour and validity. This of course is appropriate given the purpose, function and justification of academic research.

Business Research in Marketing

The belief, perspectives and perceptions of business researchers will be unique to business, and different from academic research and practitioner information gathering. That is, they will conceptualize research problems in a different way and choose research approaches that may be different from those that the other two constituents would choose. An initial understanding of the differentiation between business and academic research in marketing can be grasped by revisiting the characteristics of academic marketing research in the context of business research. A marketing academic research topic is a comprehensive piece of research on an aspect of marketing. The comprehensiveness is determined by a depth of study that may be founded on substantial and extensive consideration of prior research represented by appropriate literature. Similarly, the research progression may be expected to lead to significant outcomes that go beyond describing a certain phenomenon but also break new frontiers.

Business marketing research often focuses on topics such as writing a marketing plan, carrying out a feasibility study or examining a specific company problem (Emory 1976; Zikmund 1991). Although these may benefit greatly from the academic marketing research discipline's rigour and validity, in themselves they fall short of being academic research topics simply because of the lack of focus on elements of *depth and discovery* (Johns and Lee-Ross 1998).

Highlighting these characteristics of academic marketing research enables a clearer understanding of what concerns business and indeed practitioner marketing research. Sometimes academic marketing research may have an *applied* emphasis and focus, when it is carried out by, or on behalf of, a specific industry, market or business enterprise (Easterby-Smith et al. 1991; Hedrick et al. 1993). It may be about consumers or about business activities. As such its objectives may be to solve some specific problems or issues which will be agreed with the funding organization, which is likely to be from an industry context (Jankowicz 1995).

Such applied research is deemed here to be business research even though it is carried out by academics rather than business enterprises themselves. It is similar to the research carried out by industry/commercial *consultants*; in this case the consultants are academics. However, although it is *paid-for* research and has a specific purpose designated by the business, it will have academic or *scientific* foundations and frameworks. These are necessary in order to justify the rigour and validity of the research method and findings.

There is a whole industry that conforms to this constituency: the market research industry. Whilst much of the marketing research performed in this industry is not as rigorously examined for *correctness* as most academic research, it nevertheless must demonstrate some scientific objectiveness in order to have rigour and validity and therefore justify the cost of such research (Chisnall 1997; McDaniel Jr. and Gates 1999). Even so, the topics for this research are almost always industry and company specific and they will often contribute to marketing strategies and plans required by a business enterprise (Cooper and Schindler 1998).

Whilst contribution to marketing strategies and plans is an obvious *purpose* of business enterprise marketing research, it is by no means the only one. Indeed, many of the reasons for business marketing research are in themselves differentiators of this constituency. Much business marketing research is carried out for *political* purposes within an enterprise (Aaker et al. 1995; Deshpande and Zaltman 1982). For example, managers often commission marketing research in order to use the findings as leverage for extra funds; to justify the validity of prior decisions; to gain support for a new idea; or change company direction. Also, such research may serve simply as a 'comfort' blanket for the manager, simply to monitor events, to ensure things are stable and in control (Birn 1992). Little, if any academic marketing research will be carried out with such a purpose in mind. Rigorous academic researchers would wish not to be associated with any research project that sought to establish results that suited a purpose.

It is argued here that such political (internal) purposes lead to business research having a distinctive emphasis and aim. The stress on how the research is carried out is different, with less attention to rigour and validity and more focus on *usefulness to an agenda* (Hague 1992).

In the context of this discussion we can 'position' business marketing research a little nearer the centre of the continua in our model (see Figure 4.3).

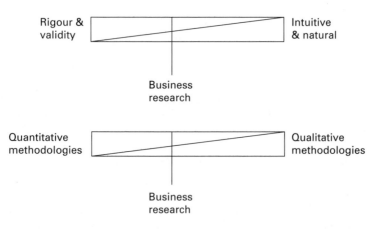

Figure 4.3 *'Positional' sense of business research*

In summary, we recognize that academic research texts and scholarly research work concentrate on business practitioners and academic researchers because they have a presupposition that they have a higher level of abstraction, are well-versed in research methods and have knowledge, expertise and resources in marketing.

Practitioner Information Gathering in Marketing

We purposely assert in this chapter that there is a third major constituency of marketing research which is different from both academic and business research, that is, practitioner information gathering. Practitioner information gathering is defined here as a process carried out by the *individual* practitioner or his/her company. It has a very specific purpose: to help *solve an immediate or ongoing problem*. The findings and results must be relevant and actionable for the practitioner/owner-manager.

The belief, perspectives and perceptions of the practitioner will be unique to his/her business, and different from academic and business researchers. That is, they will conceptualize research problems in a different way and choose research approaches that may be different from those that the other two constituents would choose.

The motivation for practitioner research is to enable the survival and development of the enterprise. Most marketing practitioners actually do marketing information gathering as part of their everyday business activity. There are several key characteristics that differentiate practitioner marketing information gathering from the other two constituencies discussed here. Practitioners can learn in a multiplicity of ways: by observing others, experimentation and research.

Marketing practitioners intuitively, naturally and qualitatively gather information. The term *gathering information* is probably more relevant to practitioners than the term 'marketing research'. However, they gather and use this information as they intuitively scan the market. They use a variety of apparently unconnected approaches to piece together a picture of market information that serves as a foundation for decision making. Much of this is based upon the underlying competencies and networks that marketing practitioners develop and use for marketing research.

Practitioners gather marketing information naturally and intuitively

Market research, as an information gathering activity, requires organization, planning and structure. Practitioners who do market research or gather information will have a market research resource of some kind, ranging from simple data gathering *systems* to personnel devoted solely to the function of information gathering. More often enterprises will commission specialist market research firms to do specific market research studies as required. Such a description depicts market research as a *formal* function of marketing with a clear purpose and role. However, it would be unrealistic to assume that this is the only way in which practitioners gather information.

Marketing practitioners use a variety of apparently unconnected approaches to piece together a picture of the market place. They use a *natural* way to understand or make sense of the human environment. For example, they may start with a hunch, react to an event or an anecdote which raises their interest in a particular issue, new idea or market. This will cause the practitioner to begin to look around for confirmation or contradiction of the developing hunch. S/he will begin to observe the market place, activities and interactions, and will talk to others in their social/work environment.

Let us illustrate how practitioners gather marketing information with a hypothetical scenario. Picture a number of typically occurring events in a day in the life of a marketing practitioner. On the routine trip to work every morning a practitioner passes the premises of one of his/her major competitors. One morning s/he notices a large billboard on the front wall of the competitor's offices illustrating a new product promotion. A mental note is made of the promotion details and his/her thought process begins to plan how to react. This marketing practitioner has intuitively and naturally gathered some market/competitor information and is opportunistically forming a competitive strategy.

In this way marketing practitioners take a naturalistic, even artistic, approach to gathering market information. The use of the term *artistic* implicitly acknowledges that artistic observations and actions are, according to Anderson (1983), 'always interpreted in the context of a priori knowledge'. This is supported by Kuhn (1970) when he states: 'What a man sees depends both upon what he looks at and also upon what his previous visual-conceptual experience has taught him to see'. Artistic in this sense relates to the notion that practitioner research will be uniquely created by the individual and related specifically to his/her business.

Therefore practitioners often carry out their own market research (information gathering), but they do it intuitively and with flexibility, and would not call it market research. Practitioner information gathering will use any method at its disposal, regardless of correctness and compatibility of method. Typically, a practitioner will gather information from a variety of sources and in a variety of ways. Concepts, rigour and validity seldom enter into his/her mind-frame. Instead the practitioner will have a *feel* for the value and usefulness of information and its source and will intuitively accept or reject information as it is gathered. Much of this information gathering may well be subconscious. A key characteristic of practitioner market research is that it is gathered haphazardly, spontaneously, opportunistically and personally. The interpretation of findings will be perceived in terms of significance and meaning, uniquely by the practitioner in the context of his/her particular business. As in art, interpretation is in the *eye of the beholder*, whether this is the artist who created the piece or the viewer of the piece; that is, an entirely personal approach for the purpose of understanding. In doing all of this, practitioners make use of their own marketing competencies and their networks. Here are some practitioner owner-managers describing how they gather information from their own perspectives:

'I will get involved in any area and I quite like to do that because that keeps me informed and involved with what's going on . . .'

'I have a notion that there is going to be a boom in our kind of business and I don't know why . . . but just listening. Sitting on committees and listening to people in high places talking to each other or talking to me.'

'it's not down to what you say. If I see a man's premises, I know what he can do and if he sees my place, he knows what I can do as well. I think that sometimes tells the story more than all the talk.'

'it is good to talk to businesses of your own size and listen to their problems. I believe there is a lot to be learned from businesses talking to businesses. Making matches and bars of chocolate at the end of the day is similar. The processes, the purchasing, the selling, the pricing . . . all that is relevant to any type of business'.

Practitioners use their networks and competencies to gather information

It is obvious from our examples above that practitioner managers use networks as an aid in collecting information that entails research for their particular organizations' needs. Networking happens haphazardly and informally; it is often spontaneous or reactive to events and opportunities; there is no overtly structured approach. To happen at all it must be interactive and interchangeable, in an individualistic and highly focused way.

Networking is a naturally inherent aspect of practitioner marketing research or information gathering, particularly in relation to marketing decisions. This is so because practitioners must go outside the firm's physical confines in order to do business and this business is a market-led activity. Thus, practitioners are gathering information through all their normal communication activities, such as interacting and participating in social, business and trade activities. Some of the characteristics of *researching by networking* are based around people-orientated activities; it is informal; often discreet; interactive; interchangeable; integrated; habitual; reactive; individualistic and highly focused on the enterprise. The way in which researching by networking is carried out is often predetermined by industry behaviours and norms through regular or irregular meeting occasions and industry activities, or in just doing routine business.

Over time practitioners develop competencies in gathering information. In doing so they will gather information in a more discriminatory manner, and become more adept at interpreting market related data. Some practitioner marketing research competencies are more fundamental than others. Core marketing research competencies consist of *knowledge, experience, judgement and communication* skills (Carson et al. 1995). Thus, the process of practitioner marketing research is that of gathering information naturally and intuitively whilst doing everyday business. Much of the information is gathered from the practitioner's network sources and his/her involvement, whether passive, reactive or proactive, with a variety of networks. The evaluation and manipulation of the process, and the use of networks and information flows is dependent upon

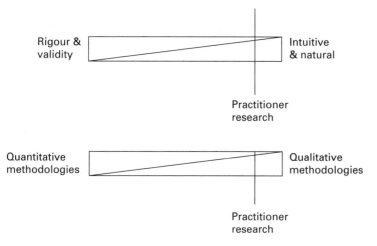

Figure 4.4 *'Positional' sense of practitioner information gathering*

the skills learned from experience. The positional sense of practitioner information gathering is illustrated in Figure 4.4.

The lower continuum positions practitioner information at the qualitative methodologies extreme. This is because the characteristics of practitioner information gathering, principally intuitive and natural, coupled with the subsequent interpretations which are individually and holistically unique and personal, make practitioner information essentially qualitative in its inherent methodologies. This is compounded by the fact that much of practitioner information gathering may not be recognized as research *per se*. Instead it is more *a way of doing business* involving qualitative interpretations and assessments towards making decisions.

Summary

The scope and nature of marketing research and gathering marketing information is immense. Marketing research is very different depending upon its purpose and constituency. Appropriate marketing research can therefore only be evaluated and chosen when considered in the light of the constituency, the context and the perspectives and perceptions of the person or organization requiring the research.

In this chapter we have described three such constituencies. The academic and business marketing research constituencies are well documented and are founded upon similar principles of scientific social science method-ological rigour and validity; indeed this book is largely a demonstration of this in the context of qualitative marketing research. Slight variance can be identified by characterizing academic marketing research as indeed being founded upon rigour and validity, whilst business marketing research can be characterized by its usefulness to an agenda which is largely directed by internal, managerial and organizational circumstances within a company, as well as providing information.

The third constituency, practitioner marketing research or information gathering, is not measured by the confines and characteristics of the other two constituencies. Its primary characteristic is to do and use marketing research information gathering for arriving at solutions and aiding decision making that ensures and enhances the survival and wellbeing of the enterprise. As such, practitioner information gathering is different to the other two constituencies. Although it is performed by a vast constituency of marketing practitioners, its value and contribution to business enterprises is important.

What is the value of the conceptual framework offered here in Figures 4.1–4.4? Academic research often acknowledges that there is a void between marketing academics and marketing practitioners. Brown explicitly states this when he writes:

> if anything, our unending search for the impossible intellectual dream (of finding 'the holy grail of marketing scientific theory') has only served to distance us from, and diminished our standing in the eyes of, those front-line foot-soldiers who battle day and daily in the marketing management trenches. (1996: 257)

The purpose of drawing attention to this third constituency of research/ information gathering in marketing is that its characteristics are not too dissimilar from the inherent characteristics and benefits of qualitative research. At the *general* level qualitative research methodologies can be recognized as inherent to practitioner research. Equally therefore, practitioner research can consciously incorporate more of the formal frameworks of qualitative research methodologies without compromising any intuitive and natural elements of the everyday process. Thus, students of qualitative research methodologies will find it *natural* to apply such concepts and methods in practitioner research and in doing business. Further, qualitative academic researchers can draw on many of the practitioner research characteristics in attempting to gain meaningful insights and understanding of marketing management phenomena.

LEARNING QUESTIONS

What is the essence of the three different perspectives of research in marketing?

What characteristic *strengths* does each perspective have?

How can practitioner characteristics aid qualitative academic researchers?

Note

The focus of this discussion on the three constituencies is on the *non*-shaded areas of Figure 4.1. It is recognized that aspects of academic and business research (and to a lesser degree, practitioner research) occur in the shaded overlapping between the constituencies. Some aspects of consumer research are not necessarily in the academic 'scientific' tradition but nevertheless achieve rigour and validity through systematic theoretically driven interpretation frameworks. For example, academic research: phenomenology (Thompson et al. 1989); semiotics (Mick 1986); similarly, business research: psychodynamics (Cooper 1991); semiotics (Valentine and Evans 1993) and phenomenology (Ueltzhoffer and Ascheberg 1999). However, in the fuller scope of marketing research, the bulk of research occurs outside these specifics of the shaded areas of the model.

References

Aaker, D.A., Kumar, V. and Day, G.S. (1995) *Marketing Research*, 5th edition, Wiley, New York.

Anderson, P.F. (1983) 'Marketing, Scientific Progress, and Scientific Method', *Journal of Marketing*, 47, Fall, 18–31.

Birn, R. (1992) *The Effective Use of Market Research: A Guide for Management*, 2nd edition, Kogan Page, London.

Brindberg, D. and Hirshman, E.C. (1986) 'Multiple Orientations for the Conduct of Marketing Research: An Analysis of the Academic/Practitioner Distinction', *Journal of Marketing*, 50, October, 161–173.

Brown, S. (1996) 'Art or Science? Fifty Years of Marketing Debate', *Journal of Marketing Management*, 12(4), 243–267.

Carson, D.J., Cromie, S., McGowan, P. and Hill, J. (1995) *Marketing and Entrepreneurship in SMEs*, Prentice-Hall, London.

Chisnall, P.M. (1997) *Marketing Research*, 5th edition, McGraw-Hill, London.

Cooper, D.R. and Schindler, P.S. (1998) *Business Research Methods*, 6th edition, Irwin, Boston.

Cooper, P. (1991) 'Comparison between the UK and the US: The Qualitative Dimension', *Journal of the Market Research Society*, 31(4), 509–520.

Deshpande, R. and Zaltman, G. (1982) 'Factors Affecting the Use of Market Research Information: A Path Analysis', *Journal of Marketing Research*, 19(1), 14–31.

Easterby-Smith, M., Thorpe, R. and Lowe, A. (1991) *Management Research: An Introduction*, Sage, London.

Emory, W. (1976) *Business Research Methods*, Irwin, Homewood.

Gibb, A.A. (1992) 'Can Academe Achieve Quality in Small Firms Policy Research?', *Entrepreneurship and Regional Development*, 4, 127–144.

Hague, P.N. (1992) *The Industrial Market Research Handbook*, 3rd edition, Kogan Page, London.

Hedrick, T.E., Bickmann, L. and Rog, D.J. (1993) *Applied Research Design: A Practical Guide*, Sage, Newbury Park, CA.

Jankowicz, A.D. (1995) *Business Research Projects*, 2nd edition, International Thompson Business Press, London.

Johns, N. and Lee-Ross, D. (1998) *Research Methods in Service Industry Management*, Cassell, London.

Kuhn, T.S. (1970) *The Structure of Scientific Revolutions*, University of Chicago Press, Chicago.

McDaniel Jr., C. and Gates, R. (1999) *Contemporary Marketing Research*, 4th edition, South-Western College Publishing, Cincinnati.

Mick, D.G. (1986) 'Consumer Research and Semiotics: Exploring the Morphology of Signs, Signals and Significance', *Journal of Consumer Research*, 13, September, 196–213.

Saunders, M.N.K., Lewis, P. and Thornhill, A. (1997) *Research Methods for Business Students*, Financial Times Management, London.

Thompson, C., Locander, W. and Pollio, H. (1989) 'Putting Customer Experience back into Consumer Research: The Philosophy and Method of Existentialist-Phenomenology', *Journal of Consumer Research*, 16, September, 133–145.

Ueltzhoffer, J. and Ascheberg, C. (1999) 'Transnational Consumer Cultures and Social Mileus', *Journal of the Market Research Society*, 41(1), 47–59.

Valentine, V. and Evans, M. (1993) 'The Dark Side of the Onion: Rethinking the Meanings of "Rational" and "Emotional Responses"', *Journal of the Market Research Society*, 35(2), 125–144.

Zikmund, W.G. (1991) *Exploring Marketing Research*, 4th edition, Dryden Press, Chicago.

Part II   QUALITATIVE RESEARCH
           METHODOLOGIES

5   Justification of a Qualitative Research Methodology

This chapter takes the foundations introduced in Part I and illustrates how they will impact upon the choice of a methodology for carrying out research in marketing and marketing management. Initially we focus on the range and scope of predominantly qualitative methodologies and their position in relation to the positivist/interpretive continuum we have described in Chapter 1 and how this impacts upon how research is carried out and analysed. The chapter then considers the characteristics and value of qualitative methodologies for research in this domain.

The Range and Scope of Qualitative Research Methodologies

The range and scope of research methods is vast (Tesch 1990). This is not diminished when focusing only on qualitative methodologies. Indeed, many positivist (quantitative) methodologies can be used qualitatively. In considering the range and scope of qualitative methodologies, it is useful to consider both the characteristics and purpose of these methodologies.

Characteristics and purpose of qualitative methodologies

The characteristics and purpose of the qualitative research methodologies described and defined in the remainder of Part II (Chapters 6–11) of this book are influenced by how they 'fit' with the overall research philosophies described in Chapter 1. Figure 5.1 illustrates methodologies in the context of research philosophies ranging across the continuum of positivist and interpretivist positions as described in Chapter 1 (Figures 1.1 and 1.2, pp. 8, 14). As indicated above, all of these methodologies can be used qualitatively, but the methodologies shown in italics, those which are primarily positivist, are outside the remit of this book. As we have established in Part I, the focus of this book is on the more *relativist/ interpretivist* methodologies; therefore Part II includes chapters on in-depth/convergent interviewing, case-based research, focus group interviewing, observation studies, ethnographic studies, grounded theory, and action research and learning.

Figure 5.1 is set in a similar framework as those introduced in Chapter 1 in terms of illustrating positivism/post-positivism at one end of a continuum and interpretivism/relativism at the other. Within this framework of overall philosophical positions we have 'positioned' a number of relevant methodologies for doing research in a marketing or business context. These are placed in relation to their overall research approach, either predominantly interpretivist or positivist. Methodologies that allow and encourage a more interpretivist approach are placed at the right side of the figure; all of these can be described as emergent studies in that they are developed over time and tend not to be one-off time specific. They can be used in any combination and may also be combined *holistically* in constructing in-depth cases of specific phenomena, such as an individual firm's marketing profiles. As we move along the continuum to the left, the methodologies allow some positivist characteristics, but can still be used as predominantly interpretivist approaches. The characteristics and

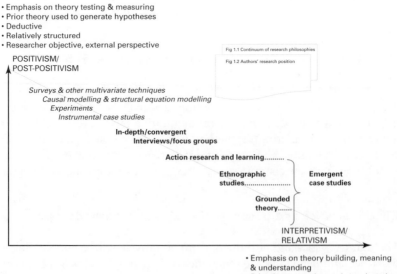

Figure 5.1 *Methodologies in the context of research philosophies*

purpose of positivist and interpretivist qualitative research are considered briefly below.

Characteristics of positivist and interpretivist research

In positivist research methodologies there is likely to be an emphasis on theory testing whereby existing theory will be tested in a specific research context: for example by taking a theoretical construct such as the marketing planning process and testing its validity in practice, using a controlled sample of designated companies. Taking the Parasuraman et al. (1985) *Service Quality Gap Model* of service marketing and testing its validity in a specific service industry context such as a five star hotel service, would be another example of 'testing' theory.

Positivist methodologies will also be concerned with objective precision in measuring outcomes. It is important that outcomes should be measured with meaningful statistical significance. Positivist methodologies will also draw on the proven foundation of prior theory to generate theories that they will test, that is, hypotheses. So for example, in addressing an aspect of cause and effect in marketing, a research hypothesis or proposition for an aspect of advertising research might state that, 'All other things being equal, an increase in advertising activity will stimulate new sales.' Theory building from prior work is not usually given as much emphasis and explicit focus as the theory testing phase of positivist research projects. The converse applies in interpretivist research projects.

Positivist research tends to be (relatively) structured in order to achieve the rigour and validity required for theory testing and measurement. Equally, structure will allow the researcher to maintain the *distance* perspective of objectivity that is appropriate for positivist research, most probably through the administration of the chosen research instrument, for example a very structured, forced choice, self-completion questionnaire used in a random sample survey.

Contrast these positivist characteristics with interpretivist research methodological characteristics. Interpretivism methodologies seek to 'build' theory as a result of empirical insights so the theory building phase of a research project is given explicit and careful attention. Prior theory may be used as a foundation and may be introduced at appropriate stages throughout the research study (in some studies relevant prior theories may be relatively limited). So for example, interpretivist research into aspects of the marketing planning process will seek to determine actual and specific planning processes in a few enterprises. Prior theory may guide or loosely frame the research but the research is not about testing this prior theory; instead it is about seeking an actual reality in a specific situation. If such research can confirm, or otherwise, a theoretical construct of *actual* marketing planning processes, in a number of cases, then theory building is occurring.

In brief the main purpose of interpretivist methodologies is to achieve substantive meaning and understanding of *how* and *why* questions in relation to the phenomena under investigation. This will require substantial inductive reasoning at any stage of the study.

Interpretivist research is often predominantly semi-structured, or sometimes entirely unstructured, in gathering empirical data, for example a researcher's ethnographic immersion in a longitudinal study of building a relationship marketing programme. The relationship building process may incorporate a variety of events that could not be predicted and therefore structured prior to the study. Clearly, such research *involves* the researcher as an integral component of the study, whereby s/he may guide and develop the research. Although our example is an ethnographic study, this kind of relatively unstructured involvement may occur in parts of, all, or a variety of other interpretivist methodologies such as those positioned in Figure 5.1.

This brief description of characteristic variances between positivist and interpretivist methodologies, coupled with our earlier discussions in Part I, serves to emphasize the value of a clear and firm research position in terms of the type of research problem that needs to be investigated. It reiterates the purpose and importance of qualitative research methodologies for specific purposes within the field of marketing research. Let us consider this further in terms of the *value* of interpretive qualitative research methodologies.

Value of Interpretive Qualitative Research Methodologies for Marketing

Here we build on the research position explained in Chapter 1 in the context of doing research in marketing by focusing on the relevance and value of interpretive research approaches. Interpretive qualitative research methods are valuable for in-depth understanding of phenomena in the marketing domain, in managerial and consumer contexts.

An outline of the value of qualitative research is given in order to demonstrate how qualitative research methods are appropriate for the marketing domain. The fundamental reason is the need to understand phenomena surrounding marketing. In seeking understanding, qualitative research methods based on the ethos of an interpretive philosophy serve marketing management decision making better than many other research methods that provide information without guidance. By the very nature of the subject, managerial performance and activities within organizations cannot be adequately studied within neatly arranged compartments in isolated and artificial settings (Fetterman 1989; Mintzberg 1979; Van Maanen 1979). For example, Mintzberg strongly argues for the use of qualitative research methods in organizational contexts when he writes that:

Measuring in real organizational terms means first of all getting out into the field, into real organizations. Questionnaires often won't do. Nor will laboratory simulations . . . what is the use of describing a reality that has been invented? The evidence of our research – of interruptions and soft data and information overload – suggests that we do not yet understand enough about organizations to simulate their functioning in the laboratory. It is their inherent complexity and dynamic nature that characterize phenomena such as policy-making. Simplification squeezes out the very thing on which the research should focus. The qualitative research designs, on the other hand, permit the researcher to get close to the data, to know well all the individuals involved and observe and record what they do and say. (1979: 584)

Similarly Das (1983) argues that longitudinal, in-depth and open-ended research designs have become almost a necessity to capture the complex and multidimensional decision making patterns within organizations.

Let us consider some fundamental aspects of interpretivist (and qualitative) research in marketing.

The characteristics of qualitative research provide flexibility and suitability for use in the interpretation of a marketing management situation. This is particularly so when carrying out research in an organizational or business context. The specific merits of qualitative methods for interpretive research are discussed further below, such as their overall focus on in-depth understanding; examination without prior judgement; focusing on *why* and *how* in addition to *what*.

Essence of in-depth understanding

Qualitative data is typically open-ended and related to a specific temporal and spatial domain. Van Maanen defines qualitative methods as

an array of interpretive techniques which seek to describe, decode, translate and otherwise come to terms with the meaning, not the frequency, of certain more or less naturally occurring phenomena in the social world. (1979: 520)

The focus of many managerial research problems is on the unfolding of the process rather than the structure; and qualitative methods are particularly suitable as they combine the rational with the intuitive approach to knowledge. The aim of qualitative studies is to gain an in-depth understanding of a situation. In-depth understanding is based on researcher immersion in the phenomena to be studied, gathering data which provide a detailed description of events, situations and interaction between people and things, providing depth and detail (Patton 1980). It is concerned with things that really happen in organizations as researchers and people experience them.

Furthermore qualitative studies are crucial in the study of managerial performance and marketing activities within and by organizations, as these cannot be adequately studied in neatly arranged compartments in isolated and artificial settings.

Examination without prior judgement

To some extent interpretive studies are about carrying out research where at one extreme 'there is no theory under consideration and no hypothesis to test' (Eisenhardt 1989: 536). Interpretive studies involve some inductive reasoning, which is a logical process of establishing general propositions or frameworks based on prior theories/studies but should not be used to constrain the development of a research study. That is, these qualitative approaches lend themselves better than quantitative tools to the production of serendipitous findings and are in many cases broader and more holistic in perspective. In some instances,

> the statistical tools instead of acting as our servants have in fact become our masters, placing constraints not only on the research methodology and specific hypothesis, but on the very thinking process itself. (Das 1983: 302)

Because of this flexibility and open-mindedness, qualitative methods allow for a variety and mixture of interpretive techniques – for example, the techniques discussed in Part II of this book. All these techniques provide qualitative data which can, as Das argues, measure 'things that really happen . . . as they experience them' (Das 1983: 304). In this sense 'qualitative data are perhaps more idiographic than nomothetic in nature' (p. 302).

'Why' and 'how' as an addition to 'what'

Interpretive studies are concerned with reaching in-depth understanding; qualitative research methods are suitable for addressing questions of *how* and *why* things occur, whereas quantitative methods are more appropriate for answering what and how many questions. Qualitative research is suitable where the research emphasis is on in-depth understanding of how, why and in what context certain phenomena occur; and what impacts upon or influences such phenomena. It is most appropriate where the explanation and understanding of behaviour or activities matter more than specific measurements, for example, a politician may be alarmed at a sudden dip in his/her quantitative poll rating, but knowing what to do about it requires input from qualitative research concerning the reasons for the decline and the deep feelings of voters.

Conversely, quantitative research is more relevant where the research emphasis is on comparison, for example *what* questions answered and compared between different companies and industries. In this context quantitative measurements are used to assess the extent of such differences or similarities and generalizations are what matter: for example, whether a government or opposition candidate is ahead in an election campaign.

Trustworthiness of qualitative findings

Is interpretivist qualitative research trustworthy? How could a researcher be sure that his/her theory reflected the respondents' reality? Indeed, can any qualitative research be trusted? And if another researcher repeated a study, would the same theory be developed? How subjective was it? Would the theory hold for researchers using the same methodology in other regions or situations? *Trustworthiness* in qualitative research is discussed using the dimensions of credibility, dependability and conformability. These terms are addressed through sound and rigorous methodological progression. Qualitative empirical findings will gain validity from these dimensions because of careful assessment and use of prior theory at various stages of the research study, and as such are unlikely to become detached from the closeness of their proximity to aspects of marketing behaviour inherent in the domain itself.

Credibility, dependability and conformability all stem from:

- careful use, interpretation, examination and assessment of appropriate literature, whether it is through referencing conceptual frameworks, prior theory or empirical results;
- careful justification of the qualitative research methodologies employed in a study and specifically their appropriateness, merits and values, all of which will have substantial previous justification in the methodological literature;
- careful structuring of data analysis to ensure full and descriptive evaluation and assessment, particularly in relation to data of key significance. This analysis will be linked back to methodological frameworks (above), prior theory from the literature, and prior theory pertaining to significant findings. All of this can be constructed into a *criteria for analysis* specific to the research study which will aim to make the data analysis and subsequent conclusions *transparent* to the reader (see discussion later in the chapter).

Many authors have attempted to produce criteria to evaluate the credibility, dependability and conformability of qualitative findings, one of the best known examples being Strauss and Corbin's (1990) list of seven criteria to evaluate how well a grounded theory study has been done. In a more general sense we consider here criteria that could apply to many other interpretivist research studies in addition to grounded theory. Techniques suggested to improve the quality of research results of interpretivist research include Denzin and Lincoln (1994), Lincoln and

Guba (1985), Patton (1990), Pettigrew (1979), Wallendorf and Belk (1989), Zeithaml et al. (1993):

- researching in the field, that is, in the natural setting of the phenomena, for example, a respondent's own surroundings;
- using purposive or theoretical sampling rather than statistically random sampling, for example where interviewees might be chosen more because of their relevance than because they were representative;
- comparing results across different contexts such as different user types;
- depth and intimacy of interviewing, like one-to-one 'conversations/ discussions';
- prolonged and persistent observation, like observations of how consumers behaved across numerous/similar retail outlets and many time periods ;
- negative case analysis, that is, asking questions designed to find exceptions to a rule in a theory that therefore invalidate the 'rule';
- debriefing by peers to help researchers sort out in their minds what they have seen and heard, which helps guard against bias and produces new insights;
- maintaining journals or memos of what was done and thought throughout the research study;
- triangulation of data from several sources, such as different interviewees and newspaper cuttings, from different sites, and from different methods of collection and analysis, for example using observations *and* interview data;
- checks by members of the group, that is, asking respondents to comment on drafts about facts and *their* interpretations of those facts;
- independent audits;
- having a number of interviewers carry out interviews, followed by interviewers discussing the meaning and interpretation of the data;
- presenting the findings from a research study to the original respondents in a focus group meeting and then inviting respondents to comment and provide feedback and discussion in relation to the findings.

The last two of these can provide interesting insights as well as corroboration. Researchers may have spent weeks or months immersing themselves in the rich data of qualitative research, so it might be difficult to find an independent auditor of that data in a short time period. And if an auditor disagrees with the researcher's interpretation of some incidents, is their interpretation necessarily better than the researcher's? By the way, it is also useful to send a draft of the analysis section of the researcher's report to respondents and ask for their comments by a particular date. Researchers can then say that if they have not heard from the respondents by that date, they will assume that the facts and their interpretations of them in the draft are credible. Doing this helps establish the validity of the research (Yin 1994).

If all of these tests of trustworthiness are carried out should qualitative research try to justify itself through statistical generalizations, that is, be concerned about testing the theory *across a population*? The answer is no, because the results of qualitative research are a function of contexts and the theoretical sensitivity and skills of the researcher. Indeed much of its value is its context-based relevance and appropriateness. A qualitative research study could cover a wide variety of respondents and settings, to try to ensure that results are transferable across that wide range. But no study can be generalized beyond its own range. Generalization beyond the data in each study will have to wait for other research studies or for a statistical survey done later on. Thus each individual study must make clear what its range of contexts is, so that later researchers will know the boundaries beyond which they may want to move. However, it must be emphasized, generalizability is not an issue *within* qualitative research studies since qualitative research methodologies have been used precisely *because* of the need to gain meaning and *in-depth* understanding and this is difficult to achieve through any method that will also enable generalizability. The specificity of qualitative research virtually excludes generalizability and because of this it is not an issue. Theory building and theory testing may go hand in hand, but they are different, although qualitative research may provide the understanding that builds the theories that may *later* be tested for generalizability, if that is relevant.

Transparency of qualitative findings

What is more significant in qualitative research studies is clear and precise evidence of transparency. In every aspect of the research it is good to demonstrate this, as in many of the techniques outlined in the above list for improving the quality of qualitative studies. Transparency is needed most in the interpretation of findings, with clear descriptions and explanations of why a given interpretation is made. The validity of this transparency can be strengthened by linking the interpretation to prior theory and to any conceptual theory building in a study. Transparency is a vital dimension in the value of interpretive qualitative research methodologies used for research in dynamic marketing circumstances.

Summary

This chapter has explored the scope, parameters and value of qualitative research in marketing. In so doing, a description of qualitative research was constructed. We have built upon the wider discussion in Chapter 1 on *the philosophies of research*. Our research position has been underlined by focusing this chapter on qualitative *research in marketing* contexts.

Given that qualitative methods are an array of interpretive techniques, they allow flexibility and variety in the study of complex phenomena in dynamic or changing environments. In order to complete the discussion on the range of possible techniques and methodologies suitable for qualitative research, some techniques often useful in a marketing and business context are summarized here.

Some of the most commonly used qualitative methods include focus group discussions, surveys, observations, conversational records, content records and in-depth interviews. The use of one or more of these different

---

Box 5.1 *Variety of qualitative methods*

An example of how qualitative methods are used in an interpretive context, and adapted from social science tradition:

Observations in business context can focus on: what impacts upon behaviour, how managers or staff act and react in certain situations, how behaviour and activities relate to or match what managers and staff say. Observations can be used to delve beyond opinions and what managers and staff say they do, and focus on actual behaviour. This will result in the collection of information on behaviour in relation to doing marketing and the participation and involvement of managers and staff.

Participation in company meetings can allow data to be gathered through observation and taking notes on how items on an agenda are discussed. For example, areas of interest might be: the importance and priorities given to some topics and not others, the criteria used to differentiate between important and less important issues, different managers' positions, opinions and recommendations in relation to each topic, and who has the final say in decision making.

Content analysis of company materials can be useful for determining the history and development of a company or departments within a company; the promotional activity and messages of the company and how they have changed over time; and the development of the product and service range.

Small surveys are useful for focusing on a number of marketing issues in researching either consumers or managers. For example, a small survey with several 'key' informants, such as business customers, in relation to aspects of the service delivery offered by a company would indicate what the most loyal or major customers liked or disliked about the service process.

Conversational analysis can be a good technique to use with different levels of staff in a marketing context. For example, conversations with service frontline staff and supervisors regarding the perception of their roles, such as dealing with customers and handling customers' complaints can help build understanding of the feelings and reactions of staff delivering the service and lead to insights in relation to improving service delivery.

Source: adapted from Gilmore and Carson 1996

methods will allow data to be gathered on verbal occurrences, visually recorded occurrences, written reports and documentation, and researcher experiential knowledge within a specific context. Box 5.1 offers a description of some qualitative research techniques or methods that are used in a company specific circumstance designed to use a variety of complementary methods to reach meaningful understanding of marketing management issues.

There are many reasons for borrowing and adapting qualitative methods from their social science background for use in marketing management situations. These methods can be readily adapted for research in any aspect of marketing within the scope represented earlier in Figure 2.2 (p. 29) in the context of the specific marketing environment or organizational characteristics.

There is a wide range of techniques available for use in qualitative research in marketing management settings (see Table 5.1). The specific techniques listed in the first part of the table have been described above in relation to their relevance for research in marketing management issues. The more comprehensive and holistic qualitative methodologies such as in-depth interviewing and convergent interviewing; case-based studies; focus group interviews; ethnographic studies; grounded theory; action research and learning are addressed in the rest of Part II. The integrative use of a variety of methods will be addressed as 'multiple mixes of methodologies' in Chapter 14.

Table 5.1 *Qualitative techniques and methods, their purpose in use*

Techniques/methods	Uses
Participant observation/contributions	as specific research techniques;
Content analysis (of printed materials/ company materials)	
Small surveys, used qualitatively	useful on their own but better when combined with other methods
Conversational analysis	
Observation	only focus on what people say, what can be observed, or what has been written
More comprehensive/holistic methodologies	
In-depth/convergent interviews/focus groups	comprehensive methodologies; allow for gathering wide range of data: allow for observation, what people say, written materials, documentary evidence; and over time, not one-off, time-specific approach
Action research and learning	
Grounded theory	
Ethnographic studies	
Case studies	

LEARNING QUESTIONS

Outline the range and scope of qualitative research methodologies.

What are the different focuses and emphases of positivism and interpretivism research methodologies?

Why is seeking an 'in-depth understanding' important in interpretive studies?

Debate the issues of *trustworthiness* and *transparency* in the context of interpretive qualitative studies.

References

Das, H.T. (1983) 'Qualitative Research in Organisational Behaviour', *Journal of Management Studies*, 20(3), 301–314.

Denzin, N. and Lincoln, Y. (1994) *Handbook of Qualitative Research*, Sage, Thousand Oaks, CA.

Eisenhardt, K.M. (1989) 'Building Theories from Case Study Research', *Academy of Management Review*, 14(4), 532–550.

Fetterman, D.M. (1989) *Ethnography: Step by Step*, Sage, Newbury Park, CA.

Gilmore, A. and Carson, D. (1996) '"Integrative" Qualitative Methods in a Services Context', *Marketing Intelligence and Planning*, 14(6), 21–26.

Lincoln, Y.S. and Guba, E.G. (1985) *Naturalistic Inquiry*, Sage, Newbury Park, CA.

Mintzberg, H. (1979) 'An Emerging Strategy of "Direct" Research', *Administrative Science Quarterly*, 24(4), 582–589.

Parasuraman, A., Zeithaml, V.A. and Berry, L.L. (1985) 'A Conceptual Model of Service Quality and its Implications for Future Research', *Journal of Marketing*, 49(4), 41–50.

Patton, M.Q. (1980) *Qualitative Evaluation Methods*, Sage, Beverly Hills and Newbury Park, CA.

Patton, M.Q. (1990) *Qualitative Evaluation and Research Methods*, Sage, Beverly Hills, CA.

Pettigrew, A.M. (1979) 'On Studying Organisational Cultures', *Administrative Science Quarterly*, 24(4), 570–581.

Strauss, A. and Corbin, J. (1990) *Basics of Qualitative Research: Grounded Theory Procedures and Techniques*, Sage, Newbury Park, CA.

Tesch, R. (1990) *Qualitative Research – Analysis Types and Software*, Falmer Press, New York.

Van Maanen, J. (1979) 'Reclaiming Qualitative Methods for Organisational Research: A Preface', *Administrative Science Quarterly*, 24(4), 520–526.

Wallendorf, M. and Belk, R.W. (1989) 'Assessing Trustworthiness in Naturalistic Consumer Research', in E.C. Hirschman (ed.), *Interpretative Consumer Research*, Association for Consumer Research, Provo, UT, pp. 115–132.

Yin, R.K. (1994) *Case Study Research: Design and Methods*, Sage, Thousand Oaks, CA.

Zeithaml, V.A., Berry, L.L. and Parasuraman, A. (1993) 'The Nature and Determinants of Customer Expectations of Service', *Journal of the Academy of Marketing Science*, 21(1), 1–12.

6   In-depth Interviewing

Interview data is a major source, perhaps *the* major source, of information for many qualitative researchers. This chapter will introduce some general principles of interviewing that can be used in the methodologies described in other chapters, for example in grounded theory and in case studies. The chapter focuses on describing interviewing approaches both from the perspective of using the interview to *build* the research database, and in terms of the importance of organizing the analysis of the data. Emphasis is given to the scope of in-depth interviews. They range from very unstructured interviews designed to discover in-depth insights and understanding, and more structured interviewing focusing on a technique called *convergent interviewing*, an approach particularly useful in business research.

In-depth Interviewing

Whatever an interview's form, its purpose is to get inside someone's head and enter into their perspective (Patton 1990) to find out things like feelings, memories and interpretations that we cannot observe or discover in other ways. The researcher should always be careful of imposing his or her own perspective on the respondent, even though researcher comments and contributions, based on prior experiential knowledge and learning, will undoubtedly enhance the overall data collection.

In-depth interviews vary in form. Reference to our continuum model (in Chapter 5) immediately indicates the scope of in-depth interviews, which can range in characteristics and uses from one extreme to another. At one end, they can be almost like an informal conversation with an individual that explores the person's perceptions of a chosen phenomenon, as in interpretivist research. Such interviews have virtually no structure or direction placed on them by the interviewer since their main aim is to explore the internal reality of the respondent. Interviews in an ethnographic study are examples of this (see Chapter 10). At the other end of the continuum interviews are more structured and directed and are a form of realism research where perceptions are interesting not for themselves but for the picture that they present of an external reality. Interviews seeking knowledge from marketing managers could be examples of this form of interview. We will try to assemble some principles of in-depth interviewing that can be used along most of this continuum of interview types.

Planning the interview

Most interviews are planned in three ways. Firstly, the *overall objective* of the interview should be sorted out within the context of the whole project. For example, it may be to explore perceptions about 'the culture of beer consumption in Belgium' or 'how international marketing relationships are established, maintained and terminated'. Secondly, an *interview guide* or protocol is then written as a memory jogger for the researcher during the interview. This guide will have some *general*, open-ended interview topics that address the overall objective, such as 'the role of beer in Belgian life'. The range of topics in an interview protocol varies as required and depending on the research objectives and the nature of the domain. Also, if multiple interviews with the same respondent are appropriate, these may begin with many topics and gradually filter down to a few key specific topics, or alternatively they may begin with identified key specific topics and gradually introduce a variety of sub-issues or new topics as they emerge. Thus, the range of topics covered in an interview or series of interviews is dependent upon the specific research objectives of the study. During the interview, these topics do not have to be addressed in the order they are written on the interview guide and so there is no need for alarm if the discussion jumps about.

Thirdly, within each of these general topics, there may be more particular *probe topics* that are raised only *after* the general topic has been raised and if the respondent has not raised or discussed them already in the context of the more general topic. For example, a topic such as an individual's beer consumption could be followed with probes such as: 'where?' 'when?' 'with whom?' 'why?'

Note that these general topics and associated probes may not have to be directly raised in the interview. Indeed, a primary skill of a qualitative researcher is to involve the respondent in a conversation rather than an interview, and the conversation may cover the general topics and associated probes without the respondent knowing they had been planned to be raised. Techniques to facilitate this conversation are outlined below. In a good interview, the topics are often covered before they have to be directly raised.

Starting the interview

After normal greetings and some general conversation about the weather or the journey to the interview, the researcher should begin the interview when he or she feels the respondent is ready. Because the researcher expects the respondent to be honest and open, the researcher should try to be the same with them. So the interview starts with a very brief outline of the purpose of the research to assure the respondent that it is important and has some benefit for them (this purpose does not need to be raised again). Because *informed consent* to be interviewed is an ethical requirement for research, confidentiality of the data and of the respondent in the report should be mentioned, and agreement to be interviewed should be confirmed. Permission to use a tape recorder should also be confirmed.

All this sounds very stilted and formal. In fact such formality can be minimized by dealing with these arrangements in a friendly manner, for example during the transition from initial pleasantries to commencement of the interview.

Note that some authors do not favour the use of tape recorders, usually because they distract both the respondent and the researcher during the interview (for example Wolcott 1990). Indeed, the 'click' when a side of tape is finished can be distracting and may suggest to the respondent that the interview is about to end. So if you do use a tape, use the longest playing one you can find, (of course, new technology should overcome this issue in the future). Moreover, some respondents simply do not like any kind of recorder to be used. However, some authors strongly recommend their use and transcription of the tapes, for example, Patton 1990. Others are between these two extreme positions, thinking that it is merely 'a matter of preference', Yin 1994: 86.

In interpretive research we prefer to try to tape interviews and also take good notes in case background noise drowns out the interview or the tape recorder does not work (a tape recorder has appeared to be working by a check of its revolving cassette and has still not recorded!). Ideally, the tape of an interview is played back at an early opportunity. We also advocate making a transcription of the tapes. This is particularly useful with regard to the first two or three interviews because they reveal how bad the notes or even the researcher probes were, and so they improve the note taking and the researcher's probes and contribution in later interviews. A common fault in initial interviews is for the researcher to talk too much, so transcription of these early interviews should almost be viewed as a necessity. The costs of having all interviews transcribed in time and in money, or paying someone else to do the transcription, often means that this is a luxury that some researchers can ill afford. So if funds are not available for transcribing tapes, some researchers merely play them back to check the handwritten notes of the interview; and to listen again for key points of interest. However, our view is that researchers should bite the bullet on this and, with patience, attempt to transcribe all interviews. They will then have much more flexibility in *processing* the data, either electronically or manually. Complete comprehensiveness is also achieved.

Managing the interview

Now the interview proper can begin. The first topic can be very broad and the language used can be similar to the respondent's own language. A way to achieve this is to encourage the respondent to talk about their experiences or tell you their 'story' in relation to the research topic. This is a good way to start as the respondent does not have to think about the *correct* response or wonder if their comment is precisely what was behind the probe; they can just start telling a story, which anyone can do. After the opening, the researcher implicitly or explicitly covers the general topics in the interview guide and their associated *probes*, always keeping the dialogue flowing in the ways described next.

Throughout the interview, the researcher follows the rules of good interviewing (Armstrong 1985). He or she:

- uses small encouragers like a murmur of understanding or 'yes?';
- maintains eye contact and smiles expectantly during pauses as if expecting the interviewee to continue;
- uses the active listening technique of *feeding back dialogue in the researcher's own words* to check his or her own understanding and to remind the respondent that what they are saying is very interesting; and
- asks non-directive questions like 'Could you please elaborate?', 'Can you give me an example?' and 'You mentioned that [repeat in respondent's words] . . . can you tell me more about that?'

In particular, it is important that the researcher:

- uses the respondent's terms rather than academic ones, for example, 'partnerships' rather than 'strategic alliances';
- allows the respondent's interests and concerns to decide the *order* in which the general topics and their associated probe questions are discussed, if the respondent seems to want to talk about them before the researcher has ticked them in the interview guide;
- goes from the general to the particular whenever possible to ensure the respondent's perspective is not overruled by the researcher's;
- never interrupts an answer;
- never asks leading questions that imply what answer is most acceptable to the researcher, for example, 'There is a lot of beer drunk around here – do you drink much?'
- never introduces his or her own ideas into the interview;
- never evaluates an answer, not even by saying 'That is interesting' for example, because doing so will start pointing the respondent away from his or her own perspective towards the researcher's perspective; and
- never worries about a 'pregnant' pause – the researcher lets the respondent fill the pause by appearing to be writing some notes.

At the end, the researcher asks if there are any other points that could have been raised and remembers to thank the respondent for their precious time. Soon afterwards, when the interviewer is some distance from the site of the interview, he/she jots down memory joggers about the interview like its date and duration, the clothes the respondent was wearing, how often they were interrupted, what the person's desk was like, what awards were on the wall, and so on.

All this may be obvious to many qualitative researchers; to others it may provide useful guidance and a framework for planning and running interviews. In order to give more depth and perspective to qualitative interviewing we include here a case example which outlines in context much of our description so far and also presents topics and probing questions which are designed to gain in-depth understanding. A further illustration is given of the purpose of follow-up interviews and aspects of analysing the data – which is the basis of our next section.

Case Example: In-depth Interview Approach for Business Managers

This study involved face-to-face in-depth interviews with the owner-managers of small companies with follow-up interviews at a later date. The objective of these interviews was to allow owner-managers to describe their views in relation to what they do, how, why, when and where.

The in-depth interviews followed a relatively unstructured pattern. The interview used the 'tell me about . . .' approach which allowed the respondents to describe their views in their own words. In-depth interviews provided an open, flexible, experiential and illuminating way to study complex, dynamic interactive situations, such as management decision making.

Such an interview technique provided all the advantages of in-depth interviewing. It allowed the coverage of a wide area of interest, allowed the researcher to become familiar with this as the research progressed; helped the interviewer identify and explore the key issues as they were revealed because of the open-ended nature of the interview protocol. In addition it allowed further probing and examining until mutual understanding was reached.

The nature of this approach allowed the research plan of action to be adaptable and flexible. Therefore it evolved with the experiential learning and development of the researcher in a relatively new research area, as new themes, ideas and topics of interest emerged. It aided researcher understanding of the whole context in which the phenomena took place, enabling the researcher to see the connections and influences upon the phenomena or topic of interest.

The language used by the interviewer deliberately excluded marketing terminology but focused instead on what the owner-manager did in relation to various aspects of business. This was a vital prerequisite for such a study. It has long been known that entrepreneurs will adapt the mode of the recipient to their views. This is particularly so if the entrepreneur has had technology transfer or prior knowledge in an area of discussion. Other entrepreneurial characteristics such as: a public need to be perceived to be in control; to be seen to be leading the company's direction and to be seen to be in charge of his/her own destiny also contribute to a situation where the entrepreneur/owner/manager will quickly respond to an interviewer in terms to which he/she thinks the interviewer will relate. As a consequence of this, the aim is for the entrepreneur to answer questions in the language in which a question is put. For example, if a question refers to marketing strategy the answer will be given using appropriate marketing strategy 'jargon'. Analysis of previous empirical data shows a significant correlation between the language of the question and the language of the reply.

To avoid such a result this study devised questions that would completely avoid the use of marketing terminology. The criteria for analysis (described below) served to 'organize' and 'group' the new data into manageable frameworks.

Some examples of question variations and extensions adopted in order to encourage the interviewee to use their own language and terminology and expand on descriptions of marketing activities are given below.

Interview questions, variations and extensions

1 How do you do business?
   1.1 How did the business grow – from here?
                                      – further?
                                      – more?
   1.2 Once the business was established [*repeat from 1.1. above*]
   1.3 Tell me how you get your business/work.

[*Further focus – by using time dimensions*]
   1.4 Describe what you have done in the past 3(6) months.
   1.5 Describe what was different about this in the previous 3(6) months.
   1.6 Describe what you will do in the next 3(6) months
   1.7 What things about your business or your environment are different today compared to last year?
   1.8 What do you think might be different about your business or your environment next year?

Issues around specific areas of marketing:

2 Product
    2.1   Describe what you (think you) offer the customer.
    2.2   How do you go about developing this offer to customers?

    Time dimensions
    2.3   What is different today . . . [*repeat 1.4–1.8*]
    2.4   Overall would you say things have developed/improved in this aspect of your business over time? [*repeat 1.4–1.8*]

3 Pricing
    3.1   What do you ask from your customers for your different offerings?
    3.2   How do you vary this in relation to different offerings?
    3.3   Has this changed in the past 3(6) months?
    3.4   Describe what you will do in the next 3(6) months.
    3.5   Given what you say you charge customers:

- Why do you think this is suitable for your customers?
- Why do you think this is viable for your business?

    3.6   How compatable is this charge with your overall desired company image?
    3.7   What are the important factors in getting your customers to accept what you want to charge them?

4 Delivery
    4.1   What are the important factors in getting your product to your customers? [*Only use after a full discussion on product*]
    4.2   [*Repeat 2.1–2.4 and 1.4–1.8*]

5 Selling
    [*Repeat where appropriate 2.1–2.4 and 1.4–1.8*]
    5.1   Describe how you get your customers to buy from you.
    5.2   Have you tried different ways over time?
    5.3   Which way works best for you? Why?

Some further guidance for questioning technique:

- Do not interrupt the flow of interviewee's response regardless of relevance.
- If an entrepreneur uses marketing jargon, ignore it if possible and use non-jargon language.
- Try and stay silent as much as possible.
- Do not engage in conversations of agreement or disagreement.
- Try to remain detached but receptive, for example nod frequently.

- Try to maintain eye contact as often as possible.
- Where possible, use encouraging phrases such as: 'Can you tell me more about . . .' and means of clarification such as: 'Tell me what you mean by . . .'

Follow-up interviews

Follow-up interviews were used as a means of investigating particular aspects of interest in more depth. They were a useful way to go back to the same respondents to discuss similar topics and focus on emerging, key issues from the initial interview. The aim is to gain further clarification, understanding and expansion in relation to particular areas of interest. This allows further questioning, with questions framed using respondents' own words and terminology. For example the follow-up interview question may begin with 'Last time you stated . . .' and continue 'can you say something more about this?' or 'can you expand on this?' or 'can you clarify what you meant by this?' Thus the follow-up interviews entail more specific probing in relation to the particular and significant areas of interest, areas of change, and focus on any 'gaps' that have been identified arising out of the first interview. At these interviews the use of 'why' and 'how' questions were particularly prominent in order to delve deeper into why and how respondents behave, think, act as they do. For example, when investigating the nature of management decision making, follow-up interviews focused on various aspects of the decision making process/activity in the following style: 'You said you gathered ideas for new products from seeing what competitors are doing – could you tell me more about that?' or 'could you describe how you. . . .'

During these follow-up interviews a combination of a critical incident technique (devising and recording key critical incidents about the research as they emerge from the data) and citation analysis (recording each time an issue or event is cited in the data) are used, where relevant, with the owner/manager to investigate various transitional elements at different stages of growth. This technique allowed respondents to be asked to 'track back' to particular instances in their work lives and to explain their actions and motives with specific regard to these instances.

Criteria for analysis

The following categories were defined and described to allow the data from the interviews to be analysed and interpreted.

'Good' marketing was defined as manifest in the tangible dimensions of good/increased sales and profits. Whilst it is possible to recognize 'good' examples of marketing activity, or in other words 'quality marketing', the question was whether this marketing activity could be assessed as being good quality in terms other than the tangible dimensions of sales and profits.

'Quality' in marketing was assessed by evaluating the *use* of marketing, that is, assessing *how marketing was performed*. This assessment determined a 'placement' of marketing along a continuum between 'negative and positive' extremes, by using terms such as:

    POOR . . . . EXCELLENT
    BAD . . . . GOOD
    NONE . . . . MUCH
    INACTIVE . . . . ACTIVE
    REACTIVE . . . . PROACTIVE

On the basis of this framework, it was possible to address the 'components' of marketing activity and to assess these in terms of their *use* and *how they were performed*. Some examples of this focus are given below.

Product-related marketing   Assessment of the quality of product marketing focused on the initial product idea on the basis that actual marketing only occurred subsequent to the idea. By positioning the assessment at this point onwards, issues such as whether the product emerged as a result of 'reaction to customer inquiry' or by some 'idea generation' policy were not of concern. Assessment therefore began with the refinement, improvement and development processes. It also took account of issues such as the number, range and scope of products and the extent of 'targeting' towards a given market niche.

Quality in product marketing was determined by a combination of the following:

1 Did any/all of these things happen?
2 How proactive was it? Either after the initial concept/idea or was activity maintained throughout the marketing of the product through to conclusion?

Price-related marketing   Price-related marketing activity was assessed in relation to price against competitors' pricing; the quality of the product that equates to price perception; and the overall image of the company. The extent of manipulation of price to aid marketing was also important. Therefore, price can be assessed in the same terms as product in terms of suitability, viability and compatibility. Specifically, in terms of the *use* of price and *how pricing was performed*.

Delivery-related marketing   Assessment and analysis were based on how the product or service was delivered, and the quality and expertise of the person(s) and systems delivering it. In particular how the delivery was managed in relation to frequency and immediacy in relation to the type of product, customer requirements and competitors' activity will be important. Quality was also assessed in terms of how the reliability of delivery is managed and ensured and how complete the delivery performance is perceived to be (by the company/manager). The interaction/communication between all parties before, during and after the delivery process contributed to the overall assessment of quality in delivery.

Selling-related marketing   This was assessed and analysed in terms of how sales people do selling, how they approach and communicate with customers. Selling was assessed in terms of the ability to execute the whole sales process – that is, the ability to create initial desire/need with sales messages, stimulate sales, manage customer contact in terms of frequency, reliability and efficiency, and contribute to relationships between sales people and customers.

Communication-related marketing   Assessment and analysis of communication involved consideration of both the use of promotional materials and the interaction/communication between all members of the company and customers. 'Good' quality in communication relates to how it is managed and carried out in terms of the use of suitable materials, the design and appearance of brochures, leaflets, etc., their focus and purpose and how they co-ordinate with the sales message. It also includes the intangible aspects of communication such as the management of staff/customer interactions, the timeliness of communication messages, and the ability to adapt messages to suit different customers' requirements and priorities.

Customer service-related marketing   Assessment and analysis took account of customer service as the integrative aspect of bringing all other marketing activity together to ensure quality in the overall marketing offer. It was assessed by the extent of after sales service (if appropriate), the scope/range of customer service (dependent upon the nature of the product/business) and its contribution to added value.

Other aspects of marketing related activity   Any other aspects relating to marketing were taken into account in the assessment and analysis of business activity. Overall, the factors identified were compared in terms of compatibility, integration and co-ordination of marketing performance.

Analysing the data

So now we have masses of words in notes or typescripts. How do we analyse all this material? Most qualitative researchers use some form of *content analysis* to analyse their data, that is, they code groups of words in their transcripts into categories. These categories are usually determined from the research topics that were the starting point for the research. Examples of codes for research about marketing strategy would be: *cost leader*, *differentiator* and *focus*, and the segments or *chunks* of the transcript that are coded could be phrases, sentences or paragraphs. In effect, the codes are keys to arranging the mass of data into patterns. 'These codes are retrieval and organizing devices that allow the analyst to spot quickly, pull out, then cluster all the segments relating to a particular question, hypothesis, concept, or theme' (Miles and Huberman 1994: 57).

Two steps are usually involved in content analysis:

- A first phase simply assigns codes to words or segments of words.
- A second phase makes comparisons and contrasts between the coded material.

The first step is sometimes called 'axial coding' and the second 'selective coding' (Neuman 1994: 408–409). In interpretivistic research, like grounded theory or ethnography, another phase called the 'open' phase *precedes* these two; in the open phase, the initial codes are found within the data itself. But for many researchers with interview data, most of the codes are known before the data is looked at, for they are based on the general topics and their associated probes in the interview guide. These in turn will have been guided and informed by the literature frameworks and conceptualizations of the research problem, aims and objectives of the study.

So let us assume that the first coding phase is the axial phase. In this *axial coding* phase the researcher goes through the data, writes the code against each paragraph or sentence, and possibly writes additional notes in the margin. New codes or new ideas may emerge during this phase, but the emphasis should be on the original list of codes.

Then in the second, *selective coding* phase the researcher goes through the data, tries to 'select' situations that illustrate themes and make comparisons and contrasts after most or all data collection is complete. For example, a researcher studying life in an office might decide to make gender relations a major theme. In selective coding s/he goes through her/his field notes looking for differences in how men and women talk about dating, engagements, weddings, divorce, extramarital affairs, or husband–wife relations. The aim is to make generalizations about these topics that summarize the similarities and differences between what people are saying.

Whichever coding procedure is employed, this stage serves best in 'organizing' the data according to the topics and sub-topics of the research.

In analysing this data further, it is common in qualitative research to itemize anecdotal evidence of a significant issue surrounding a research study. This approach is indeed beneficial in illustrating empirically the depth of perspective on a particular issue. There is a natural tendency in using anecdotal evidence to present 'evidence of extremes' which emphasizes contrasts or degrees of perspective. Sometimes though, anecdotal evidence cannot present the full scope of perspective in an extensive qualitative database. Similarly, because the anecdote is taken from one specific source, transferability to other sources is limited. A useful mechanism for overcoming these limitations is for the researcher to devise *criteria for analysis* (see case example). These criteria are taken directly from the interview protocol which, as we have said, is based on the research rationale, aims and objectives, and literature insights. The researcher's experiential knowledge and learning established from the research progression and prior studies contribute significantly to devising the criteria for analysis. The combination of experience, learning, study frameworks and insights enables the researcher to construct an *interpretation framework* around an issue. This can take a number of forms. It may simply be a description that says, if such and such occurs then this means that it can belong to an interpretation of significance or non-significance. The continuum concept (used in various forms throughout this text) can also allow data 'meaning' to be nominally positioned on a scale of extremes on a variety of dimensions, for example, good/bad, none/many, active/non-active, etc. The parameters are many but they will always have pertinence to the specific research study and the data gathered. Our case example gives an illustration of marketing criteria for analysis in use.

In summary, interviews are used to find out the perspectives inside someone's head. This is no easy task and each person we interview will be a little different from the previous person. But if we plan for the interview, start and manage its flow with skill and analyse it with care, we will find out very interesting things for our research projects. We have suggested a framework called 'criteria for analysis' as a means of careful analysis beyond that of anecdotal evidence. To illustrate the use of in-depth interviewing further, consider how the general principles above can be applied in the form of interviewing called 'convergent interviewing'.

Convergent Interviewing as an Application of the Principles of Interviewing

In the early stages of most research projects, not much is known about the topic area or the issues within that topic area that are worth investigating. Convergent and divergent in-depth interviewing, or convergent interviewing for short, is a methodology that allows a relatively structured approach to sorting out what needs to be done in a research project in the early stages. That is, it is a technique for collecting, analysing and interpreting qualitative information about people's attitudes, beliefs, knowledge and opinions through the use of a limited number of interviews with experts that converge on the most important issues within a topic area. The methodology uses normal in-depth interviewing techniques of market research but adds a procedure to analyse the interview data. In brief, each interview goes through the complete process of design, data collection, interpretation and back to redesign. In some ways it is like grounded theory, but it is not as complex or common.

Convergent interviewing can be used in the planning stages of a survey within a well-established topic area, but is particularly useful in qualitative research about a topic area which has no established theoretical base or methodology (Dick 1990: 4). Moreover, it can be used in established areas where the *researcher* happens to know little and wants to 'get up to speed'.

Consider an example. Woodward (1997) was investigating how brand equity was measured in services. Although the literature about measuring brand equity of goods was extensive, little was known about measuring the brand equity of services. Before conducting a survey, she had to find out what was done in the real world. So she arranged to personally interview three consultants in her region and two by telephone in the country's capital city, to find the major issues involved. Her first interview's questions were based on her limited, initial reading. She asked questions like 'Is there a difference between the marketing of goods and services?', 'Can brand knowledge of a service be made up of brand awareness and image?', and 'What would be an interesting service brand for me to study?' As the interviews proceeded, she added questions based on the previous interviews and on her increasing knowledge of the branding literature. After five interviews, she had a good idea of the critical issues involved in her study and lots of examples of service brands – she was confident she was on the right track for the rest of her research project.

The rest of this section is very closely based on the ideas of convergent interviewing's developer, Bob Dick (1990), and incorporates the ideas and words of reports by several others who have refined the process for marketing research (Batonda 1998; Nair and Reige 1995; Woodward 1997). We will define convergent interviewing and then give an example. The processes of convergent interviewing are described: planning the first interview, conducting the interviews, and analysing the interview data. Finally, its strengths and limitations are discussed, and it is compared with focus groups, an alternative qualitative technique often used at different stages of a research project.

What is convergent interviewing?

Essentially, convergent interviewing is a cyclic series of in-depth interviews with experts that allow the researcher to refine the questions after each interview to *converge* on the issues in a topic area: it is a series of 'successive approximations' (Dick 1990: 3) arising from a continuous refinement of method and content. For example, when the first interview is done, the researcher may have only three or four questions about the international marketing practices of computer services firms. From the analysis of this and succeeding interviews, the researcher will gain more and more questions, combined with more understanding of the topic area. Probe questions are developed after each interview, about important information where agreements and disagreements among the respondents are tested for explanation.

At its beginning, each interview is almost completely unstructured. It then proceeds into more specific questions, to which the researcher adds as s/he conducts more interviews, and differences and similarities of attitudes and opinions begin to emerge. The flexibility of convergent interviewing arises out of this continuous refinement of content and process.

The power of this qualitative method is:

- its combination of an unstructured *content* of topics, because its unstructured questions do not determine the answers;
- a *structured process*: its rigorous data collection and analysis procedures reduce the suspicion that might otherwise attach to in-depth interviews; and
- a *dialectical process*, where convergence and divergence of views is tested after each interview while you try to 'disprove your emerging explanations of the data' (Dick 1990: 11).

Given this last point, perhaps we should call this convergent interviewing method 'convergent *and divergent* in-depth interviewing', but that would be too much of a mouthful even though it would be more accurate.

The major attraction of convergent interviewing for researchers is the rigorous but flexible processes it provides to help refine a research project's focus in its early stages, by talking with knowledgeable people. The processes are reasonably straightforward and the crucial in-depth interview skills can be learned and practised by the researcher over two or three days (Armstrong 1985: 28–31).

Planning for convergent interviews

There are several steps involved in planning a convergent interview (Dick 1990: 12–14):

- deciding how many people to interview and who to interview,
- arranging for the interview with the respondent,
- determining the time and setting of the interview,
- determining the opening question, and
- determining probe questions for the specific information required.

Firstly, consider the people who will be interviewed. Dick (1990) suggests that a small, heterogeneous selection of people should be interviewed. In marketing research, this means the selection is not a random, representative sample but is a collection of relevant people that are chosen purposively, that is, chosen to provide *relevant* rather than representative information about the purpose of the research project. More precisely, in qualitative research selection terms, the selection follows the principles of maximum variation and snowballing (Patton 1990). The first person interviewed should be someone who can direct the researcher to other knowledgeable people. This person is often someone who is active in professional bodies or an academic who has strong links with consultants and government policy makers.

How many people should be involved, that is, how big should the sample be? Dick (1990: 25) suggests that the sample size should be data-driven and that it should contain at least 12 interviewees. However, he works in the field of organizational change and development. In contrast, marketing researchers have found that 'stability' in the matrix (shown in Table 6.1 below) can occur with as few as six in-depth interviews. A stable pattern of agreements and disagreements between respondents occurs, and the disagreements can be explained. Beyond this 'stability number', increases in understanding are small and not worth the cost of the time spent in further interviewing.

One way of reducing the required number of respondents is to use *prior theory*. Dick (1990) suggested going into organizational change and development research without any prior knowledge. However, in marketing research, the researcher should start reading the literature about the phenomenon before the first interview and continue reading it while the interviews are proceeding, 'enfolding' the literature around the findings as they emerge from the interviews. Having prior knowledge helps in the selection of interviewees, and allows the opening and probe questions in the first interview to be more effective and efficient. It also helps the researcher to make more believable encouraging noises during the interview, as well as helping the researcher recognize when something important has been said. Rapport and interview dynamics are thus assisted through a sharing of concerns. In brief, prior theory is precious.

The other steps involved – the planning, timing and setting of the interview; the opening topics/questions; and managing the interview – are similar to those for in-depth interviewing addressed in the earlier part of the chapter, so now we turn to the final step of data analysis.

Analysing the interview data in the context of convergent interviews

We have described in some detail how analysis of qualitative interviewing data may be carried out. It would be fair to suggest that our earlier descriptions could be positioned towards the interpretive extreme of our continuum. The analysis of interview data for convergent interviews belongs much further along the continuum towards the positivist frameworks that are concerned with aspects of demonstrating rigour, validity, process, structure, etc. Let us now explore analysis of interview data for convergent interviews.

At the end of each convergent interview, a detailed summary of the key issues raised, in order of priority, is drawn up. This summary can be up to two pages long, includes the words of the interviewee, and is preferably written within one hour of the interview during or after listening to the tape recording.

After this summary is made, the issues can be assessed in terms of their agreement or disagreement with earlier interviews. Dick (1990) suggests that only issues about which there is agreement should be included in the probe questions of later interviews (hence his use of the term 'convergent' to describe this method). However, in our experience, disagreement among interviewees can be as enlightening as agreements, and so we include *all* the important issues in all the interviews, as the interviews and their analyses proceed one after another. Of course, this procedure can become cumbersome if too many issues are included, but we use the respondents' priority ratings and our own understanding, gained from reading the literature, to narrow in on the important issues. Table 6.1 is an example of the matrix that is the basis for the discussion of the data analysis in the final report.

In Table 6.1, respondent A confirmed one issue (1) suggested in the literature and raised another (2). In the next interview, respondent B agreed about one of these but disagreed with the other. She then raised issues 3 and 4 and so they were probed for agreement or disagreement in later interviews. Note that in the interview with D, there was no time to discuss issue 6 even though a probe question had been developed for that purpose. Nevertheless, D had raised issue 7 early in the interview.

The precise form of Table 6.1 will vary from research project to research project. For example, a column may sometimes include numbers

Table 6.1 *An example matrix of agreements and disagreements about issues in five convergent interviews*

Respondent	Issue						
	1	2	3	4	5	6	7
A	yes	yes	–	–	–	–	–
B	agree	disagree	yes	yes	–	–	–
C	agree	disagree	agree	agree	yes	yes	–
D	agree	disagree	agree	agree	agree	–	yes
E	agree	agree	agree	disagree	agree	agree	agree

like the average life of a network in years, or it may include the names of brands. Whatever is included, the table is only the starting point for the data analysis because the *reasons* for the entries in the table are more important than the entries themselves and so these reasons are included in the report. For example, here is part of Woodward's (1997: 127) report of her interviews with marketing consultants about brand equity (with small changes for the purpose of being succinct):

Question 3 asked 'Do you agree with brand equity and how could it be represented by a consumer's knowledge of a brand?' First raised with respondent A, all respondents agreed that brand knowledge could determine brand equity. However, respondent D stated that points-of-difference, relevance, popularity and esteem were also required. Nevertheless, these four terms are all linked to image that, along with brand awareness, is a dimension of brand knowledge. In conclusion, all respondents agreed with this part of the brand equity concept.

Some researchers have used the table format to group issues together. Others have used the table as the starting point for understanding the dimensions of the phenomenon being studied. These dimensions would have caused the disagreements to occur; for example, the disagreements may have occurred because some respondents were referring to small businesses and others were referring to big business.

In conclusion, by carefully analysing the data from convergent respondents, later interviews can be improved and a deeper understanding of the phenomenon being studied can be gained.

Convergent interviewing – strengths and limitations

What are the strengths and weaknesses of convergent interviewing in marketing research and how does it compare with the alternative methodological techniques? The strengths of convergent interviewing should be particularly obvious. Its cyclic nature allows refinement of both questions and responses over a series of interviews; moreover, it is in the early, exploratory stage of a research project that the learning curve is steepest and most refinement needs to be done. Thus convergent interviewing allows a researcher to obtain relevant and important information that other researchers may have overlooked or not sought.

However, convergent interviewing has some limitations too, like all research methodologies. Firstly, it is essentially a theory building/framing technique and is best used in conjunction with or built upon frameworks or conceptual models from prior literature and with other techniques like case-based research or surveys. Secondly, the costs in time of considering all the information thrown up in each interview can be large. Usually, the benefits exceed the costs because the respondents are asked to select the high priority issues and the use of prior theory helps to sift the wheat of important issues from the chaff of unimportant ones. Finally, the interviewer is part of the data collection process (Dick 1990) which may lead to bias in the results or can contribute to the strength of the method if the interviewer develops experiential knowledge and becomes an 'expert' in the research topic (this issue was discussed in Chapter 1).

Summary

This chapter has outlined a variety of procedures for planning and conducting in-depth interviews. It highlighted different approaches within the scope of unstructured and structured emphasis and outlined aspects of analysing the interview data, ranging from using anecdotal evidence to creating 'criteria for analysis' and using convergent interviewing.

In conclusion, we believe in-depth interviewing (whichever method is used) is a powerful research technique for interpretive research. It is a useful method for exploring new and under-researched topics, including those that are new only to the researcher. Its overall strength is its ability to gather rich and meaningful data, analysis of which will lead to a significant depth of understanding that would be difficult to achieve by using any other method alone.

The importance of in-depth interviewing is manifest in its often integral presence in many qualitative research methodologies; as will be seen in the following three chapters.

LEARNING QUESTIONS

What is the key advantage of the in-depth interview method?

Describe the steps involved in doing in-depth interviews.

What additional benefits are derived from the *convergent interviewing* technique?

References

Armstrong, J.S. (1985) *Long Range Forecasting*, Wiley, New York.

Batonda, G. (1998) 'Dynamics of Overseas Chinese/Australian Business Outwork', PhD thesis, University of Southern Queensland, Toowoomba, Australia.

Dick, B. (1990) *Convergent Interviewing*, Interchange, Brisbane.

Miles, M.B. and Huberman, A.M. (1994) *Qualitative Data Analysis – An Expanded Sourcebook*, Sage, Newbury Park, CA.

Nair, G.S. and Reige, A. (1995) 'Using Convergent Interviewing to Develop the Research Problem of a Postgraduate Thesis', *Marketing Educators and Researchers International Conference Proceedings*, Griffith University, Gold Coast.

Neuman, W.L. (1994) *Social Research Methods: Qualitative and Quantitative Approaches*, Allyn and Bacon, Boston.

Patton, M.Q. (1990) *Qualitative Evaluation and Research Methods*, Sage, Newbury Park, CA.

Wolcott, H.F. (1990) *Writing up Qualitative Research*, Sage, Newbury Park, CA.

Woodward, T. (1997) 'Identifying and Measuring Customer-based Brand Equity and its Elements for a Service Industry', PhD thesis, Queensland University of Technology, Brisbane, Australia.

Yin, R.K. (1994) *Case Study Research – Design and Methods*, 2nd edition, Sage, Newbury Park, CA.

7   Case-based Research

Here is a story of how case-based research could be done. It shows that the research is driven by an original research problem and often consists of two stages: an exploratory stage and a confirmatory/disconfirmatory stage. The story concerns a practising manager who grew to love this sort of research (Teale 1999):

> John was the owner-manager of his insurance broking firm and had done a survey of his customers about his business's customer service quality. But he thought the picture he gained from the survey was too abstract and static. He wanted to know how and why customers' views of quality service changed over time and how he and his team could tap into that process. Case-based research was the most appropriate methodology to use. He read some of the literature about customer service and did some convergent interviews with industry consultants and a very experienced broker in another area. From this exploratory information, he drew up an initial theoretical model of what he was looking for, and wrote an interview protocol based on the model. Then he used that interview protocol as a template to investigate eight individual cases – these cases involved the relationships between the supplier of policies and a broker, and between a broker and the end-consumer. Most of his data about each case was gained from in-depth interviews with managers in firms that supplied insurance products, with managers in other broker firms, and with end-consumers. He also gathered data from brochures, trade magazines and from interviews with consultants and government regulators, to triangulate the picture he was discovering. He then compared the eight cases and built a final theory of how the relationships grew and what influenced each stage of that growth. 'I learned a thousand times more from this case-based research than I did from the survey', he said. ' This is how managers like research to be done and the results can be easily applied by managers.'

In discussing this powerful research methodology, this chapter explains how to do case-based research primarily by using interviews but with other sources of data included such as company brochures, newspaper and magazine articles, and observation. Although our focus is on case-based research within marketing management, the principles are the same as those used, for example, in evaluating education programmes (Patton 1990) or other consulting work (Yin 1994). The chapter is based on Perry (1998).

Why Use Case-based Research?

In contrast to the case-based research in this chapter, cases are familiar to marketing educators and their students as a *teaching device*. For example, the Harvard Business School's cases are widely used so that students can be emotionally involved and learn action-related analysis of real, complex situations (Christensen and Hansen 1987). Although cases can also be used as a research methodology (Easton 1982; Parkhe 1993; Tsoukas 1989; Yin 1994), there are varying opinions on how this can be achieved in a rigorous manner for research at doctoral level. One survey of PhD dissertations in six fields concluded that case studies were very inappropriate in postgraduate research – a judgement based on descriptive case *stories* with little rigour. To balance this view, the case study methodology is widely used for doctoral dissertations in Sweden and Finland, for instance. This chapter will show how case-based research methodology *can* be used rigorously.

There is evidence to support the claim that managers and other researchers will benefit from our rigorous, structured procedures to research complex, contemporary topics relevant to their current or future work, and about which little academic research has been published. Recent examples of topics studied by case-based researchers are marketing on the Internet, business re-engineering and customer service, home banking, marketing of community museums, and organizational accountability of the marketing communications function. In brief, rigorous case-based research is not only possible, but it is increasingly widespread.

The chapter has two main parts. Firstly, case-based research's strengths are explained. The issue of levels of induction and deduction is also covered. Secondly, how to implement the case-based methodology is examined, including decisions about how many case studies and interviews to use.

Theory Development in Marketing Management Research

Types of research problems that drive case-based research

The case-based research methodology usually tends to address *research problems* within the interpretivist paradigms rather than the positivist paradigm (Perry et al. 1999). Put simply, the research problem is usually a 'how and why?' problem rather than a 'what' or 'how should?' problem. Any prescriptions about the *best* way of doing things that a case researcher wants to make are made *after* doing the research and are speculative – they are placed in the 'implications' section of the report rather than the 'conclusions' part. Because the research problem that is the focus of a case-based research project is a 'how and why' one, it usually involves a relatively complex, social science issue about which little is known. Examples of appropriate research problems for case-based research are:

- How and why is relationship marketing implemented in a modern accounting practice?
- How and why does the marketing infrastructure of a foreign country impact on the internationalization process of manufacturers of industrial products?
- How and why do Australian high value-added manufacturing companies develop their market entry modes into China?

So, case-based research can be explanatory, theory-building research which incorporates and explains ideas from outside the situation of the cases. That is, this sort of case-based research is *extrinsic* rather than *intrinsic*: 'we will have a research question, a puzzlement, a need for general understanding and feel that we may get an insight into the question by studying a particular case' (Stake 1995: 3). Yin (1994: 18) gives examples of the how and why research problems in case-based research and shows how they are different from survey research:

> 'how' and 'why' questions [in case-based research are] . . . explanatory . . . such questions deal with operational links needing to be traced over time, rather than mere frequencies or incidence . . . If you were studying 'who' participated in riots, and 'how much' damage had been done, you might *survey* residents, examine business records (an archival analysis), or conduct a 'windshield survey' of the riot area. In contrast, if you wanted to know 'why' riots occurred, you would have to draw upon a wider array of documentary information, in addition to conducting interviews.

But note that the answer to the 'why' part of the research problem/question is not based on an experiment that shows that A directly causes B, as a match directly causes gunpowder to explode. In social science phenomena, there are few direct A to B causality links because any links are strongly influenced by the context. For example, whether the installation of extra lights in a car park influences the crime rate in the car park depends on the 4 Ps of the *context* – place (where), period (time), people and process.

Consider more closely the 4 Ps of context in our lights and car park example. Whether lights affect the crime rate depends on the *place* of the car park. If it is in an affluent suburb, what little crime does occur may be reduced; but in low-income, high-crime areas with inadequate policing, crime might be unaffected. Similarly, if most car parking occurs during the *period* of daytime, lights may not affect the crime rate. Furthermore, if the *people* who might steal cars are hardened criminals who have successfully stolen cars before, the existence of lights will not deter them; but if the people are inexperienced, the lights might deter them. In brief, treating people as independent, standardized objects is inappropriate because doing so 'ignores their ability to reflect on problem situations, and act upon this' (Robson 1993: 60). That is, the issues are longitudinal over time, as well as being investigated at a particular point in time. Finally, consider the core *process* of lights shining on cars. If the cars in the car park are expensive products like Mercedes cars, lights may not deter would-be criminals; however, if the cars are old and inexpensive, the lights may make the payoff not worth the risk of being caught. This car park and lights example illustrates the complex cause-and-effect links within the context of a complex, social science situation that case-based research can investigate. These links grounded in the context of a situation are sometimes referred to as 'causal tendencies' or powers (Bhaskar 1978: 20).

In conclusion, case-based research is especially appropriate for these practical business situations (based on Yin 1994: 23):

- a *contemporary* phenomenon *within* its dynamically changing, real-life context; where
- the boundaries between the phenomenon and the 4 Ps of its context (place, period, people and process) are not clear-cut; and
- multiple sources of evidence are used (for example interviews and documents)

In the example at the beginning of this chapter, John's complex customer service problem exactly fitted these characteristics. In brief, case-based research is used for *particular* types of problems.

Unit of analysis

After deciding on the appropriate research problem, the next step is to decide on the unit of analysis, that is, what constitutes a *case*. Deciding this issue is related to the research problem. If the research is about what a *person* can do, then the unit of analysis is an individual. But case-based research is often more appropriate for the more complex situation involving two or more people and/or their organizations. Thus case-based research has been done about the relationship between two businesses (as in the example of John above), about the relationship between two individuals, about decisions, about programmes, about organizational change, about laws and about neighbourhoods. Deciding on the unit of analysis can sometimes be a confusing process, and to finalize it often requires some long discussions with a colleague.

Sometimes researchers use small cases as *part* of a big case that is the unit of analysis for a study. For example, in a study of organizational change within the marketing departments of a corporation, it might be useful to analyse the individual marketing departments of each strategic business unit of a corporation. These parts or sub-cases are called *embedded cases* because they are embedded in the bigger unit of analysis. The important issue is that each of the embedded cases must be considered and compared with other embedded parts of the same big case, *before* the big cases can be compared. For example, the strategic business units within each corporation have to be analysed to find the pattern within each corporation, before the corporations can be compared.

Another consideration for using embedded cases in a study is operationality. Sometimes the unit of analysis may be so abstract that the findings may have no practical implications for managers unless embedded cases are included. For example, if a study's unit of analysis is international marketing networks or 'cobwebs' between many interlinked buyers and suppliers, then the findings may have no usefulness for those individual buyers and suppliers unless the relationship between two or three of them is studied in more depth as an embedded case.

So the research problem usually determines the unit of analysis in case-based research but sometimes embedded cases are included for operational reasons.

How much prior theory?

Although case-based research can have elements of theory building and theory testing, there is controversy about how much theory building or *induction* compared to theory testing or *deduction* should occur in the research. (This will also depend on the availability of relevant prior theory.) Views range from almost pure induction through to almost pure deduction and are illustrated in Figure 7.1 (Teale 1999). Here induction starts on the left-hand side, that is, prior theory is not used to structure the very exploratory research that is used to start to *build theories*. Deduction is at the right-hand side, with prior theory being used to give direction to the *testing of theories* that have been built up before the main data collection period. In this section, we argue that often a useful form of case-based research is the middle road involving both induction and some very limited deduction. We start with initial theory building on the left-hand side of Figure 7.1, and then move to what we call theory confirming/disconfirming in the middle. The final theory testing stage is left to later researchers. The term 'theory confirming/disconfirming' is used to distinguish the middle stage from the clearly 'theory testing' stage on the right-hand side of Figure 7.1.

Let us begin our argument for using both theory building and a confirming/disconfirming stage in case-based research, by discussing the

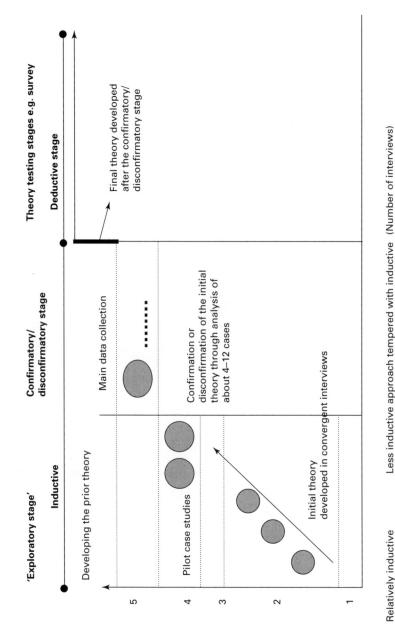

'Exploratory stage'

Inductive

Confirmatory/
disconfirmatory stage

Theory testing stages e.g. survey

Deductive stage

Developing the prior theory

Main data collection

Final theory developed
after the confirmatory/
disconfirmatory stage

Confirmation or
disconfirmation of the initial
theory through analysis of
about 4–12 cases

Pilot case studies

Initial theory
developed in convergent interviews

(Number of interviews)

5

4

3

2

1

Relatively inductive
approach

Less inductive approach tempered with inductive
features of pilot case studies and interviews

Figure 7.1   *Example of prior theory in theory building research*

pure theory building or *induction* view. For example, Dyer and Wilkins (1991) downplay deduction such as investigation of particular constructs and cross-case analysis and instead focus on the deep structure of *rich descriptions* of the context within which social events occur. Indeed, they think that case studies should be mere stories and not have any theorizing associated with them at all. Eisenhardt (1989: 532, 536; 1991) describes a process that has inductive features such as 'flexible and opportunistic data collection methods' that allow additions to questions in an interview protocol *during* the series of interviews. Moreover, she thinks that the initial research problem 'may shift during the research' as data is gathered, and 'research is begun as close as possible to the inductive ideal of *no theory* under consideration and no hypothesis to test'. That is, the literature is enfolded around the data *after* it has been collected – literature is used as little as possible prior to data collection. The left-hand side of Figure 7.1 represents Eisenhardt's position.

In contrast to the induction view above, Yin (1993: xvi) is close to the theory testing, confirming and/or disconfirming, *deduction end* of the induction–deduction continuum. He has a very tight structure set up before interviews are begun, with 'the posing of clear [and precise] questions . . . [and] the use of theory and reviews of previous research to develop hypotheses and rival hypotheses; the collection of empirical data [is] to test these hypotheses and rival hypotheses'. He is explicit in arguing against changes in direction after the research has begun and for a standard, consistent interview protocol to be used in *all* interviews. John in the example above used his interview protocol as a template in all his interviews in this way.

Figure 7.1 illustrates these differences between induction and deduction in case-based research, that is, between 'indigenous concepts' derived from the *data* and the 'sensitizing concepts' from *prior theory* which the analyst brings to the research (Patton 1990: 391). We will use John's case-based research to illustrate the points that Figure 7.1 raises. The left-hand side of the figure shows the more inductive or 'exploratory' approach (Yin 1993: 5) to case-based research. Here John used the literature and convergent interviews to provide sensitizing concepts to ensure he stayed on the track he wanted to stay on, and was not sidetracked by indigenous concepts thrown up in his later case interviews. Indeed, the first case on the left-hand side of the figure is almost *all indigenous* concepts and is analogous to grounded theory. But after the first case, data collection and analysis of the later cases is informed by preliminary concepts from the preceding cases and from prior theory, for without this structured process of accumulating sensitizing concepts, 'researchers who set out to practise the precepts of grounded theory frequently went aground in uncharted analytical terrain' (Jensen and Jankowski 1991: 68).

The *disadvantages* of the inductive, left-hand side of Figure 7.1, approach for researchers are that the cases are difficult to compare with each other (because there are different interview questions for each case) and so data analysis is difficult to do. John, being an inexperienced researcher and also a practical manager who wanted to solve a problem relevant to his own firm, therefore did not think his study was solid enough with just a first, inductive stage. He used the inductive, exploratory stage of his research to build a preliminary model of customer service that was a foundation for a second, more deductive stage. The second stage allowed him to use all his cases to confirm or disconfirm this preliminary model.

The researcher who uses only one inductive stage in a case-based research project may run the risk of drifting away from his or her already crystallized literature review or even 'rediscovering' existing theory, and thus not answering the client's problem or not making a new contribution in academic research. Indeed, Yin explicitly warns against the more flexible approach, saying it is not well documented in operational terms and is fraught with dangers, especially for postgraduate students with limited experience of scientific or management research. Furthermore, Miles and Huberman (1994: 17, emphasis added) have stressed the importance of '*prestructured research*' for new qualitative researchers working in areas where some understanding has already been achieved (which is the situation for much marketing management research).

Combining induction and deduction: the role of prior theory

The discussion above of 'exploratory' (induction) and 'confirmatory' (deduction) case-based research might suggest we need to decide for one or the other in an 'all or nothing' choice. But that suggestion is incorrect: a *mixture* of induction and deduction is often required.

In practice, it is unlikely that any researcher could genuinely separate the two processes. Pure induction without prior theory might prevent the researcher from benefiting from existing theory, just as pure deduction might prevent the development of new and useful theory. Parkhe (1993: 252, 256) argues that 'both extremes (of induction and deduction) are untenable and unnecessary' and that the process of ongoing theory advancement requires 'continuous interplay' of the two.

Similarly, Miles and Huberman (1994: 17) conclude that induction and deduction are linked research approaches and that tradeoffs might be made between 'loose' and 'tight' *initial* theoretical frameworks – the former is more locally focused and site-sensitive while the latter is more economical and facilitates comparison between sites.

Thus, although the right-hand side of Figure 7.1 is separated from the left-hand side, our *most* preferred approach in a research project is a blend of the two approaches in a case research project. A discussion of how the confirming/disconfirming stage may be replaced with another exploratory stage is provided later in this chapter. This blending can be done in three ways. Firstly, an early stage of convergent interviews with practitioners is almost always incorporated into the research design while the prior theory from the literature is being reviewed (Nair and Riege 1995). Secondly, one or two pilot studies are done to fine-tune the interview protocol, before the major data collection stage. These pilot studies are not a pre-test or 'full dress rehearsal' of the interview protocol (Yin 1994: 74); they are an integral part of the whole protocol writing process. Thus both the convergent interviews and the pilot interviews can provide the prior theory for the development of the interview protocol to be used in the second stage of the project. Thirdly, the interviews in the confirming/disconfirming stage *begin* with unstructured questions and not with the probe questions developed from the prior theory, as noted below. In brief, prior theory is developed from the literature *and* from pilot studies and/or convergent interviews, *before* it is used to develop the questions for an interview protocol that will be standard across most of the interviews in the case-based research project.

Incidentally, let us consider how this issue of the level of prior theory could apply in a thesis. In the literature review part of a case-based thesis, small initial models of theory drawn as boxes and lines are developed. Furthermore, the prior theory provides a focus to the data-collection phase in the form of *research issues* that help to focus the literature review. That is, the literature review is the same as in a 'traditional' thesis, charting the body of knowledge and identifying gaps. But the gaps are not expressed as precise, testable, closed yes/no propositions or hypotheses, but as general broad, open research issues (Yin 1994: 21) that will be used as section headings in the data analysis and concluding chapters of the thesis. Examples of such research issues are:

- How does an accounting practice move from transaction marketing to relationship marketing?
- What is the role of the marketing manager in a modern relationship orientated accounting practice?
- How do contextual influences impact on export marketing strategy selection?
- How and why are export marketing strategies adopted?
- How is the effectiveness of export marketing strategies measured?

In conclusion, our preferred position seeks an appropriate blend of induction and deduction in case-based research, for 'each is necessary for the other to be of value' (Emory and Cooper 1991: 62).

Implementing the Case-based Research Methodology

Given that a blend of induction and deduction appears to be the most preferred position, how can it be implemented? This section details some of the specific practices of case-based data collection and analysis: interview questions and protocol, selection and number of cases, analysis of data and the case study database and protocol.

Interview questions/topics in an interview protocol

As noted in the previous chapter, we have found the starting question in an interview should invite the respondent to simply tell the *story* of their *experience* of whatever the research is about – for example, 'What is the story of your experiences of leading strategic marketing planning workshops?' This question does not ask the respondent to *think* – so it does not make them apprehensive about being on trial.

Although the interviews start in this general way as *inductive* by the interviewee, the analysis of the interview data will involve some *deduction* or confirmation/disconfirmation of prior theory by the interviewer/ researcher. That is, the researcher/interviewer has some prior theoretical issues that must be discussed and considered in the data analysis part of his or her report. Some probe questions about the research issues must be prepared in case the interviewee does not raise them in the early, unstructured parts of the interview. However, one hopes that the answers to the probe questions are provided in the discussion so that the questions are not required. The probe questions usually always start with 'How . . .?' and can definitely *not* be answered with 'yes' or 'no'. Care should be taken to phrase the probe questions using the words or 'jargon' used by the interviewee – for example, 'link' rather than 'inter-organizational network' – and not to show what answer is preferred by the interviewer. Other techniques for the unstructured parts of the interviews are noted in our chapter on interviewing. In brief, probe questions form the major part of the prepared interview protocol (Yin 1994) that is used to provide a reliable framework for later cross-case analysis of data.

The questions/topics in the interview protocol are not precisely the same for all respondents in the first convergent or pilot interviews leading up to the main stage of case-based research, but they *are* the same in that main stage. That is, the prior theory for the middle of Figure 7.1 is developed from the literature or from some convergent interviews or some pilot studies, and then informs all data collection protocols *equally*.

It is sometimes useful in interview protocols to include Likert-scaled frameworks summarizing the overall perceptions of a respondent of the issue addressed in each question, to be answered by the interviewer (Yin 1994: 69) during or after the interview. These frameworks can be used *after* some broad questions have asked for the respondent's own views of issues. These scales assist in writing up the data analysis chapter of a report. For example, a Likert scale from 'formal' to 'informal' can summarize discursive answers about how strategic market planning is carried out, for each case. However, the Likert-scaled framework must not interfere with the core research issues/topics of the protocol and most importantly with the richness of the interview method and respondents' responses.

Principles of selecting cases

Procedures for interviews for each case were discussed above, but how many cases are required? And how are they selected? Principles for answering these two questions are developed next, before details are presented in later sections. Consider the question of the number of cases first. A researcher can use just *one* case when

- one or more of the three justifications listed in Yin (1994) apply (critical, extreme or unusual cases; these three justifications are discussed below), and
- the appropriateness of two or more theories can be tested with the case.

Nevertheless, more than one case is most common in case-based research because having several cases allows the extra dimension of cross-case analysis to be used which may lead to richer theory building for some studies. But how should these several cases be selected? The principle underlying the answer to this question is *replication*. In other words, the several cases should be regarded as 'multiple experiments' and not 'multiple respondents in a survey', and so replication logic and not sampling logic should be used for multiple-case studies (Yin 1994: 45–50). That is, relevance rather than representativeness is the criterion for case selection (Stake 1994). Careful choice of cases should be made so that they either:

- produce *similar* results for predictable reasons, that is, **literal replication**; or
- produce *contrary* results for predictable reasons, that is, **theoretical replication** (Yin 1994).

In John's research, he predicted from the brokers' level in the distribution chain that they would say roughly the same thing (literal replication), and that the end-consumers would say different things from the brokers (theoretical replication). This issue of theoretical and literal replication is discussed further below.

Other researchers support this replication method of case selection and highlight the inappropriateness of random sampling – for example, Eisenhardt (1989: 537) states that the 'random selection of cases is neither necessary, nor even preferable'. Patton (1990) lists 15 strategies of 'purposeful sampling' (in contrast to 'random sampling'), which can be used to select cases. Of these, 'maximum variation' sampling is the most appropriate for our analytical and general purposes. Maximum variation sampling includes very extreme cases – for example, a researcher investigating company turnarounds found that an outside-the-boundaries case, which had continued to decline and had *not* turned around, provided valuable insights into the turnaround process.

Number of cases

Turning from the general principles of case selection above, let us consider the issue of the precise number of cases in more detail. There are no precise guides to the number of cases to be included – 'the literature recommending the use of case studies rarely specifies how many cases should be developed. This decision is left to the researcher' (Romano 1989: 36). In a similar vein, Eisenhardt (1989) recommends that cases should be added until 'theoretical saturation' is reached, and Lincoln and Guba (1985: 204) recommend sampling selection 'to the point of redundancy'. Patton (1990: 181) does not provide an exact number or range of cases that could serve as guidelines for researchers, claiming that 'there are no rules' for sample size in qualitative research. However, their views ignore the real constraints of time and funding in most research and so some guidelines must be given as to how many cases are required in case-based research.

For a start, consider research with just one case. Having only one case is justified if it meets *at least one* of these three criteria (Yin 1994):

- the case is a *critical* one for confirming, challenging or extending a theory because it is the only one that meets all the conditions of the theory (an example is how the United States government acted during the international nuclear incident described below);
- the case is rare or *extreme* and finding other cases is so unlikely that research about the situation could never be done if the single case was not investigated (a clinical psychology case sometimes fits in this category);
- the case provides *unusual access for academic research*, and unless the case is investigated, an opportunity to examine a significant social science problem may be lost; an example is where the access to his/her firm can allow a researcher to see how strategic marketing planning is actually done in the real world (with all the confidential information, power politics and human weaknesses that usually prevent academic researchers from finding out the real story about it).

If you can justify just one case for one or more of these reasons, it is also preferred that there be *two or more theories* to be tested on the information in the case. This classic example shows the power of the *explanatory* use of a single case study:

This strategy was followed by Graham Allison in *Essence of Decision Making: Explaining the Cuban Missile Crisis* (1971). The single case is the confrontation between the United States and the Soviet Union over the placement of offensive missiles in Cuba. Allison posits three competing organisational theories or models to explain the course of events, including answers to three key questions: why the Soviet Union placed missiles in Cuba in the first place, why the United States responded to the missile deployment with a blockade, and why the Soviet Union eventually withdrew the missiles. By comparing each theory with the actual course of events, Allison shows how one provides the best explanation for this type of crisis. (Yin 1994: 16)

Let us consider the more usual situations where Yin's three criteria do not apply. Other authorities on case-based design have attempted to recommend a range for the number of cases. For example, Eisenhardt says:

> While there is no ideal number of cases, a number between four and 10 cases often works well. With fewer than four cases, it is often difficult to generate theory with much complexity, and its empirical grounding is likely to be unconvincing. (1989: 545)

But there are somewhat different views. Although some researchers advocate a *minimum* of two cases, the usual view is that four cases should be the minimum – 'in practice, four to six groups probably form a reasonable minimum for a serious project' (Hedges 1985: 76–77). For the *maximum*, Hedges (1985) sets an upper limit of 12 because of the high costs involved in qualitative interviews and the quantity of qualitative data which can be effectively assimilated. In the same vein, Miles and Huberman (1994: 30) suggest that more than 15 cases makes a study 'unwieldy'. In brief, the widest accepted range seems to fall between 2 to 4 as the minimum and 10, 12 or 15 as the maximum.

Number of interviews

Turning from the number of cases to the number of interviews, our experience and anecdotal evidence suggests that 30 or so interviews are required to provide a credible picture in a reasonably sized research project. The interviews could involve about three interviews at different hierarchical levels within 10 case organizations, for example. However, more than one interview in a small business is difficult, so interviewees researching case studies in these case organizations would include interviews in the 'context' of case organizations such as industry associations, consultants and government advisers, to bolster the number of interviews. Also the research could take a longitudinal approach by carrying out follow-up interviews with owner-managers at a later stage to investigate how things change over time; or by presenting early findings to the respondents and allowing them to comment further on the research questions and findings to date.

In conclusion, a researcher should use the above guidelines for the number of cases and interviews as *starting* points for research design, and then possibly use this quotation from Patton to justify not slavishly following a rule:

> The validity, meaningfulness and insights generated from qualitative inquiry have more to do with the information-richness of the cases selected and the observational/analytical capabilities of the researcher than with sample size. (1990: 185)

However many cases are used in a study, they should be arranged to cover a range of types based on theoretical replication. Here are some examples of how the range of theoretical replication has been used:

- high to low experience/effectiveness of strategic marketing planning into China from Hong Kong;
- high to low experience/effectiveness of market penetration into China from Australia, or from Eastern Europe to the European Union;
- high to low experience/effectiveness of firms' internationalizing into world markets; and
- different approaches to carrying out strategic planning, from rational through to interpretive approaches.

Some research designs can become multidimensional blends of theoretical and literal replication. One investigation of trading companies had one dimension of 'country' (that is, Australian and Taiwanese) and another dimension of 'size' as measured with a multi-item index composed of firm size, number of products and number of countries of export. Figure 7.2

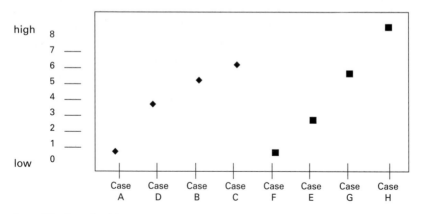

Figure 7.2 *Example of theoretical and literal replication of case studies, using the dimensions of 'country' on the horizontal axis and 'firm size' on the vertical axis*

illustrates the resulting arrangement of cases, with four cases from Australia and four from Taiwan, ranging from small-sized to large-sized firms. In another international marketing example, after some convergent interviews and piloting of her interview protocol, a researcher decided on three dimensions of theoretical replication (which had been discussed in the literature review): type of industry, country traded with, and size of firm. She selected two types of industry, two countries traded with, and 'high' and 'low' levels of size of firm. Her research design showed the blend of theoretical and literal replication of Figure 7.3, with 16 cases and two interviews in each case. In Figure 7.3, there are two cases in each cell, indicating there are two cases in each of the two types of firms, the two sizes of firm and the two countries traded with.

Dimension 1: Industry				
Manufacturing		Services		
Dimension 2: Size				
	Big	Small	Big	Small
Dimension 3: Country				
Japan	X X	X X	X X	X X
New Zealand	X X	X X	X X	X X

The 16 cases are indicated with X

Figure 7.3 *Example of a research design based on three dimensions of theoretical replication and literal replication*

Analysis of data

After selecting cases and conducting interviews, the researcher must analyse the data. It is customary for *case* analysis always to precede *cross-case* analysis (Miles and Huberman 1994; Patton 1990) because the case analysis provides the data for the cross-case analysis. However, it is during the cross-case analysis that the researcher can most clearly display his or her analytical capabilities and escape the 'mindless' description of many case study theses (Adams and White 1994: 573). Thus description near the beginning of the data analysis part of the report can be restricted to less than about half a page per case, with other descriptive material relegated to appendices or the database. In contrast, in the cross-case analysis, the report emphasizes reasons why differences occur, with an explanation of why a difference was found. Quotations from interviews are used frequently to justify conclusions about differences between cases in the cross-case analysis.

For their cross-case analysis, most qualitative researchers use some form of content analysis initially to analyse their data, that is, they code groups of words in their transcripts into categories. These categories usually are determined by the research issues that were the starting point for the research. 'These codes are retrieval and organising devices that allow the analyst to spot quickly, pull out, then cluster all the segments relating to a particular question, hypothesis, concept, or theme' (Miles and Huberman 1994: 56). Examples of codes for research about marketing strategy might be 'cost leader', 'differentiator' and 'focus', and the segments or 'chunks' of the transcript that are coded could be phrases, sentences or paragraphs. (Content analysis is described in more detail in Chapter 6.)

This use of prior theory to provide codes shows that prior theory is emphasized again in the data analysis part of the report of case-based research. The prior theory is also used to provide a tight structure to categorize the interviews into subsections of report of the data analysis. As noted above, theoretical replication is the key to the selection of cases, but it is also the key to the rigorous reporting of case data analysis. For each interview question, the cases can be placed along the horizontal axis, with a Likert-scaled summary position of each on the vertical axis. Then the cases are analysed in turn, with an emphasis on *cross-case analysis*. On every question, the researcher is hypothesizing an association between the context incorporated in the axis of theoretical replication, and the answers to the interview question. For example, in the Australian/ Taiwanese study, is a firm's country and its size associated with the firm's use of formal or informal market research (Figure 7.4)? It does not matter whether this association is proven or not – the association is merely being used to generate insights during the cross-case analysis. Comparing Figure 7.2 with Figure 7.4 shows that neither country nor size explained the answers, and so the cross-case analysis continued on to examine the answers to the interview question in detail to find *other* explanations for why the answers varied. Figures like Figure 7.4 for each interview question

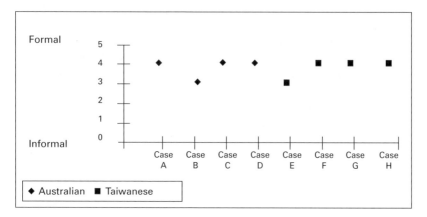

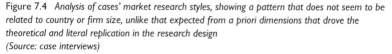

Figure 7.4 *Analysis of cases' market research styles, showing a pattern that does not seem to be related to country or firm size, unlike that expected from a priori dimensions that drove the theoretical and literal replication in the research design*
(Source: case interviews)

supplemented by occasional case-ordered figures like some of those in Miles and Huberman (1994: Chapter 7), usually provide sufficient insights in the data analysis phase.

A more interpretive approach to case study use in business research

This chapter has described a relatively structured approach with *post-positivist* characteristics (as we described them in parts of Part I), to carrying out case study research in business arenas. However it is often more appropriate to use the case study approach in a less structured way, allowing the research to develop and evolve over time. This is particularly so in a 'single' case study or an embedded case study.

If we refer back to Figure 7.1, the initial approach can be similar to the one described for the early or 'exploratory' stage. Prior theory can be used to develop ideas and constructs for the research focus. Such a study could begin by looking at aspects of managerial activity or how managers make decisions in a particular company or industry. After some searching of the literature and maybe some observations and discussions with relevant managers the early findings could provide the researcher with further directions in which to progress the study such as focusing on particular aspects of managerial activity or looking at specific aspects of decision making.

However, at this stage it may not be the aim of the research to enter a *confirmatory* and *disconfirmatory* stage for the main data collection. Instead of confirming/disconfirming a number of similar issues with different managers or companies, the research may instead want to focus on a more in-depth study of specific areas/issues. These could be revisited over a period of time: for example, to see how decisions are followed through to implementation within a company or industry, how decisions change over time or how managers actually ensure that plans are carried out. Such a study would still collect data in the form of observation notes, interview transcripts, follow-up interviews or discussions with key people involved, collection of documentary evidence such as minutes of planning meetings, internal communications, memos to staff and maybe external information on competitive activity.

The emphasis of such a study would be to illustrate in-depth knowledge and understanding of specific aspects of managerial activity and decision making in a particular context: how it varies and is followed through, how it depends on other members of staff, where it works well and does not work, and how it depends on different internal and external contexts.

The issue of case 'samples' and number of cases would not be important in such a research focus. The 2 by 2 matrix of companies in different regions, with different levels of involvement or characteristics, would not be important in relation to the nature of a research problem which would be served better by focusing on in-depth understanding of the reasons why managers do what they do. Consideration and justification of how many cases to include and how many interviews to carry out in order to achieve 'sufficient' data would not be relevant. Instead the key requirement would be to carry out the research until understanding is reached and the researcher has sufficient data to analyse in appropriate depth.

This data could be analysed by using 'codes' or content analysis using phrases and headings derived from the prior theory or literature frameworks described above. It could be further analysed and categorized by using criteria for analysis (described in Chapter 6) to assess the levels of activity or performance. More specifically it might be analysed by using a 'conceptual framework', originally derived from prior theory in the literature and adapted to take account of the specific industry or company characteristics discovered in the early or exploratory stage of research. The dimensions of the conceptual framework would then provide the 'codes' or 'labels' under which to consider the data. Further assessment and analysis of these codes, labels and descriptions of data should lead to a further stage of categorizing the findings into different levels, priorities or aspects of activities or performances that can then be explained or justified in context. In effect the research will construct a 'descriptive model' of actual happenings in context which can, if necessary, be compared with the conceptual framework. Such an approach to case analysis offers a different and in many ways a more in-depth focus to theory building, particularly in the comparison of the conceptual and descriptive models. This in turn can be used for further studies seeking replication of the theory.

Case study database and the case study protocol

The penultimate tricks of the trade of case-based research are the case study database and the case study protocol (which is different from the interview protocol discussed above). An aspect of assessing the quality of case-based research is in the ability to view the evidence from several angles. Thus sources of information like magazine articles, company brochures, company reports and office plaques should be used along with interview transcripts and notes to help make the reported data analysis more credible. All of these items should be kept in boxes, drawers or folders as they create a 'case study database' that can be accessed to check out the accuracy of the reported data analysis. Details of the items in this database could be presented in an appendix of the report and the whole database should be made available to any reader who may want to check the accuracy of the reported data analysis.

Finally, the creation of a 'case study protocol' which provides a summary of the whole project is valuable. It can be used to train interviewers when several interviewers are being used. Of course, it will include the interview protocol, but it also includes a summary of the project's aims and prior theory, and an outline of what the project report will look like. The case study protocol is used to ensure that the interviews are similar and the results are therefore reliable.

The interview protocol will provide a framework for 'criteria for analysis' which also stems from the research issues, aims and objectives and built upon prior theory. These criteria allow the researcher to build codes that are precisely focused on the research purpose. A detailed description of criteria for analysis stemming from interviews is given in the case example in Chapter 6.

Summary

Prior theory from the literature review, pilot cases and convergent interviews is linked to the cases through practices of data collection and analysis that include:

- the open research issues at the end of the literature review;
- the relatively more specific interview probe questions used to 'flush out' quotations and ideas about aspects of those research issues, after more open questions have been posed;
- appropriately selected cases;
- scales and codes used by the interviewer to summarize answers to the probe questions; and
- further analysis to compare cases against *a priori* expectations based on the theoretical replication range of the research design.

This chapter has described a case-based research methodology that operates from within a structured qualitative paradigm. It emphasizes the building of theories but also incorporates prior theory, and so is a blend of induction and deduction. How to use the methodology was described, starting with the appropriate research issues, through selection of cases and analysis of their data based on theoretical and literal replication, to evaluating the research's quality. The development of trustworthy knowledge requires the careful documentation of procedures by researchers and the guidelines developed for case-based research in this chapter contribute to this objective. In conclusion, the case-based methodology is a rigorous, coherent one based on justified philosophical positions, and is appropriate for researchers, whether they are doing academic or industry research.

LEARNING QUESTIONS

What are the main strengths of case-based research?

Outline the steps in theory building using case-based research.

Outline the characteristics of confirmatory/disconfirmatory and in-depth case-based research.

What are the key factors to consider when constructing and implementing case-based research methodology?

References

Adams, G. and White, J. (1994) 'Dissertation Research in Public Administration and Cognate Fields: An Assessment of Methods and Quality', *Public Adminstration Review*, 54(6), 565–576.

Bhaskar, R. (1978) *Realist Theory of Science*, Harvester, Brighton.

Christensen, C.R. and Hansen, A.J. (1987) *Teaching and the Case Method*, Harvard Business School, Boston.

Dyer, W.G. and Wilkins, A.L. (1991) 'Better Stories, not Better Constructs, to Generate Better Theory: a Rejoinder to Eisenhardt', *Academy of Management Review*, 16(3), 613–619.

Easton, G. (1982) *Learning from Case Studies*, Prentice-Hall, New York.

Eisenhardt, K.M. (1989) 'Building Theories from Case Study Research', *Academy of Management Review*, 14(4), 532–550.

Eisenhardt, K.M. (1991) 'Better Stories and Better Constructs: The Case for Rigor and Comparative Logic', *Academy of Management Review*, 16(3), 620–627.

Emory, C.W. and Cooper, D.R. (1991) *Business Research Methods*, 4th edn, Richard D. Irwin, Boston.

Hedges, A. (1985) 'Group Interviewing', in R. Walker (ed.), *Applied Qualitative Research*, Gower, Aldershot.

Jensen, K.B. and Jankowski, N.W. (eds) (1991) *A Handbook of Qualitative Methodologies for Mass Communication Research*, Routledge, London.

Lincoln, Y.S. and Guba, E.G. (1985) *Naturalistic Inquiry*, Sage, London.

Miles, M.B. and Huberman, A.M. (1994) *Qualitative Data Analysis – An Expanded Sourcebook*, Sage, Newbury Park.

Nair, G.S. and Riege, A. (1995) 'Using Convergent Interviewing to Develop the Research Problem of a Postgraduate Thesis', *Proceedings*, Marketing Educators and Researchers International Conference, Griffith University, Gold Coast.

Parkhe, A. (1993) '"Messy" Research, Methodological Predispositions and Theory Development in International Joint Ventures', *Academy of Management Review*, 18(2), 227–268.

Patton, M.Q. (1990) *Qualitative Evaluation and Research Methods*, Sage, Newbury Park, CA.

Perry, C. (1998) 'Processes of a Case Study Methodology for Postgraduate Research in Marketing', *European Journal of Marketing*, 32(9/10), 76–85.

Perry, C., Riege, A. and Brown, L. (1999) 'Realism's Role among Scientific Paradigms in Marketing Research', *Irish Marketing Review*, 12(2), 16–23.

Robson, C. (1993) *Real World Research: a Resource for Social Scientists and Practitioners-researchers*, Blackwell, Oxford.

Romano, C. (1989) 'Research Strategies for Small Business: A Case Study', *International Small Business Journal*, 7(4), 35–43.

Stake, R.E. (1994) 'Case Studies', in N.K. Denzin and Y.S. Lincoln (eds) *Handbook of Qualitative Research*, Sage, Newbury Park, CA.

Stake, R.E. (1995) *The Art of Case Study Research*, Sage, Thousand Oaks, CA.

Teale, J. (1999) 'Influences of Service Quality on Relationship Development and Maintenance in the Australian Financial Services Industry: An In-depth Study', PhD thesis, University of Southern Queensland, Toowoomba, Australia.

Tsoukas, H. (1989) 'The Validity of Idiographic Research Explanations', *Academy of Management Review*, 24(4), 551–561.

Yin, R.K. (1993) *Applications of Case Study Research*. Applied Social Research Methods Series Vol. 34, Sage, Newbury Park, CA.

Yin, R.K. (1994) *Case Study Research – Design and Methods*. Applied Social Research Methods Series Vol. 5, 2nd edn, Sage, Newbury Park, CA.

8   Focus Group Interviewing

Focus group research is among the most widely used research tools in the social sciences. In the past it was associated with market research, where it was regarded as the predominant form of qualitative research (Advertising Research Foundation 1985). But it is also used in marketing management research, for example, a manager may get his team together to brainstorm ways of solving a problem. This chapter will look at this very popular form of qualitative research first by defining it and justifying its use. Then we develop a set of steps that can be followed by researchers using focus groups.

Example

As we go through the chapter, we will use an example of a marketing management focus group set up and run by Marilyn:

> Marilyn was empirically investigating how small business managers used networks in their international marketing. She recruited four groups of about six managers – two groups did not do any international marketing and two were experienced international marketers. Recruiting participants from her own and her colleagues' business networks took several weeks, but she eventually rounded up enough people to come along to sessions that started at 5.30 p.m. and finished about 90 minutes later, in an office that had free parking nearby. The audiotapes were transcribed and from the transcripts she discovered many new ideas for later parts of her research.

Definitional descriptions of focus groups are given in this part of the chapter. Although groups have been used in aspects of social science research for some time (Stewart and Shamdasani 1990) the term *focus group* was first used in the classic *The Focused Interview* (Merton et al. 1956), when some of the procedures that are now accepted as common practice in focus group interviews were established.

Now focus groups are used extensively across a wide variety of disciplines. For example, in addition to consumer marketing research, focus groups are used in studies in communication, human resources, public health; the film industry to test new films; political science including the instance of focus groups being used by an American president's political advisers to evaluate possible character assassination by a political foe. Focus groups, of course, are widely used across the whole spectrum of marketing management research.

Definition of focus groups

The main characteristic of focus group research is the simultaneous involvement of a number of respondents in the research process to generate the data. The distinguishing feature of focus groups is the explicit use of the *group interaction* to produce data and insights that might be less accessible without the interaction found in a group (Morgan 1988). Indeed, the focus group is one of the few research techniques in which participants are encouraged to interact.

Thus a focus group can be described as a research technique that collects data through group interaction on a topic or topics. Although this definition is broad, it does address three key elements of focus groups. Firstly, it differentiates focus groups from other group meetings where the primary purpose is not to collect ideas as data, for example therapy groups, education and decision making groups. Secondly, it encompasses the notion of group interaction as opposed to group interviews such as nominal groups and Delphi groups (see note at the end of the chapter), that do not include interactive discussion to the same degree. Finally, it incorporates the active role of the researcher as a catalyst or moderator in addressing the research problem.

The use of focus groups as a research methodology can be justified in relation to four main points: collection of information; depth of understanding; flexibility and group interaction. A secondary point we will discuss is savings in time and money.

Collection of information

Focus groups are particularly useful when they produce new results that would not be possible with other standard methods. The strength of focus groups is not limited to listening to what people have to say, although this can be important in guiding future marketing, but in generating insights into the sources of complex behaviours and motivations. Focus groups may be used differently according to the purpose of the research and the background of the researcher, as discussed below.

In traditional social science research, literature and research based on *positivist* philosophy, focus group research is often described as most useful and appropriate in the exploratory and developmental phases of research where little is known about the phenomenon of interest. Thus, this sector of research is about:

- obtaining general background information about a topic of interest;
- generating research ideas that can be submitted to further research and testing using other approaches;

Alternatively, traditional social science researchers may use focus groups for:

- interpreting previously obtained quantitative results.

Marketing practitioner research is concerned with specific marketing issues in relation to corporations and business activities, so common focus group research would be useful for:

- stimulating new ideas and product concepts;
- diagnosing the potential for problems with a new programme, service or product;
- generating impressions of products, programmes, services, institutions, or other interests.

Interpretivist social science researchers may make any or all of the above common uses of focus group research. However, remembering that qualitative research is about *understanding* phenomena, the greatest use of focus group methodology for interpretivist researchers is about:

- learning how respondents talk and construct their own understanding about the phenomenon of interest.

In the main, focus group research will seek to gain insights into meaningful constructs of phenomena which emerge out of sharing and discussing issues, exchanging opinions, revising perceptions and highlighting commonalities and differences.

Note that the heading of this section purposefully uses the term *information*, rather than *data*. This is a further definitional aspect of focus group research in that information can be deemed to have a broader and deeper meaning than data; involving some level of interpretation. Information may be deemed to represent *knowledge* whereas data may not represent knowledge or indeed understanding. It is this dimension of information gleaned which is one of the most significant justifications for focus group research methodology.

Depth of understanding

Qualitative research methodologies enable greater understanding of specific phenomena. All research findings will contribute to better appreciation of a phenomenon but greater understanding is generally achieved only through qualitative research methods. Focus groups are one method that help to achieve this. The difference between focus groups and other qualitative methodologies is that they bring together a group of individuals who may be either heterogeneous or homogeneous, in an *interaction* of views that collectively aims to achieve a balance of meaningful information and opinions. Focus groups will generate greater depth of information on an issue than a general count of single opinions gleaned from a survey.

Closely aligned to depth of information is the strength of collectivity. The strength of focus group research is its emphasis on the *participants'* own comparisons between variables and ideas rather than the catalysts' or moderators' speculations about comparisons. This is achieved through the researcher's ability to ask the participants for comparisons and views rather than aggregating individual data so that the researcher can speculate about whether participants differ. We return to the issue of *researcher's ability* below.

Flexibility and group interaction

The most important feature of focus groups is their ability to reveal complex behaviours and motivations and this is a direct result of the interaction within the group. This interaction has been termed the *group effect* (Carey 1994) or *synergy* (Keown 1983), or simply *group dynamic*. The real issue of interactive comparison may be in the *quality* of the ideas. The factor which makes the discussion in focus groups greater than the sum of separate individual opinions gleaned from interviews is that participants both query each other and explain themselves to each other. That is, *interaction* is a unique strength of focus groups and should improve the quality of the ideas and opinions generated.

Consider Marilyn's example: as a result of the location of the interviews, the mobility of participants at 5.30 p.m., and in the flexibility of their schedules Marilyn thought that despite a possible reduction in the number of ideas, her focus groups were still more logistically efficient than individual interviews.

Efficiency of running focus groups

An often postulated factor is that savings in time and money are a positive feature of focus groups, as the same number of participants can contribute in similar or less time in a group setting than in individual interviews. Furthermore, there are fewer audiotapes, thus leading to savings in their transcription and analysis. However, Morgan and Krueger (1993) caution against the notion that there are savings in time and money, suggesting that recruitment and analysis are especially likely to be expensive and time-consuming, unless the participants are already at hand. This caution may not be relevant for studies about the consumption of fast moving consumer goods because participants are easy to find, but it should often be heeded in research about business-to-business marketing and in marketing management research about how managers behave. Certainly Marilyn in the example above found that co-ordinating the schedules of busy managers around a session time was a tiresome business involving many phone calls.

The message is clear on this: a researcher should not engage in focus groups on the basis of saving time and money. The positive research rationale for focus groups does not need to take account of such savings. The issue is the *appropriateness* of the methodology. Thus, even though for Marilyn bringing together busy managers was difficult, the purpose of doing so far outweighed any difficulties.

Framework for Focus Group Research

All research methodologies, including focus groups, benefit from a rigorous framework and prior planning. Useful guidelines may be followed in the planning and undertaking of the groups and in their data analysis and reporting. Table 8.1 (p. 122) shows our framework, the discussion of which represents most of the remainder of this chapter.

Step 1: defining the problem

Quality is affected when the purpose of a focus group is not clear. Thus the first step in preparing for a focus group is to gain a thorough under-standing of the problem or issue and to express it as a concise question or issue for discussion. For example, Marilyn's problem/question was, 'What are the structures and processes of the networks used by Australian small businesses, in their internationalization?' Although Marilyn's question is concise, it has several inherent topics which may require individual discussion in the focus group, for example *elements* of networks; *use* of networks; and *forces for change*.

Step 2: establish the groups and plan for the sessions

The next stage requires the researcher to determine the number of groups, the number of participants in each group, the length of each session, their siting and timing, and finally the recruiting of participants.

Step 2.1: determine the number of groups

Selection for focus groups is purposive rather than random or convenience selection. In purposive selection, participants are selected for their suitability and ability to provide insights that are *relevant* to the particular study even though they are not necessarily *representative* of the frequencies of different types of people in the population as a whole. The more important issue is whether the focus group has characteristics of heterogeneity or homogeneity. If the issue is largely unframed or determined, a heterogeneous group will enable broad and general discussion and a wide variety of opinions to be expressed without prejudice or pre-judgement. Most focus group research, however, will seek some element of homogeneity, so that opinions stem from some element of commonality amongst participants. This can be as simple as commonality of age group, lifestyle, consumption patterns, expertise or experience. For example, all of Marilyn's groups were small business managers.

Referring again to purposive selection, the number of focus groups to be conducted depends upon the nature of the issue being investigated, the number of distinct market segments and the number of new ideas generated by each successive group. A secondary factor may of course be time and cost but this should not be a primary concern for restricting the number of focus groups to be researched. A general guideline is to continue conducting focus groups until little additional information is gained and the moderator can predict what is going to be said in the next group. This occurs usually after three to four groups. Where the research is exploratory in nature or with the purpose of simply *seeking new ideas* about a topic, this is usually the number of groups required. Where more detailed information is needed, up to about 8 or 12 focus groups might be undertaken. By the way, while there are no general rules concerning the optimal number of groups, the more homogeneous the groups are in terms of background, the fewer that are needed. Increasing the number of groups does not ensure increased accuracy.

After deciding on the number of groups, it is useful to produce a recruiting protocol to screen potential participants on, for example, standard demographics like management experience, age or gender. *Homogeneous* participants will be expected to get along easily and it is hoped they will be able to get over their lack of familiarity with each other quickly so that they can concentrate on the issues that the moderator raises. An alternative is to allow focus groups to *self-select* so that members know each other and will talk openly to the group about the issues, for example a group of managers in the same distribution channel who communicate regularly with each other and who perhaps have become friends over time.

Whilst focus group participants may be *experts* in a field, their deliberations are about issues outside their immediate sphere of responsibility and influence. Marilyn's focus groups of small business managers discussed issues of international marketing: these could be situation specific to the individual manager's own firm, and lead to discussions on individual opinion arising out of specific experience. The pooling and sharing of opinions enhances the profile of the issue being discussed and may also widen the scope of perspective.

Where focus group participants are brought together as non-experts, for example as consumers of household products, then it is the variety of opinions that will make most contribution to greater understanding of specific issues. Take an example of a producer/marketer of pre-cooked savoury pies. Research such as surveys incorporating store/shelf counts and street interviews will result in meaningful data about the most popular brands, pie fillings, buying patterns, and so on. However, focus groups will allow the pie producer to *test* new fillings, glean opinions on *why* certain types of pie are preferred, determine the reasons for preferences on image, price/value, variations of pie size, etc. Such information is a result of interaction of opinions and not simply a singular response to given stimuli. In other words, whatever the construction and constituency of a focus group it will allow greater depth of information on an issue compared to a general count of single opinion gleaned from surveys.

Given this requirement for group homogeneity, focus group research often involves at least four group interviews: two of one set of participants (for example, advertising copywriters) to allow cross-checking of the results of each of the two interviews, and two of another set of participants (for example, marketing managers).

In her study, Marilyn settled on four groups of small business people. To ensure she identified *international* marketing practices, two of the groups did not do international marketing and two did.

Step 2.2: determine the number of participants in each group

There is no consensus in the literature as to the number of participants in each focus group. Numbers range from 6 to 12, with some suggesting 8 to 12 participants (Stewart and Shamdasani 1990). Other researchers suggest 6 to 8 (Daume 1988) and 8 to 10 (Calder 1977). Even 20 participants has been suggested (Hess 1968); however, groups larger than 12 are usually not recommended due to the constraints large numbers put on each person's opportunity to share insights and observations.

Internationally the trend is towards a lower number of participants, presumably to allow greater interaction. For example, in Canada, where traditionally eight to ten people have been used in groups, group size is now typically five to six respondents. In the United States the trend is also towards smaller numbers of participants where groups now range from 6 to 8 respondents instead of the traditional 10 to 12 (Harris 1995). A similar trend is occurring in Australia and the UK. Thus the spread of the number of respondents now appears to range from a lower limit of five to an upper limit of eight.

Marilyn aimed for six when recruiting seven for each session to cover a *no-show*. For one session, only five turned up but she went ahead with the session nevertheless and found it worked satisfactorily.

Step 2.3: decide on the length of a session

Once a session begins, sufficient time needs to be taken to establish rapport with participants and to fully explore the issues at hand. Thus a focus group may last from one to three hours, although a duration of 1.5 to two hours is typical. Marilyn planned for her groups to last about 1.5 hours because her and others' experience showed that business people started to get restless by then.

Step 2.4: select the site

Although focus groups have been held almost anywhere, the venue should be neutral and one in which participants feel comfortable and at ease. Furthermore, the venue should be convenient and easily accessible. For example, Marilyn found that free, convenient parking was a key consideration.

For a focus group to be successful, the immediate physical environment is just as important as the venue. The environment should be free of distractions and as relaxed as possible to encourage informal *off the cuff* discussion. The most common option is a quiet room with circular or round conference table, which allows participants to lean forward and be less self-conscious about their bodies. Others prefer a living room atmosphere with coffee tables and easy chairs.

Step 2.5: decide on the timing of sessions

The actual time of day that a focus group is held can affect the extent to which participation is achieved. For example, early evening (5.30 to 7.00 p.m.) was the most appropriate time to conduct the sessions for Marilyn's small business owner/managers. The primary justification for this timing is that holding the sessions after normal business hours minimizes disruption to the daily routines, thus removing a possible obstacle to attendance. Additionally, early evening appears to be the optimal time in terms of both the degree to which group members stimulate each other's thoughts about a topic and also the extent to which participants enjoy the focus group. Nevertheless, breakfast, lunch, and mid-morning or afternoon can be appropriate for marketing management focus group research, and evening after dinner has been suitable for consumer research.

Step 2.6: recruit the participants

Recruiting participants for consumer focus groups can often be carried out by specialist firms that have lists of people in various categories. Alternatively, a variety of techniques can be employed in recruiting participants. These generally involve some kind of survey or trawl of a population and selection and invitation of those that match the demographic profile of the study in question. For marketing management research, recruiting is often more arduous again. In the example, Marilyn had to find participants from her own and colleagues' business and professional networks.

Participants are recompensed in some way for attending commercial consumer focus groups. Marilyn thought it would be insulting to pay her business people a small attendance fee and so she gave each of them a beautifully wrapped gift of a bottle of boutique wine (all at a cost of less than the usual fee for focus groups, as it turned out).

Step 3: select the moderator and assistant moderator

The quality of focus group research depends almost exclusively on the abilities of the moderator/facilitator/catalyst because the moderator is the instrument in the focus group interview. Here we emphasize the use of the researcher as the moderator, and also discuss the role of the assistant moderator.

The use of *professional moderators* is advocated by some authors (for example Stewart and Shamdasani 1990). Being a good scholar or researcher does not necessarily make a person a good moderator. Moderators must possess a number of skills: a genuine interest in hearing other people's thoughts and feelings, an ability to express their own feelings, to be animated and spontaneous, and to have a sense of humour, empathy, the ability to admit their own biases, insightfulness about people, and the ability to express thoughts clearly and to be flexible (Langer 1978). Phew!

However, instead of using a professional moderator, most academic researchers using focus groups take on the role of moderator. This is justified because researchers have the appropriate skills, particularly when there is a need for the moderator to be very familiar with the topic of discussion, and thus able to put all comments into perspective and follow up critical areas. Indeed because this requirement is inherent in the nature of research in business and management the researcher should always try to carry out the role of moderator. In the example of Marilyn, because she had been trained as a market researcher and knew more about the topic than anyone else available, she was able to justify acting as moderator herself.

We recommend having an *assistant moderator* if one can be found. Although the subject is not often addressed in the literature, the advantages of having an assistant moderator are numerous. Primarily an assistant prevents the moderator from being distracted by housekeeping duties and environment issues, thus enabling total concentration on the discussion. For example, the assistant moderator can take care of the refreshments, control the audio equipment, and make notes about the proceedings and participants' reactions. His or her notes and comments are helpful in the post-meeting analysis of each session.

Step 4: conduct the focus group discussions

A number of issues are involved in successfully conducting focus group discussions. These include the level of moderator involvement; number of topics in a session; wording of topics/questions; pre-testing the interview protocol; and running the beginning, the middle and the end of session. Each of these will be discussed in turn. Table 8.1 is an example of Marilyn's moderator's guide to illustrate many of these issues.

Table 8.1 *Framework for focus group research*

1	Defining the problem/issue/topic
2	Establishing the groups and plan of sessions
2.1	– determine the number of groups
2.2	– determine number of participants in each group
2.3	– decide on the length of a session
2.4	– select the site
2.5	– decide on the timing of sessions
2.6	– recruit the participants
3	Selecting the moderator and assistant moderator
4	Conducting focus group discussions
4.1	– determine the level of moderator involvement
4.2	– decide on the number of topics in a session
4.3	– word/identify questions/topics for discussion
4.4	– pre-testing the moderators' guide
4.5	– run the beginning, middle and end of sessions
5	Analysing the information

Source: based on Stewart and Shamdasani 1990 and Keown 1983

Step 4.1: determine the level of moderator involvement

The level of the moderator's involvement is governed by the objectives of the research and the structure of the groups. What is the purpose of the moderator? Earlier we discussed the importance of how the researcher raises topics and asks questions. Of course a focus group research moderator will have a topic or range of topics for discussion, many of which will be stimulated by appropriate questions. However, the focus group researcher is best considered not as an interviewer but as a *catalyst* for discussion. The true ability of a focus group researcher is being able to introduce a topic in such a way that participants are stimulated to respond. A further skill is in managing the balance of opinions. Every focus group will have a variety of personality types. Some will be extrovert or dominant and perhaps *jump in* with opinions frequently and early. Others will be introvert or be inclined to think privately about an issue and may or may not offer their opinions to the group. All types of personality have a value in focus group research: the skill on the part of the researcher/moderator/catalyst is in controlling the extrovert/dominant personality and ensuring meaningful contributions by introverts/private thinkers without them feeling threatened by this experience. Any new focus group researchers must be acutely aware of their role and function. Experiential learning will enable a focus group researcher to stabilize discussion to achieve a proper balance of participants' opinions. Experiential knowledge will also ensure that the researcher does not dominate the focus group through too much involvement and direction.

The moderator can control the group dynamics so that the desired high level of involvement is planned and achieved. This control prevents one person dominating the conversation, as well as allowing stimulation of quiet respondents to participate. Furthermore, unproductive discussion can be carefully interrupted without imposing the moderator's personal biases or putting words in the respondents' mouths.

In brief, the moderator needs to strike a balance between having too much structure, which prevents the participants' own ideas surfacing, and not enough structure, allowing some participants to dominate and some research issues or topics to be ignored.

Step 4.2: decide on the number of topics in a session

The number of topics covered impacts on the level of moderator involvement: it contributes towards what defines a structured or unstructured interview and thus high or low involvement by the moderator. But there appears to be little consensus as to what constitutes a structured group interview. For example, five broad topics have been considered as quite structured (Lederman 1990), but at the other extreme, 17 questions have been described as relatively unstructured (Byers and Wilcox 1991). As noted below, we suggest that the number of topics covered remains in balance between structure and no structure.

In addition, it is not necessary to adhere rigidly to the order of topics and the moderator may adjust the sequence according to the flow of the discussion. As well as having the freedom to rearrange the order of topics, the moderator needs to be involved, to ensure that all topics and surrounding issues are discussed. This prevents problems that may occur with low levels of moderator involvement, such as failure to discuss some topics, and difficulties in analysing disorganized data.

Deciding on the number of topics to be addressed in a session is often difficult to judge, as one group may react quite enthusiastically to a topic whilst another group may be uninterested, affecting the length of the session. Generally the accepted guideline is that there should be fewer than 12 topics – 'in practice most interview guides consist of fewer than a dozen' (Stewart and Shamdasani 1990: 62). More precisely, 10–12 topics are often appropriate. Marilyn's focus groups had 11 questions/topic areas, which are presented within her notes for the groups (Table 8.2).

Table 8.2 *Example of a moderator's guide*

Notes
Take extension cord, tape player and blank tapes
Fix labels on tapes
Take name tags
Take refreshments
Arrange gifts
Take notepaper and pen for everyone
Sandwiches, orange juice and tea and coffee on arrival
Name tags – first names only

Agenda for focus groups
Introduce assistant moderator
Before starting – explain housekeeping items
  1. Session taped to assist recording and analysis of data
     All participants shall remain anonymous in the report
  2. No right or wrong answers – purpose is to generate open discussions
  3. Ideally, only one person to speak at a time – if you have a sudden brainwave, jot it
     down and raise it when you can
  4. Be as spontaneous as possible
  5. Please speak up

Start tape

Ice-breaking session
Explain that each person (including the assistant moderator) will be asked to introduce
themselves and give a little background about what they do and their company, but first give
some history about yourself.

Explain the purpose of the discussion and itemize each topic grouping that will be covered.

Topics/questions for focus groups
  1. Ask for thoughts on the following topic/question to be written on individual sheets: as
     well as interacting with customers, a business must interact with suppliers, distributors
     and actual or potential competitors:
     (a) what has been your experience with interacting with people in these other
         organizations?
     (b) in your opinion has the experience been good or bad, and why?

  2. What has been your most successful experience and why?
     Suppliers
     Distributors
     Competitors – actual or potential

  3. What has been your worst experience? Why?
     Suppliers
     Distributors
     Competitors – actual or potential

  4. If I suggest the term 'network' to you – how would you define a network?

  5. Which networks are most important to you? Why?

  6. Which networks have you recently established or joined?
     How – e.g. through colleagues or broker?
     Why – e.g. age of organization, enter new markets?

  7. Which networks have you recently terminated?

Table 8.2 *continued*

8. How do networks influence the marketing activities of your business? Why?

9. Do you think networks have stages in their life? If so, what are various ways of progressing through these stages?

10. [*Give some warm up for this*] Are international marketing networks different to domestic ones? How?

11. Any other comments about networks?

Debriefing
Explain more about the research
Thank participants and present gifts

Another approach is to develop a rolling interview guide, where the list of topics is revised for the next group, based on the outcome of the previous group. This method may result in difficulties when trying to make comparisons between groups. But this difficulty may be far outweighed by the progression of in-depth understanding.

Step 4.3: identify questions or topics for discussion

Quality data is directly related to quality topics, which typically follow a prescribed format so that the maximum amount of useful information can be gained. Consequently, extreme consideration and careful forethought need to be given to the wording of the topics in the sessions. Furthermore, the way questions are addressed can place respondents in embarrassing or defensive situations.

Quality topics for focus groups are those which are *open-ended*, so providing a stimulus to the participants. Start with some very general issues and then funnel in to more specific ones. If the researcher decides to use questions, as in Marilyn's case, these should begin with key words such as *what, which* and *how*, as shown above. *Why* questions must be used cautiously in recognition that respondents often rationalize answers when asked 'why' or may become defensive. Therefore, *why* issues are best addressed as discussion points, coupled with phrases such as, 'could you explain that a little more' and similar probes. This approach indicates to the respondents that the moderator is interested not only in facilitating the discussion but also in the complexity of their answers.

Step 4.4: pre-test the moderators' guide

As for quantitative surveys, the focus group interview guide or protocol should be pre-tested to eliminate obvious problems. This allows the nature and wording of the interview topics to be evaluated to ensure that the wording of the questions is appropriate, to ascertain whether the topics are easily understood, and finally to ensure that the questions will elicit discussion. Marilyn piloted her protocol on three experienced focus group moderators and five business friends.

Step 4.5: run the beginning, middle and end of the sessions

The beginning of sessions is crucial as it sets the tone for the rest of the session and thus affects the outcomes. A stiff formal opening can inhibit discussion and stifle the dynamics in a group. So focus groups often provide refreshments and snacks for the participants prior to the commencement of the sessions. The sessions should begin close to the expected start time with a friendly and open welcome. The introduction should include an overview of the topic, explaining the ground rules and engaging in some form of *ice-breaking* activity or shared experience to facilitate group dynamics. For example, ask each person to introduce the person next to them to the whole group after a short discussion between pairs of participants.

The ground rules for focus groups are fairly standard. Respondents need to be assured that all participants will remain anonymous in the subsequent report, and that there are no right or wrong answers. Because the sessions are tape-recorded to assist in data analysis and reporting, ask individuals to speak up and that only one person speaks at a time. If a person has a thought while another person is speaking, ask that they make a note on the paper provided and enter the discussion at an appropriate point.

Although some focus groups can consist of people who already know each other, it is a general assumption that better information is obtained when participants are strangers. This may not be possible in much research with managers, but it may pay to try to include some people from outside the group of managers who know each other. Thus ice-breakers or introductions will occur. Introductions assist in creating a congenial group atmosphere that fosters self-disclosure. Marilyn showed participants how introductions could be done by introducing the assistant moderator to them and then asking the assistant moderator to introduce her. These introductions were beneficial because they not only broke the ice but also resulted in participants networking with each other immediately the sessions finished. She also provided name tags to wear and arranged name signs in front of positions at the table.

Whilst the beginning of the session is the most difficult, the flow and direction of the conversation *after the start* can be unpredictable. Two techniques helpful in soliciting additional information are the probe and the five-second pause (Krueger 1988). Probing eliminates the tendency of people to simply agree with what other participants have stated, for example, 'What has been your experience, Shirley?' and 'Have you any comments on this issue, John?' Similarly a pause often prompts additional points of view. Other techniques of non-evaluative interviewing (noted in

Chapter 6) are not to interrupt, not to introduce the moderator's own ideas and to practise active listening. The moderator should not evaluate a person's contribution by saying something like 'That was interesting.' People who do not receive these positive evaluations may feel that what they have said was wrong or unappreciated. 'OK' might be the limit of evaluations.

If theory testing is one of the objectives of the focus groups, participants can be asked to comment on and make suggestions about a conceptual model developed for the research which summarizes *a priori* the main features of the topic of discussion. Doing this provides the opportunity to obtain real-world feedback from the participants about a theoretical framework.

However if theory building is one of the objectives of the focus groups, it is even more important to avoid using questions to lead the discussion, but to raise discussion topics and allow participants to speak freely about these. In this case, the main contribution of the moderator would be to encourage further discussion and clarification by saying as little as possible but by using positive body language to encourage respondents. If any interjection is required it should be limited to encouraging statements such as 'Tell us more about that.'

Then, before finally concluding the sessions, some time can be allocated to a debriefing session where more information is given about the research if it is appropriate and to allow further clarification of points and issues. For example, the moderator may want to ask for any other comments about the research topic and then ask for suggestions about who else he/she should contact who would be knowledgeable about the research topic. This approach not only allows the conceptual framework to be refined, but also stimulates thoughts and ideas from some participants which may not have previously been mentioned in the discussion.

The conclusion of the focus group session provides another opportunity to gain information. Rather than just thanking participants and dismissing them, a summary of the main points helps to confirm the moderator's perception about the proceedings. Of course, any participants' payments or gifts are made then, too.

Step 5: analyse the information

Analysis of the information is also a challenging part of focus group research. This section discusses the content analysis part of focus group research and then briefly addresses the question of whether the moderator should also be the analyst.

Content analysis can be performed either with the assistance of computers using software programs such as NUD*IST, or by manually coding the data. That is, it reviews the focus group transcripts attaching tags or labels to 'chunks' of data to enable objective and systematic counting and recording procedures. A chunk can be anything from a phrase, a sentence or sentences to whole paragraphs.

The actual creation of the codes can be achieved in three ways. Firstly, the research can develop a provisional *start list* of codes prior to conducting the fieldwork. This list may come from the conceptual framework, the list of research topics or key variables. For example, Marilyn's codes included elements, forces for change and uses of networks. Secondly, a more inductive approach is to delay deciding on the codes until the data is collected, and then examine it for ideas, themes and key concepts that could be codes – a method known as open coding (discussed in Chapter 6). This is a particularly insightful approach in achieving deep meaning and understanding of issues. A third way is a combination of both methods.

The researcher who moderates the groups is often the analyst in the research, as noted above. This can be justified on the basis that this person would have a better feel for the data than an external analyst, as moderators have had first-hand exposure to each of the discussions, have observed the interactions of participants and are likely to have had the most intensive exposure to the problem at hand (Krueger 1988). In addition it is sometimes valuable to utilize researchers who might not have been the moderator on a specific focus group but nevertheless are experienced moderators in themselves, to analyse the transcripts. This can often lead to different interpretations or identification of issues overlooked by the moderator in his/her own analysis.

When the analyst writes his or her final report, quotations are used to substantiate the findings and conclusions made about the patterns in the data.

Limitations of Focus Group Research

Researchers should be mindful of focus groups' limitations, as focus groups can be very easily misused. Limitations, like strengths, are linked to process issues and the generalizability of the findings. Process issues relate particularly to achieving focused interactions in the group, the impact of the presence and role of the moderator, and the impact of the group itself on the data. Each of these issues affects the data generated.

Process issues

Two main points arise when discussing process issues. The first is the extent to which group members affect each other and the second is the effect of the moderator on the group. Each of these will be addressed in turn.

Despite the best efforts of moderators, groups may suffer from uneven participation brought about either by the impact of an overly enthusiastic respondent dominating the conversation, or by an aggressive respondent intimidating others in the group. Indeed, focus groups can be influenced by an emerging mentality as the group interacts about a topic (Morgan 1988), and that may suppress the views of some people.

In some situations, individuals may be more honest with an outside interviewer than with peers in a focus group. For example, Marilyn found that focus group interaction might have biased her findings. In later individual interviews, she found results that contradicted some focus group findings about the importance of various types of networks. Apparently business people were willing to divulge views about their competitive strengths in the relative privacy of an individual interview, but they would not do that in a focus group. The lesson here is to recognize that in a homogeneous group, such as one consisting of small business managers where issues of competition and confidentiality are present, some topics will be inappropriate in a focus group.

In addition, the very presence of the moderator can have the paradoxical consequence of disrupting the group dynamics (Agar and MacDonald 1995). The moderator's presence and probing, which are inherent features of focus groups, may produce group processes that might not otherwise occur. Furthermore, the moderator may unwittingly bias results by emitting cues or signals about what may be favourable or unfavourable responses. However, moderator training and experience will help minimize these problems.

Generalizability of the findings

Focus groups are most useful when they produce new results. However, the results of focus groups are not generalizable to the larger population, as the participants may not be truly representative of the target population. Therefore focus group researchers should concentrate on analytic generalizability, if this is desired, rather than statistical generalizability.

Summary

Focus groups are an extremely useful and often cost-effective method of gathering insightful aspects about a research topic. Efficiency can be enhanced by following a clearly defined framework similar to the one described in this chapter. The contemporary view of an appropriate number of respondents in each group is five to eight. A critical element of successful focus groups is the moderator, who must be careful not to bias participants' responses. Rigorous attention needs to be paid to the wording of topics and how and when they are introduced. Potential problems with wording and flow can be avoided through the use of pilot studies. All stages of the focus group discussion – the beginning, the middle and the end – are of equal importance.

In conclusion, focus groups are a versatile research methodology but can be misused unless a well thought-out planning process is followed.

LEARNING QUESTIONS

What are the advantages of using focus group interviewing for interpretive research?

Outline the steps involved in the planning of focus group interviews and illustrate the value of planning each step.

What are the limitations of focus group interviews and how can a researcher overcome these?

Note

Nominal groups are groups in name only. The members are interviewed individually and summaries of responses are provided to the other members of the group. Such groups are useful when it is too difficult to congregate members together at a mutually convenient time or location. Delphi is a specialized application of the nominal group technique. Delphi (derived from the Greek literature 'Oracles of Delphi') is used when focusing on the future (Stewart and Shamdasani 1990: 22–23).

References

Advertising Research Foundation (1985) *Focus Groups: Issues and Approaches*, Author, New York.

Agar, M. and MacDonald, J. (1995) 'Focus Groups and Ethnography', *Human Organization*, 54(1): 78–86.

Byers, P.Y. and Wilcox, J.R. (1991) 'Focus Groups: a Qualitative Opportunity for Researchers', *Journal of Business Communication*, 28: 63–78.

Calder, B.J. (1977) 'Focus Group Research and the Nature of Qualitative Marketing Research', *Journal of Marketing Research*, 14(Aug.), 353–364.

Carey, M.A. (1994) 'The Group Effect in Focus Groups: Planning, Implementing and Interpreting Focus Group Research', in J. Morse (ed.), *Critical Issues in Qualitative Research Methods*, Sage, Thousand Oaks, CA, pp. 225–241.

Daume Jr., H.C. (1988) 'Focus Groups Don't Have to be Expensive', *Marketing News*, 22(24 Oct.), 23 and 26.

Harris, L.M. (1995) 'Technology, Techniques Drive Focus Group Trends', *Marketing News*, 29(5) 27 Feb., 8.

Hess, J.M. (1968) 'Group Interviewing', in R.L. King (ed.), *Proceedings of Advances in Consumer Research*, American Marketing Association, Chicago.

Keown, C. (1983) 'Focus Group Research: Tool for the Retailer', *Journal of Small Business Management*, 21 (April), 59–65.

Krueger, R.A. (1988) *Focus Groups: A Practical Guide for Applied Research*, Sage, Newbury Park, CA.

Langer, J. (1978) 'Clients: Check Qualitative Researchers' Personal Traits to Get More; Qualitative Researchers: Enter Entire Marketing Process to Give More', *Marketing News*, 12(8), Sept., 10–11.

Lederman, L.C. (1990) 'Assessing Educational Effectiveness: the Focus Group Interview as a Technique for Data Collection', *Community Education*, 39, 117–127.

Merton, R.K., Fiske, M. and Kendall, P.L. (1956) *The Focused Interview*, Free Press, Glencoe, IL.

Morgan, D.L. (1988) 'Focus Groups as Qualitative Research', *Qualitative Research Methods*, 16, Sage, Newbury Park, CA.

Morgan, D. and Krueger, R.A. (1993) 'When to Use Focus Groups and Why,' in D.L. Morgan (ed.), *Successful, Focus Groups: Advancing the State of the Art*, Sage, Thousand Oaks, CA.

Stewart, D.W. and Shamdasani, P.N. (1990) *Focus Groups: Theory and Practice*, Sage, Newbury Park, CA.

9 Observation Studies

This chapter outlines the scope and nature of observation studies in the context of qualitative research. It considers the circumstances when observation is appropriate in a research study, and why. In particular, we aim to illustrate and emphasize the value of observation studies for research in the context of marketing management.

Definition

Observation is based on watching what people do, looking at their behavioural patterns and actions and at objects, occurrences, events and interactions. In its purest form it involves collecting data without questioning or communicating with people: we can call this non-participant or passive observation; or taking the role of a 'complete observer' (Gill and Johnson 1991). There is also participant observation that allows more interaction and communication with people in a research setting. Becker and Geer's definition highlights the specific characteristics of this approach and how it can be distinguished from 'pure' observation:

> By participant observation we mean the method in which the observer participates in the daily life of the people under study, either openly in the role of researcher or covertly in some disguised role, observing things that happen, listening to what is said, and questioning people, over some length of time. (1957: 28)

We discuss participant observation in more depth later in the chapter.

Observation can be used where data is accessible, that is, actions, occurrences and interactions must occur where access can be gained by a researcher. The researcher needs to be aware that the particular phenomenon of interest is likely to arise in a certain context or circumstance. To some extent, these actions need to occur frequently and repetitively in order to allow time for patterns and habits to be observed (McDaniel and Gates 1999). Action to be observed must take a relatively short time so that it is possible for someone to observe and record it.

Traditionally observation has been used in consumer research. For example, common uses of observation have been to understand consumer buyer behaviour, consumers' responses to stimuli such as marketing activity or interactions; or emotional reactions in different situations. Observation studies are very useful for watching people's behaviour, actions, habits or patterns in specific situations or contexts.

In particular, observation studies have been widely used in the development of new product or marketing concepts: for example, observing how specific consumers use new products such as observing children play with prototype toys. Observation studies are also very useful in service settings for observing service processes and performances, and the extent and nature of customer–staff interactions in different situations (Grove and Fisk 1992). Furthermore, observations have been integral to the practice of *mystery shopping*, a method widely used in retail and services outlets where an individual acting as a customer experiences how staff interact with them and observes other relevant dimensions of service in a retail/service location. Again, we discuss this in more detail later in the chapter.

Appropriateness of observation studies

Observation studies are appropriate where a study aims to confirm actions in a discreet manner without involving the subjects explicitly. They are also useful where the researcher's purpose is to expand his/her perspective, where the aims and objectives of a study or research require knowledge and understanding of a variety of perspectives in relation to a particular area of study in an unobtrusive or covert circumstance.

Observation studies are also appropriate when respondents may act unconsciously or find it difficult to articulate their views, for example patterns or habits in ritualistic or repetitive behaviour (Denscombe 1998). Often consumers on a shopping trip would find it difficult to recall which shops they visited, how long they had spent in different shops, how long they spent comparing brands or evaluating products before selecting items. Therefore the use of observation studies would be very relevant for research with such a purpose.

However, observations are inappropriate for the measurement or assessment of people's 'internal' values, such as feelings and beliefs. They primarily record observable behaviour and not intention.

Positivist/interpretivist approach to observation

Traditionally in positivist research, the use of observation studies has been as a preliminary technique, usually for exploratory research at early stages in order to refine research techniques and protocols. They have been used predominantly in consumer research and in retailing contexts. In such a circumstance observations would adhere to positivist strictures such as being part of a formulated research process, planned systematically, recorded systematically, used to *count* the number of phenomena, subject to checks and controls.

In interpretivist research, observation studies can play a wider, more integrative role in the context of the overall research purpose. They can be used widely in managerial and organizational contexts and in more comprehensive marketing situations. Therefore they are valuable for research in management where they can be used in a more holistic manner either throughout a research study or longitudinally for interpretive research purposes. Observation studies used in interpretivist research may in fact form the sole research method that is designed to gain in-depth insights and understanding of specific practices. Such studies may involve ethnographic dimensions and are likely to be longitudinal in order to observe and monitor changes and developments.

Either or both positivist and interpretivist philosophies may be inherent in different types of observation research depending on the researcher's philosophy and aims. Let us consider some of these different types.

Different Types of Observation Research

Traditionally observation studies can be carried out in a number of different ways using a number of different techniques. These are summarized briefly in this section.

Structured or unstructured

Structured observation occurs where the researcher has a research protocol designed for the research (McDaniel and Gates 1999). That is, where there are specific factors that the researcher needs to observe, such as the size and layout of an office and the number of managers in the office, or the layout of a retail store and the position of key demand product items.

Unstructured observations, in contrast, have no specific focus: the researcher might want to record everything they observe in a new situation but have no pre-formed ideas of what should be observed. It is a useful method for exploring and clarifying the focus for the next stages of a research study or to contribute to the design of an observation research protocol for a more in-depth or a longitudinal study. For example unstructured observation studies would be useful in a circumstance that is new to a researcher, where they may need to expand their perspective on the phenomena of interest. In the past we have used this technique in the development of a number of studies that required understanding the complexity of a large variety of service dimensions in different situations. Firstly in trying to identify all the service variables involved in a ferry travel service we, as researchers, travelled as passengers in order to observe and record the details of each service area and points of interaction between customers and company staff in a typical return journey. The outcome of this unstructured approach was to use the data to design an observation tool/protocol for assessing the marketing and service dimensions of different ferry services in Northern Europe. Further development of this research led to the construction of in-depth interview protocol for use with travelling customers.

Human or mechanical

Observation can be conducted by human or mechanical means (Grove and Fisk 1992). Observations using mechanical means are common in consumer research. For example, closed circuit television sets have been used widely to observe consumers' buying behaviour. Mechanical counting can occur in relation to the sales of specific products or brands in retail outlets. Observations of the packaging in consumers' bins is used to record the products and brands they buy (called 'garbology'!) (McDaniel and Gates 1999). Traffic census involve both the mechanical counting of cars at specific road junctions, at specific times of the day and week, coupled with human observation of *type* of vehicles.

Human observations are much more relevant to research carried out in a managerial or organizational environment. These are more appropriate when the study is not interested in simplistic information only, such as a count of people, objects or activities. Instead human observation is vital for recording more descriptive data that involves the behaviour of individuals or groups of people, the context of the behaviour, variations in activities and possible reasons for the behaviour. Human observation is much more flexible and appropriate for business research involving human interactions and decision making.

Natural or contrived

The options here are in relation to whether the phenomena of interest can be observed in a natural context, and if not, whether a situation or scenario can be contrived to research a particular phenomenon. Traditionally, contrived situations have been used for consumer research: for example setting up a variety of store layouts without disrupting real stores, in order to evaluate the potential of new store layouts in terms of how customers use them and how much they spend. Similarly, contrived situations include the use of store-like settings where participants are invited to compare the packaging and branding of competitive products.

Many phenomena of interest to researchers in managerial research require to be observed in a natural setting, as there is little value in researching managerial activities and behaviours in contrived or unrealistic situations (Johns and Lee-Ross 1998). Indeed, many studies have emphasized the value of observation studies in managerial research mainly because managers and managerial activities occur in specific places such as the *natural* setting of an organization. Such activities, if they are to be researched, need to be observed in context rather than in isolation (Mintzberg 1979). Traditional methods and approaches of using observation studies in consumer studies (as opposed to participant observation, consumers as participants and mystery shopping which are described later) can be adapted and refined to suit observations in business or organizational settings. Take, for example, the use of observation studies for monitoring how consumers use retail outlets, in terms of store layout, choice of products and brands, and how various marketing and merchandizing activities impact on their shopping behaviour and amount of money they spend. Using their managerial knowledge and experience, marketing managers can use observation studies as a natural and ongoing method of collecting data, as an everyday activity in relation to how consumers respond to various marketing activities. Indeed as managers become more experienced in this they can develop the skill for observing and improving the management of customer–staff interactions and ways of dealing with complaints or unsatisfactory situations in service delivery or customer interactions.

Furthermore, observation studies of managerial activities in specific contexts are an appropriate and useful means of gaining understanding of how managers manage. For example, observation studies focusing on what managers do during their working day, how managers make decisions, who they talk to, how they delegate activities, and how marketing actions are implemented would provide very rich data on the managerial situation in a given context. Much of the renowned management theorist Mintzberg's early work in organizational studies was based on observations. For example, his doctoral dissertation involved a study of the work of five managers using structured observation (Mintzberg 1970). During this study Mintzberg observed what each manager did for a week, recorded systematically whom the managers worked with, when, where, for how long and for what purpose. He used this data to induce a set of characteristics and roles of managerial work (Mintzberg 1973).

Similarly, observation studies are widely used for research in the travel industry. For example, ferry companies have used observation studies to record customers' vehicle registrations. They use this information to ascertain where people travel from, which ferry route they use and at which times of the day, week and year.

Disguised or undisguised

Should people know if they are being observed or not? Ethically it is important that people are not involved in some aspect of research without their prior knowledge (Jorgensen 1989). However, the counter side of this argument is that if they knew they were being observed they might change their behaviour and the research would be of little value. There are many examples given in past studies of how this can happen. For example, studies where people's TV viewing habits were observed noted that their habits change during the first few weeks of being observed, before they finally revert to their normal habits. Thus, if this method is to be used, it should be carried out over a long time period. However, if the identity of those being observed remains anonymous, then disguised observation may be acceptable.

In managerial research this dilemma of disguise is less likely to be an issue. The value of carrying out observation studies in managerial or organizational situations is to observe managers and employees in their work settings and in many cases this involves observations of subconscious activities which are *natural*, instinctive and ritualistic. Clearly the managers' and organizations' permission would be sought before embarking on such research, and a longitudinal element will enable managers to absorb observers into the everyday circumstances of their environment.

Participant observation

Participant observation is where the researcher becomes closer to the research situation and actually participates in the research setting or phenomena (Blumer 1969). The participant observer can behave in a completely covert fashion by operating *under cover* (Delbridge and Kirkpatrick 1994). Indeed often the success of the research depends upon the researcher remaining undetected. If no one knows about the research in the research setting, then it is assumed that everyone will act in a normal way and thus preserve the naturalness of the setting. Otherwise there is the possibility that the people may hide or disguise some phenomena, situations or behaviour. Covert observation reveals such events by doing the research secretly. This method has been well used by social scientists in studies of inmates in clinical wards, mental institutions, juvenile detention centres and prisons, and has been widely used in studies of *inadmissible* activities such as drug taking or prostitution. In such studies aspects of the culture or subculture's *normal* or acceptable behaviour would remain hidden because researchers using other methods would not get this close to the situation. The value of participant observation is that data is gathered through the researcher's experience of events and situations. By experiencing things from the insider's point of view the researcher becomes aware of the crucial factors in a given scenario and the values and priorities of the people involved.

Yet it is also possible, and often preferable, for the researcher's role not to be secret. In some situations everyone involved may be aware of the researcher's purpose and will have no reason to feel threatened by it or have need to change their behaviour because of his/her presence. There are situations where the researcher's role will only be known by some *gatekeepers* such as top or middle management but may not be known to others in the situation. The purpose here is to gain access and permission for the research but not spoil the *naturalness* of the setting by informing everyone involved in the phenomena under study. In such cases the researcher may keep some distance from the group under study and this may be appropriate if the researcher lacks the expertise or personal credentials to take on a *role* in the research context.

Often in managerial research the participant is predominantly an observer. This is where everyone knows the identity of the participant as a researcher. This may take the form of *shadowing* individuals or groups for a specific length of time or while a particular scenario is carried out. This type of participant observation has the advantage that the consent of all involved can be gained and also that the specific information required can be explicitly sought out.

Participant observation is an important and integral part of ethnographic studies (see Chapter 10). It is a fundamental aspect of *in-dwelling* in a research setting that is the foundation of ethnographic studies. Given that ethnography emphasizes the importance of understanding things from the point of view of those involved, participant observation allows the researcher to *live with* the people under study in the same surroundings and situational context. In this case, participant observers will want to maintain the naturalness of the setting as much as possible and not want to intrude with their values, demands, research tools or experimental designs. Observation research can sometimes serve as a specific tool within a wider research methodology such as an ethnographic study.

The meaning of actions and reasons behind the phenomena are the focus of participant observation, where the emphasis will be on reaching an in-depth understanding of the situation. It will aim to achieve deep insights, which can describe the subtleties, complexity and contrasts of the phenomena under study.

However, there are different degrees of involvement or immersion for the participant observer role (Jaeger 1988). At one extreme the researcher will *live* in the research setting for a longitudinal time period and play a role such as one of the employees or contributors to a situation. Or the researcher could visit the research setting sporadically such as once a week, for a number of weeks or for a few days in every month, bi-monthly, or quarterly over a longitudinal period. Another approach is for the researcher to visit or *hang around* with a group of people frequently or infrequently rather than being a *member* of the group. However, this must be carried out often enough and over a long enough period to allow the researcher to gain insight and reach an understanding about the phenomena under study.

Mystery shopping

Mystery shopping is a term used for researching phenomena related to customers' experiences of shopping (McDaniel and Gates 1999). It may be to gather data about a store, its layout, merchandizing, product ranges and so on or about experiences of the customer–employee interactions. This means that the research may include both observations and conversations or interactions with staff. Note the word *conversations* as opposed to *interviews*; interactions should be limited to conversations as a customer to a staff member. The purpose of such studies is really about the *front line* interactions with customers and everything the customer experiences in a retail, hotel or other service outlet. They are widely used in the hospitality industry by trade researchers and evaluators. The people who allocate star ratings to hotels and restaurants and writers who are restaurant critics act as mystery shoppers.

Consumers as participant observers

Observation studies can be constructed as survey questionnaires or self-completion forms for consumers of retail service situations. We have all had the opportunity to participate in customer service or service quality surveys, for example restaurant or hotel survey forms where we are asked to record our opinions or experience of various service dimensions. There is a variety of ways in which such information can be gathered, for example:

- forced choice self-completion questionnaires;
- open ended questions seeking opinions;
- a positional tick in a schematic scale which may use numbers or graphics, such as
  Very bad   1   2   3   4   5   Very good
  Very bad   ☹   ☺   Very good

Such information can provide a valuable database of consumer observations on aspects of customer service that can then be evaluated and used to seek ways of improving service delivery and service quality.

How to Prepare for Observation Studies

The purpose of any type of observation study is firstly to learn about and secondly to analyse or assess a situation or context. Observation requires considerable time to be spent in the field. The researcher(s) need time to prepare and organize for the research and time at all stages of the research.

For example, it takes time to gain entrance, understand what is going on, gain trust, define parameters and develop understanding and insights (Bogdewic 1992). It will also require time to analyse the situation, revise and review the situation and write up the final report.

In early stages the researcher should try to get an overall feel for the situation, that is search for a *holistic* observation or perception (Shaffir et al. 1980).

Some thought must be given to how to make field notes, what to note, how often, when, where and what detail should be included. We recommend that the researcher should keep a detailed diary of all events and should develop a framework or protocol for gathering data early on in the study when an initial understanding or knowledge of the key phenomena have been achieved. This framework should be flexible enough to allow the collection of new types of information and more detail as the research progresses. In tandem with the recording framework it is a good idea to utilize other data recording mechanisms such as pictorial records using a picture and/or video camera and if appropriate an audio recorder. Similarly, gather any literature that outlines and describes the concept or facility such as floor guides, layout brochures and any promotional or factual material.

Value of observation studies

The value of observation studies is that what actually happens is recorded. Compared with the limitations of surveys or interviews where questioning approaches must be used, which recognize that the nature of question wording and interviewing can be restrictive, observation studies generate actual data, as observed by the researcher.

Some might argue that such observation is biased according to the researchers' perspective or stimulus. However, such prejudices can be negated by using several observers, longitudinal timescales and by constructing an observation *protocol* or instrument. This protocol or instrument can take a variety of forms, for example using the layout of a shopping mall complex that allows the researcher to plot and record the actual consumer purchase points. Another example would be to create a key point observation instrument which allows the recording of actual happenings at each key point, say a hotel's reception, restaurant, or other service areas. (We return to this protocol/instrument in our examples below.)

Our discussion in Chapter 4 on *domains* of marketing research offers critical perspectives on the value of observation research. In the *practitioner* research domain, as this chapter demonstrates, observation research is a powerful, easy to use and valuable research tool, which can serve management in its decision making and help to improve standards, particularly in relation to customer service and service quality dimensions.

In the marketing research industry and academic research domains, observation research studies are commonly viewed as preliminary research tools, or as confirmatory mechanisms of wider studies (as outlined earlier in the context of how observation studies are used by positivist researchers). However, it is our view that observation research when utilized in academic research studies can be a powerful tool in its own right as a mechanism for qualitative research. Although observation studies still need to emerge from their *supporting* role and function, there is every scope for extensive observation studies in the marketing management domain in both confirming existing marketing phenomena and in gaining new insights into new marketing phenomena.

Examples of observation studies in marketing management practice

Two examples of how observation studies have been used in practice are given below. One example is in a retail setting and the other is in a service setting.

A retail merchandising and catering complex

Alan, the Managing Director of a large retail merchandizing and catering complex was keen to know the consumer patterns of usage at each of the service points in his complex. Specifically, these included five catering units ranging from snack and fast-food outlets to full restaurant service; three bars for drinks and beverages; and one large retail merchandizing store offering a variety of gift and value items.

Initially observation studies observed patterns of usage including areas of congestion and queuing, under-used space, aspects of ambience, suitability of layout, convenience and efficiency. As a result of these regular, passive non-participatory observation studies, Alan was able to make adjustments to the layout of the complex and alter some product and service ranges. Much of the observation was carried out by Alan and his service managers, who were able to observe, from suitable vantage points, all that was necessary within the scope of the efficiency objectives and decision making requirements.

The next stage of Alan's customer service and service quality improvement drive was to gauge the service interactions of specific service points. To do this he needed participant observers who were unknown to his service staff and managers. Hence he utilized observers as *mystery shoppers* who engaged in all aspects of the service interaction and reported on their expectations and experiences. The findings here allowed Alan and colleagues to address specific service interactions and to discuss with staff the best ways to improve specific and overall levels of service quality and delivery.

Such a mystery shopping study could only be utilized to a certain extent before staff became resentful of a continuous *big-brother* syndrome that increasingly appeared to *blame* them for certain aspects of non-delivery. For example, when a particular unit was very busy to the point of overcrowding, service delivery levels inevitably declined and staff felt they were being blamed for this. Alan's solution was to establish levels of service delivery and service quality in agreement with staff and to revert to non-participation observations, which used the agreed criteria as benchmarks. Variances from the benchmarks allowed Alan to focus on issues such as manning levels and customer interaction efficiencies to overcome deficiencies. Staff responded positively to this and proactively suggested service improvements as appropriate.

Alan continues to engage in periodic non-participation observations based on known benchmarks of interaction performance. These observations serve to monitor and maintain the levels of service delivery and service quality now expected by Alan's customers.

The ferry travel industry – a wider mechanism for comparative evaluations using observation studies

An example of our observation protocol designed for the study of the services marketed on board car ferries in Northern Europe is shown in Figure 9.1 (this example is taken from Gilmore 1997). The design of the protocol was based on what should be observed, where, when, and how these observations should take place.

In this case the protocol was based on the necessity and value of carrying out observations of all elements of marketing activity in service settings, that is taking account of both tangible and intangible marketing dimensions in a relatively complex service delivery.

The purpose of the observation study was to carry out a comparison of each major ferry company's marketing activity in relation to the facilities and quality on the major Irish, UK, Northern European and Scandinavian routes. The Northern European ferry companies studied included operators of Irish, UK, Dutch, French, German, Swedish and Finnish origin.

Observations of the facilities on board and customer–staff interactions were carried out at the beginning, during and end of each sailing time. These were carried out by researchers and immediately followed by extensive data recording. Thus the similarities and differences in the level of service on board each of these company's ferries was observed in relation to physical facilities, choice and range of product/service, information available, staff accessibility to customers, communication and interaction with customers and customer response to products/services.

Physical facilities – this included observations of the style of ferry layout and spaciousness of the ferry and how these contributed to the freedom or otherwise of passengers' movement. The number of service outlets was also taken into account.

	Beginning	during	end
PHYSICAL FACILITIES Style of layout Spaciousness of ferry Number of service outlets			
CHOICE AND RANGE OF PRODUCTS/ SERVICES Range of food offered Range of shop products Range of beverages Range of entertainment			
INFORMATION AVAILABLE Visual promotion to customers Verbal promotion to customers Tannoy announcements Guidance signs Information leaflets			
STAFF ACCESSIBILITY In restaurant/s In bar areas In entertainment facilities In shop/s			
COMMUNICATION AND INTERACTION Courtesy/politeness Helping customers Competency of staff			
CUSTOMER RESPONSE TO PRODUCTS/ SERVICES Use of restaurant/s Use of bar areas Use of entertainment facilities Use of shop			

Figure 9.1 *Observation tool*

Choice and range of products/services – observations focused on the range of food offered in the restaurants and cafeterias, the range of products in the on-board shops, the range of drinks in cafeterias and bars and the range and scope of entertainment for each age group observed on board.

Information and advice available – Visual and verbal communication and promotion to customers, tannoy announcements, guidance signs and information leaflets were all aspects of the information and advice observed on board.

Staff accessibility to customers – This involved observing the presence of staff when they were required for delivering a service to customers in the various outlets on board such as the restaurants, cafeterias, bars, entertainment facilities and shops.

Staff communication and interaction with customers – This included observing the courtesy and politeness shown, whether staff helped customers, and the competency of staff in carrying out their jobs.

Customer behaviour/response to the product and services – Customer responses were observed in relation to all the on-board products and services offered such as the extent of use of the restaurants, bars, entertainment facilities and shops.

During each sailing observations were made in relation to these aspects of on-board service delivery and recorded, with descriptions and examples of occurrences. Again, the monitoring of these observations was carried out at the beginning, during and the end of each sailing to take account of service consistency. The level of these offerings and activities was measured on a five-point schematic scale where a rating of 1 denoted the non-existence or a very low level of that element whereas a rating of 5 denoted a high level. These ratings were used as guidelines only and were justified and explained by the descriptions of and comments on what was observed and how this resulted in such a comparative rating.

After the fieldwork had been carried out *criteria for analysis* were developed which were based upon the service dimensions above and the extent to which these were delivered (see our description in the case example in Chapter 6, pp. 80–84).

Summary

Observation studies can be used in a variety of ways and for a variety of purposes. This chapter has outlined these and focused on their application in the context of marketing management research. In this context we believe that observation research is not simply a *first touch* methodology for larger studies but can be an integral interpretivist tool in reaching deep and insightful understanding of *real* phenomena which provide meaningful and usable data for marketing managers and qualitative researchers alike.

LEARNING QUESTIONS

What is meant by observation research and what is its context in the wider research domain?

Outline different types of observation studies.

What is the value of observation research for marketing managers? Give some examples.

References

Becker, H. and Geer, B. (1957) 'Participant Observation and Interviewing: A Comparison', *Human Organisation*, 16(3), 28–35.

Blumer, H. (1969) *Symbolic Interactionism: Perspective and Method*, Prentice-Hall, Englewood Cliffs, NJ.

Bogdewic, S.P. (1992) 'Participant Observation', in B.F. Crabtree and W.L. Miller (eds), *Doing Qualitative Research*, Sage Publications, Newbury Park, CA, pp. 45–69.

Delbridge, R. and Kirkpatrick, I. (1994) 'Theory and Practice of Participant Observation', in V. Wass and P. Wells (eds), *Principles and Practice in Business and Management Research*, Dartmouth, Aldershot, pp. 35–62.

Denscombe, M. (1998) *The Good Research Guide*, Open University Press, Buckingham.

Gill, J. and Johnson, P. (1991) *Research Methods for Managers*, Paul Chapman, London.

Gilmore, A. (1997) 'Marketing in the Northern European Ferry Industry: An Overview of On-board Activity', *Journal of Vacation Marketing. An International Journal*, 3(3), 207–220.

Grove, S. and Fisk, R.P. (1992) 'Observational Data Collection Methods for Services Marketing: An Overview', *Journal of Academy of Marketing Science*, 20(3), 217–224.

Jaeger, R.M. (1988) *Complementary Methods for Research in Education*, American Educational Research Association, Washington, DC.

Johns, N. and Lee-Ross, D. (1998) *Research Methods in Service Industry Management*, Cassell, London.

Jorgensen, D.L. (1989) *Participant Observation: A Methodology for Human Studies*, Sage Publications, Newbury Park, CA.

McDaniel Jr., C. and Gates, R. (1999) *Contemporary Marketing Research*, 4th edn, South-Western College Publishing, Cincinnati.

Mintzberg, H. (1970) 'Structured Observation as a Method to Study Managerial Work', *Journal of Management Studies*, February, 87–104.

Mintzberg, H. (1973) *The Nature of Managerial Work*, Harper & Row, New York.

Mintzberg, H. (1979) 'An Emerging Strategy of Direct Research', *Administrative Science Quarterly*, 24 December, 582–589.

Shaffir, W.B., Stebbins, R.A. and Turowetz, A. (1980) *Fieldwork Experience*, St Martin's, New York.

10 Ethnography and Grounded Theory

This chapter introduces two techniques that epitomize qualitative research in that they collect data that is deep, rich, thick. Ethnography and grounded theory are especially appropriate for research in marketing because they can be used to investigate the people oriented aspects of marketing phenomena. We will start with ethnography because it uses many qualitative methods such as going into the field to collect interview and observation data which we have described in earlier chapters. We then move on to grounded theory and introduce additional issues of qualitative research such as coding, bias and trustworthiness as we do so.

What Is Ethnography?

Ethnography is a form of qualitative research originally developed by anthropologists and sociologists to describe a society, group or culture. Its aim is to answer research questions about understanding and describing a group of interacting people. Essentially, the researcher becomes immersed in the group, that is, *goes native* and *lives* with a small group of people in a specific setting to record, categorize and code what is going on to provide a holistic picture of the group (Sanday 1979). Classic ethnographic studies have involved researchers living with and describing a wide variety of social groupings such as nude bathers, professional gamblers, street gangs, police in police cars, and doctors and nurses in hospital emergency wards. In addition, ethnographic studies have been done of managers in their work setting. For example, one researcher worked in four small businesses for more than a year, making notes of everything he could, including hastily written transcripts of morning tea banter, recordings of telephone conversations and an analysis of 660 invoices (Stockport and Kakabadse 1991). An example of a marketing ethnographic study is in Dunnett and Arnold (1999) and is summarized as follows:

> Jane wanted to investigate how the strong organizational culture of the retailing giant Wal-Mart impacted upon customer satisfaction.

After some weeks of phone calls and letters to Wal-Mart managers, she was allowed to join the company as a regular peak-time associate, working less than 28 hours per week. She went through the same training and socialization programmes as all Wal-Mart Associates did, and had the same responsibilities, work patterns, benefits and pay as they did. Her data was her experiences and discussions with other associates who thought she was an ordinary associate like them. She found that the values of the founder, Sam Walton, drove the organization in many ways, like having posters with Walton quotations about the importance of customers in back hallways used only by staff, and the use of first names for everyone who worked there to foster a team culture devoted to customer satisfaction. She herself found that this culture made her forgive nasty customers in a way that she would not forgive people outside her Wal-Mart work, for example. However, she found the customer-first culture was not consistent when she found it hard to be a people greeter at the store entrance when she had to check what goods customers brought into the store. She concluded that her direct experience of Wal-Mart's culture showed that organizational culture did indeed affect customer satisfaction.

Throughout all ethnographic studies, several characteristics are common (Hammersley and Atkinson 1983):

- the culture that drives the behaviour of people in a small group is studied in its everyday setting and contexts;
- the researcher participates in the group for a long period, so that he or she has to live two simultaneous lives, one as an insider in the group and the other as an outside observer of the group;
- observations and relatively informal interviews are the major sources of information, although other sources can be used; for example, literature.
- the data is gathered in a relatively unstructured way so that data collection is *played by ear* and flexibly covers as much of the everyday life of people as possible;
- the masses of data that are rich descriptions of the group are analysed to extract the meanings and functions of the group's behaviour and the report takes the form of verbal descriptions and explanations.

Consider a rather realistic scenario. You think hardly anything is known about how marketing managers *actually* make decisions (in contrast to what the textbooks say about how they *should* make decisions, and to how some managers *say* they make decisions). An ethnographic study would be one way that you could find out how they actually make decisions in their everyday settings, as Jane wanted to do at Wal-Mart. The usual steps to go through from the start to the end of an ethnographic research project in an unfamiliar setting are listed next. But note that if you do ethnographic research in your own familiar work setting, then not all the early steps below will be necessary. However, if you study your own work setting, you may be so familiar with it that you might overlook some aspects that an outsider would not. Thus it is often wise to avoid doing an ethnographic study of your own workplace unless it is the only access to a suitable site that you are likely to get. The usual steps are as follows (Neuman 1994):

- select a site where the group interacts, for example, their offices and meeting and common rooms, or Jane's shopfloor at Wal-Mart;
- find a gatekeeper who has formal or informal power to provide access to the group, for example the group's manager who is on the advisory board of your university or the managers at Wal-Mart that Jane contacted;
- build trust among group members about you and your project and negotiate with them how you will gather data; this step may take several weeks from when Jane entered her group as a trainee at Wal-Mart, for example;
- observe the group through watching, listening and behaving as a group member, for example at weekly meetings of the group and at their strategic planning retreats;
- find key informants within the site who are very familiar with it and are willing to talk in great detail about it and provide a platform for you *to bounce your impressions off* about it, for example a secretary or the employee who has worked in the department the longest;
- conduct interviews with group members, even if they are the lunchtime discussions that Jane used; these participants are selected by *snow-balling*, that is, each participant is asked who else might be able to provide more information about incidents or processes, and those people are then interviewed and also asked who else might be able to provide more information;
- take notes, either at the site or away, and when an incident happens or afterwards (being able to write and type fast are handy traits for an ethnographic researcher, as well as good memory);
- handle the ethical dilemmas of ethnographic research such as whether to tell the members *all* the objectives of the research, or whether to discuss confidential information with a key informant, or whether to report illegal activities observed in the group; these concerns did not seem to worry Jane in her Wal-Mart research but may worry a researcher of a smaller number of people; and
- write up a report that communicates what are the rules for conduct within the group, and the reasons for them in the form of meanings and interpretations. This is a particularly difficult aspect of ethnographic research because of the problems associated with constructing a suitable framework for analysis and interpretation, especially if no

prior framework has been used or constructed. Hence the importance of building on prior research which may provide such a framework, or alternatively using other research as the framework for some of the analysis and interpretation of an ethnographic study.

Conclusions about ethnographic research

It should be clear that ethnographic research is not easy to do. The researcher has to immerse him or herself in the field over a long period of time and also try to be an impartial observer. Thus it produces wear and tear on a researcher's emotions, personal life and ethical frameworks. Nevertheless, it can provide descriptive data about small groups inter- acting that cannot be gathered in any other way. Since the output is essentially just a description of the one group it is difficult to extrapolate the findings to other groups. That is, one ethnographic study's findings may not easily translate to generalizable *theory* about how various aspects of marketing are linked. However, findings of an ethnographic study can become more generalizable by making reference to other appropriate research and literature and considering the similarities and differences. Similarities will reinforce the validity of the findings; differences may suggest the existence of new insights which may require or enable further research.

The key advantage of ethnographic research is its *closeness* to the *reality* of the topic under investigation. As such it can provide significant *under- standing* of the phenomena being researched as well as produce new, previously unrecognized phenomena and insights.

Our next technique, grounded theory, has this characteristic of limited generalizability to other specific situations, too, because grounded theory expressly sets out to develop theories about social phenomena from the same, specific, in-depth sort of data that is collected in ethnographic studies. That is, it is based on interviews and observations in natural settings that are collected in ways that evolve as the research proceeds. However, grounded theory studies emphasize their own form of theory more than many ethnographic studies and so can often offer greater and deeper insights into phenomena. This is its major advantage, which far outweighs any methodological limitations of generalizability. Indeed, such generalizability is not an issue in choosing grounded theory; the research objective of grounded theory is not concerned with this in the first place.

What Is Grounded Theory?

At one time, the quantitative methods of individual psychology were being used to test *grand theories* in sociology. The outcomes of this sort of research were disappointingly abstract and stale to two US sociologists, Barney Glaser and Anselm Strauss. They wanted sociology to build new theories about social processes, rather than merely test inappropriate theories. Indeed, they wanted to let the actual data of social phenomena produce the theories, that is, theories that were grounded in the everyday experience of the social processes *between* individuals, rather than let a theory decide what data was to be collected and how it was to be analysed. In *The Discovery of Grounded Theory* (Glaser and Strauss 1967), they developed a method of analysing data that built its own theories while data was being collected, rather than testing hypotheses about theories that had been determined before the data collection began. The methodology has since been widely used in sociology and many other areas like psychology, nursing, education, social work and anthropology, and in recent times in management and business research.

One would expect it to be used in marketing, too, because much marketing involves social processes between individual consumers or marketing managers, that is, it aims to identify the concerns of social actors and the strategies they use to resolve those concerns. It has been used successfully to analyse consumers' perceptions about women's clothing in the workplace (Kimle and Damhorst 1997), and advertisements (Phillips 1997). Nevertheless, its use in marketing has been limited, for example, marketing PhD theses that have used grounded theory could probably be counted on the fingers of two hands; it 'has largely been excluded from the discourse about interpretive and postmodern methodologies' (Goulding 1998: 50). This neglect of grounded theory in marketing may have been caused by the controversies among grounded theorists, their jargon and the complexity and apparent subjectivity of their methods.

This chapter aims to introduce the basic processes used in grounded theory in as straightforward a way as possible, while also facing up to its controversies, jargon (shown in **bold**), complexities and subjectivity.

An example of grounded theory

To begin, consider this example of grounded theory research. It is about an Australian consumer research study that illustrates many of the key ideas of grounded theory as it goes through the steps of data collection, data analysis and final theory generation. This example is summarized from Pettigrew 1999:

> Simone was investigating the *perceptions* of consumers that underpinned the reality of their beer consumption. As well as observing people drinking in hotels and clubs, she interviewed men and women in those hotels and clubs. Some women refused to talk with her when she came up to them with the request for 'casual chat about a few things for a research project', while some men considered her

request quite close to normal mating behaviour in the hotel or club. Between *each* interview, she analysed the interview data, line by line, to code or categorize ideas about the social processes she was uncovering. After each interview, she considered who would be the best type of person to interview next to provide a clearer picture of the phenomenon, for example, a well-dressed couple, a teenage girl or a middle aged mother. Gradually a consistent picture emerged through a series of interlinked and hierarchical codes like 'alcohol/beer/brands/brand names/Australian' and 'culture/people/types'. While she was doing the interviews, she wrote memos to herself about the patterns she was discovering in her data, and also began to read the literature about consumption in general but not about beer consumption in particular.

Eventually, her interviews were not unearthing new insights and so she stopped them. Based on her interview data analyses and her reading, she then built a theory that drinkers believed in four untrue *myths*:

- all Australians drink beer;
- taste is the primary reason for drinking beer;
- beer consumption is a totally enjoyable activity; and
- consumers are completely in control of their consumption decisions.

So the overriding issue for beer drinkers was *image management*, with drinkers managing an image of themselves within their social processes.

The essence of grounded theory

Simone's story illustrates many of the key processes of grounded theory. Grounded theory's interview and observation data is collected in the field, like ethnographic data. But grounded theory and ethnography are different from some other qualitative techniques. Firstly, grounded theory starts analysis as soon as data starts to be collected, and does not wait until all the data has been collected. The theory is built while the data is being collected. Secondly, this analysis builds theory in a very laid down and *hierarchical* way, instead of the more simple and straightforward way of *content analysis* used merely to describe strategies used by consumers in focus groups, for instance. A grounded theory attempts to explain social phenomena by showing links between diverse facts, as well as merely describing those facts.

Next, the continuous steps of data collection and analysis continue until saturation is reached. It does not stop at some predetermined point as in other methods, for example after four focus groups have been run or after data about a (given) number of case studies has been collected. Finally, there is extremely limited prior theory involved, unlike the prior theory that is used to develop the interview protocol in case study research or the questions or discussion topics that a moderator takes into each focus group.

Steps in Grounded Theory Research

Data collection

With this background, let us turn to the steps involved in a grounded theory research project. Firstly, the data can be transcripts or notes of interviews with individuals or groups, observations or documents. But the data collector should try not to impose a prior framework on the perceptions of meanings, definitions or interpretations that respondents provide. That is, the interviewer must not contaminate the meanings of the respondents with his or her own meanings. So interviews of individuals and groups will usually appear to be *conversations* where the interviewer operates at the same level as the respondent, usually in *the field* like Simone's hotels, and engages in a 'real conversation with "give and take" and empathetic understanding' (Fontana and Frey 1994: 371). A grounded theory researcher will not have an interview protocol, but may have a short list of probe issues that grows as the number of interviews increases. Analyses of these will unearth issues that need to be checked in later interviews. These probe issues may or may not come from prior knowledge or research.

Schism of philosophy

This issue of prior frameworks has caused a schism between the two 1967 founders of grounded theory. In 1990, Strauss (Strauss and Corbin 1990) said that grounded theory research should begin with the formulation of a *research question* before the first interview: for example, Simone's question was effectively 'What is the culture of beer drinkers?' Then, after the data from each interview has been collected, Strauss and Corbin said the *coding* of each interview should look at the specific **constituent elements** or **coding paradigm** of the data, that is, **causal conditions, phenomena, context, intervening conditions, strategies of action and interaction,** and **consequences.** This relatively prescriptive approach was too much for Glaser. Glaser is a purist and said that the data itself must say what the research question is, and that patience by the analyst will eventually allow the data itself to determine how it should be coded. He asked Strauss to withdraw the book for revision and then pronounced on the morality of what he was doing: 'Strauss' book is without conscience, bordering on immorality' (Glaser 1992: 3). It seems that two denominations of grounded theory had appeared.

There is no consensus among grounded theorists as to which of the two approaches provides the best theories of social phenomena (Kools et al. 1996). Given this uncertainty, our own view is that marketing researchers may prefer the pragmatic Strauss approach described in Strauss and Corbin (1990) or alternatively the purist Glaser (1992) approach. It simply depends on the nature of the research and the issues under consideration. Human beings cannot help but bring their own preconceptions to a research project; indeed most researchers in marketing will have accumulated substantial prior knowledge about aspects of marketing, so will have preconceptions. It may be best to make those preconceptions known in the up-front, explicit statement of a research question and an explicit explanation of a coding process. This statement will be especially appropriate in marketing management research where the research is usually being done for some purpose, like investigating adherence to the marketing concept in a workgroup, for instance. Most researchers will focus their attention in areas where they already have some knowledge. To claim that knowledge can be erased, so that a researcher's mind can become a clean slate, seems unlikely to be possible.

That is, however much any qualitative *methodology* may try to erase the researcher's influence, the qualitative *epistemology* means that the effect of the interaction of researcher and reality cannot be erased. There will always be *some* interaction between human subject and human researcher in effective qualitative research. In other words, a qualitative researcher *has to generate* data rather than merely collect it. In qualitative research, the value-free, always reliable, *one-way mirror* of positivism between subjects and a researcher cannot be achieved. Indeed, it may be inadvisable even to seek this one-way mirror, for developing a two-way rapport between an individual interviewer and the respondents will always influence interview results for the better. A more knowledgeable coder of interview data cannot help but provide more insightful codes than an ignoramus. In brief, grounded theory is essentially interpretivist research about people's perceptions that drive their social/marketing behaviour, and the epistemology of interpretivism requires that the researcher must be a participant in reality, even a passionate participant. De Burca and McLoughlin (1998: 96) sum up the major concerns relating to the development of knowledge about social science reality, that this schism raises: 'the main problem with grounded theory is how it glides and glosses over its ontological and epistemological assumptions'. However, as an interpretivist methodology seeking new and meaningful insights, it is an extremely powerful tool.

An *experienced* grounded theory researcher may be able to abstract much of his or her own self from the process and the results, as Glaser hopes for. But most researchers will find that the guidelines provided by Strauss, or those which they may have created for themselves to suit their research purpose, ensure that they do not become too *distant* from their sources of rich data and wander off into terrain that they know nothing about or are not interested in, or into terrain that will not provide the desired outcome of a new contribution to knowledge.

Data analysis

After the *first* interview and before the next interview is begun, the data is **coded**. Almost always, this coding is done with software like NUD*IST or ETHNOGRAPH. There are three levels of coding for each interview: open, axial and selective. Firstly, the researcher goes through **open** coding of each line of the transcript to see what it is about, giving each incident (*not* each person) a **concept** code like Simone's *alcohol* or *beer* codes, usually using Strauss' constituent elements above as a guide to thinking about what and how to code. That is, researchers try to develop the codes to *fit inside* the data, and do not force the data into the codes.

Secondly, the researcher moves to the **axial** coding phase, going through the transcript to see the connections between the coded lines, and to sort the lines into several higher-level clusters of **categories** according to obvious fit, like Simone's 'alcohol/beer/brands/brand names/Australian'. In this phase, the researcher is trying to link everything together in several hierarchical levels, with fewer and fewer categories in each higher level. This phase is what grounded theorists call the **constant comparison** step, where there is a constant comparison between the themes found in incidents described in the data and emerging theoretical concepts. These themes can be either similarities or differences in the data, which are then used to develop further categories into which the data can be slotted.

Finally, there is the **selective** coding phase, carried out at the end of the project. In this phase, all categories are brought together into the final core category. Simone's five myths and core category of image management are an example of the outcome of her final selective coding phase. The top-level category of image management is called the **core category** by grounded theorists. It is the major concern of the social respondents and explains most variation in the data and to which other variables appear to be related.

In brief, as each interview and its analysis proceeds, the researcher is trying to increase the number of hierarchical levels of categories and at the same time reduce the number of categories in each of those higher and higher levels.

But how is this building of higher and higher levels of categories of theory actually done? The first way is for the researcher to write a constant stream of **memos** to him or herself about the ideas and how they interrelate, even if it means interrupting a coding session to do so, as Simone did.

The second way is to start selectively reading literature about the topic. Note that this reading may be about the issues in general and not just about the specific area being analysed, thus providing a wider perspective than reading only previous theories in the literature. For example, Simone read about consumption in general while analysing her data, but did not read about *beer* consumption until she had developed her core category of image management. (By the way, pragmatic Strauss suggests that this reading be done, but purist Glaser insists on *no* reading of the literature at all until the one final, core category has been identified in the data. Again, the choice is that of the researcher.) This reading of the literature is best used merely to inform the theory generation process and not to direct it. It is simply another informant and like all sources of information in grounded theory, it has to be fitted into the emerging patterns of several levels of categories.

Selecting respondents and ending data collection

After *each* interview has been coded and analysed in the ways described in the two paragraphs above, the researcher starts a process of **theoretical sampling** to decide on the type of person who should be interviewed next. The next type of person to interview (age/type/location etc.) should provide incidents that add to the understanding of the theories that are evolving in the analyses – 'sampling on the basis of concepts that have proven theoretical relevance to the evolving theory' (Strauss and Corbin 1990: 176). Thus Simone considered the type of drinker, for example a teenage girl, that would further her emerging understanding of the phenomenon. This sampling is not stopped at a predetermined number as it may be in a survey, but is stopped when information from respondents becomes repetitive and no new themes or levels of categories are emerging from the analyses – the research becomes **saturated** with information. In practice, the number of respondents before saturation is reached is often between 8 and 24, but not always (Riley 1996, cited in Goulding 1998).

Conclusions about grounded theory research in marketing

Despite grounded theory's relative neglect by marketing researchers, it does provide some opportunities. The three necessary characteristics of a research problem that would be appropriate for this technique are as follows:

- the research should be intrepretivist, that is, it should focus on the concerns and perceptions of the people involved because they are the driving forces of the phenomena involved: research about national or organizational cultures (consumers or corporations), or about symbols (brands), would fit this characteristic;
- the research should be about complex social processes between people; most research about marketing networks would fit this pattern as would much research about what marketing managers do; and

- there should be virtually no existing theories about the phenomena (because most previous research has been descriptive perhaps), or existing theories are demonstrably inadequate for example, how marketing planning is done in small businesses, and how marketers sell blocks of seats to companies before a concert (Parry 1998).

If all these characteristics exist and the decision to use grounded theory is made, researchers should be careful of two things. Firstly, they should carefully use the technique as described above and by Strauss and Corbin (1990) or Glaser (1992), and not use another technique such as content analysis and say that any resulting description is a theory that was generated from the data, and so can be called a grounded theory. They should show they are aware of the schism in grounded theory and justify their choice of the Strauss or Glaser position along appropriate lines.

Secondly, they should note that the *report* of the research will be different from the *research process* itself. In particular, the report will start with the research problem or question that the report addresses, and then it will review the literature before the data collection and analysis. Then the data collection and analysis will be described one after the other. However, the research process may actually have started before the research problem or question has been fully clarified and much of the data will have been collected and analysed before the literature was read. Moreover, the data collection and analysis will have been done together and not one after the other.

Summary

In brief, grounded theory is a complex and time-consuming technique, and its potential to help understand some aspects of some social marketing processes has not been realized. Similarly, ethnographic studies are also complex and time-consuming. However, the benefits of *closeness* to a *reality* and the depth of understanding that can be achieved, which may also lead to new insights, far outweigh the disadvantages. They deserve to be used more widely in research situations where appropriate.

LEARNING QUESTIONS

What is meant by ethnography and when is it appropriate to use it as a research methodology?

Grounded theory is based on two perspectives. Glaser and Strauss (1967) and Strauss and Corbin (1990) outline the merits of both.

How does grounded theory differ from ethnographic studies?

References

De Burca, S. and McLoughlin, D. (1998) 'Business Network Research: a Grounded Theory Approach', in P. Naude and P. Turnbull (eds), *Network Dynamics in International Marketing*, Pergamon, Oxford.

Dunnett, A.J. and Arnold, S. (1999) 'Falling Prices, Rising Morale: the Impact of Organizational Culture on Customer Satisfaction at Wal-Mart', doctoral colloquium, the Marketing Academy, Stirling University, Scotland, 6 July.

Fontana, A. and Frey, J.H. (1994) 'Interviewing', in N. Denzin and Y. Lincoln (eds), *Handbook of Qualitative Research*, Sage, Thousand Oaks, CA.

Glaser, B. (1992) *Basics of Grounded Theory: Emergence vs Forcing*, The Sociology Press, Mill Valley, CA.

Glaser, B. and Strauss, A. (1967) *The Discovery of Grounded Theory: Strategies for Qualitative Research*, Aldine, Chicago.

Goulding, C. (1998) 'Grounded Theory: the Missing Methodology on the Interpretivist Agenda', *Qualitative Market Research: an International Journal*, 1(Nov.), 50–57.

Hammersley, M. and Atkinson, P. (1983) *Ethnography Principles in Practice*, Tavistock, London.

Kimle, P.A. and Damhorst, M.L. (1997) 'A Grounded Theory Model of the Ideal Business Image for Women', *Symbolic Interaction*, 20(1), 45–68.

Kools, S., McCarthy, M., Durham, R. and Robrecht, L. (1996) 'Dimensional Analysis: Broadening the Conception of Grounded Theory', *Qualitative Health Research*, 6(3), 312–331.

Neuman, W.L. (1994) *Social Research Methods*, Allyn and Bacon, Boston.

Parry, K.W. (1998) 'Grounded Theory and Social Process: a New Direction for Leadership Research', *The Leadership Quarterly*, 9(1), 85–105.

Pettigrew, S. (1999) 'Culture and consumption: a study of beer consumption in Australia', PhD thesis, University of Western Australia.

Phillips, B.J. (1997) 'Thinking Into It: Consumer Interpretation of Complex Advertising Images', *Journal of Advertising*, 16(2), 77–87.

Riley, R. (1996) 'Revealing Socially Constructed Knowledge through Quasi-structured Interviews and Grounded Theory Analysis', *Journal of Travel and Tourism Marketing*, 15(2), 21–40.

Sanday, P.R. (1979) 'The Ethnographic Paradigm(s)', *Administrative Science Quarterly*, 24, 527–538.

Stockport, G. and Kakabadse, A. (1991) 'Using Ethnography in Small Firms Research', Small Firms 91 conference.

Strauss, A. and Corbin, J. (1990) *Basics of Qualitative Research: Grounded Theory Procedures and Techniques*, Sage, London.

11   Action Research and Action Learning

The term 'action research' was invented and introduced by the eminent social scientist Kurt Lewin over 50 years ago (Lewin 1946). Since then, it has become acclaimed and criticized. There are several reasons for such controversy. For example, the label of action research is rather broad, often left undefined, and used in different ways. This has led some academics who are less convinced of the merits of qualitative research methodologies to suggest that fuzzy categorizations of types of research are subsumed under the label of action research. Nevertheless, action research is *essentially about a group of people who work together to improve their work processes*. For example, action research could occur if a small team or task force was set up in a marketing department to reduce their company's time in getting a new product to market. Another example would be the series of meetings involved in setting the incoming year's budget for a department so that it was more successful than it had been this year. Yet another example would be a group working with a consultant to run new computer software and incorporate it into their daily processes. That is, action research often occurs in management even though it may not be called that and it may not explicitly follow the procedures of action research.

The term 'action learning' is widely used in education and training throughout Europe; in North America, the term widely used is 'experiential learning'. Both equate to the same approach to learning. Sometimes the term 'discovery learning' is used in the same context.

In this chapter we try to clarify some of the ambiguities surrounding action research, and discuss the merits and limitations of this approach. Firstly, we describe the four core elements of how to do an action research project, including the involvement of the researcher in the project. Against this background, we closely inspect how action research has been defined, and identify its specific characteristics as a basis for establishing the domain of action research. Finally, potential benefits of action research are identified, with emphasis on the requirement for the action researcher to produce valid and useful knowledge. Some attention is given to action learning, how it differs from action research while maintaining significant similarity with action research. (Parts of the chapter are based on Gronhaug and Olson 1999.)

Definition of Action Research

First let us try to put action research into the context of scientific research. Lewin's (1946) seminal contribution emphasized the importance of making use of scientific knowledge to make social improvements, indicating that a main purpose of doing social science research should be its usefulness to society. Lewin himself conducted large-scale studies followed up by well-founded programmes to improve people's eating habits. In a similar vein, business firms conduct research to gain insights as a basis for initiating and implementing purposeful actions, for example, to improve their competitive position, to exploit discovered opportunities and/or to handle threats. Market research, for example, is often conducted to gain insights and/or clarify alternatives as a basis for purposeful actions. So, as we have already noted above (see Chapter 1), Lewin (1951) emphasized that science consisted of two aspects: 'general laws' that did not refer to any one particular situation, and their 'application in action' taken to improve a particular situation.

Consider these two aspects in more detail. Lewin's general laws can be seen as context-free scientific knowledge. But to suggest actions to improve any particular context or situation, situational knowledge is needed in addition to knowledge about general laws. Thus action research is essentially about how to apply general laws to improve a situation. The reader may get the impression that Lewin's perspective on action research applies only to social science knowledge with the aim of changing and improving specific situations, but he also considered action research to be an important way to acquire insights about any social system. For example, through such research one may observe unexpected reactions, and/or discover problems not previously thought of, which may initiate further theorizing and testing. In a similar vein, marketers through their field activities may acquire new insights, resulting in reconstruction of their 'market realities' (Zaltman 1997).

Action research was hailed as an important innovation in social science inquiry, and subsequent investigators have built on Lewin's ideas. In his original contribution he did not explicitly define the term 'action research'. Rather the intended meaning was reflected through description of purpose and procedures for doing such research. However, Rapoport has framed probably the most commonly used definition of such research:

> Action research aims to contribute both to the practical concerns of people in an immediate problematic situation and to the goals of social science by joint collaboration within a mutually acceptable ethical framework. (1970: 449)

Closer inspection of this definition and the discussion above reveals that action research:

1 emphasizes the importance of both scientific contributions and the solving of practical, real-life problems;
2 focuses on the common values and standards of researchers and clients (these value standards – even though important – are usually not explicitly taken into account in *traditional* research);
3 represents an intensive research strategy (which also may be the case, but need not necessarily be so, in traditional research);
4 involves some aspects of collaboration between researcher and client which is paid almost no attention in prototypical, traditional research where there is a one-way mirror between the researcher and the objects being observed;
5 is longitudinal and emphasizes gradual learning and improvements (although the learning aspect is crucial in traditional research, much of the research literature focuses on the single study. In *real life*, however, the focus is often on longitudinal knowledge creation and learning);
6 assumes that the researcher needs contact and interaction with clients to really know their problems and influencing factors, that is, the *total situation*. As such, this represents a deviance from the distant and objective, one-way mirror ideal of traditional research. This may also explain the strong anti-positivistic attitude reflected in much of the action research literature (for example, Peters and Robinson 1984; Reason 1994; Susman and Evered 1978).

From the preceding discussion, action research represents an intensive approach, involving cycles of actions and reflections, emphasizing understanding and learning. The underlying assumption is that it takes time for the actors to acquire new knowledge, or more precisely, to change their cognitive structures in such a way that their reality constructions change. The emphasis in action research is on 'double-looped learning' (Argyris and Schon 1974) where the actor's cognitive structure or *world view* must be altered if he or she is going to initiate change for improvements.

Elements of Action Research

How is action research done? The following example will illustrate four of the elements of action research before we go into each element in detail.

Lewin's action research work began in the Second World War. A story from shortly after the war illustrates what action research is. In 1945, Reg Revans suggested the development of a staff college for coal mine managers in the United Kingdom where managers would talk in groups about their problems and solve them, but without experts or lecturers to tell them what to do! The college was not set up, but the coal mine managers met anyway to work together upon their operational problems, such as how to maintain unfamiliar American machinery, and how to deploy men at the start of a shift when absenteeism was high. No experts were available to guide them but they did have technical manuals for some of the equipment. After each meeting, the managers would try an idea from the group in their workplace and then report back to the group to discuss the result, and then come up with a better idea to try. Eventually, they wrote a manual of procedures as a report of what they had done and learned. They had been successful because they had worked together incrementally to improve how they carried out work activities.

This story illustrates the four elements of an action research project. It involves a group of people:

- using a spiralling circle of activities that involve planning, acting, observing and reflecting upon what had happened;
- doing these activities to try to improve workgroup processes of action;
- helping to solve complex, practical problems about which little is known; and
- producing at least one report about what was found.

Let us consider each element in turn.

Element 1: a spiral of planning, acting, observing and reflecting

The *explicit* framework of any action research project can be compared to a spiralling series of circles. Each circle consists of *action, observation* and monitoring, *reflection* and evaluation, and *planning* for the next circle. Figure 11.1 illustrates these circles, each one spiralling out of the preceding one.

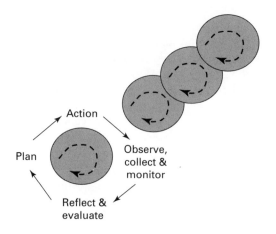

Figure 11.1 *Action research theory: problem identification circles*

From Figure 11.1, an action research project has four interlinked stages:

- Deciding what the problem is and then *planning* to do something about it. Identifying what the problem is can sometimes take a period of time and so in the first few spirals, the plan does not necessarily attempt to solve the problem, but merely to learn more about it.
- Putting the plan into *action*. For example, this action could be pilot tests of a new product or trial of a new sales training method.
- Collecting data to *observe* and monitor the results, for example diaries, documents, agendas and minutes of meetings, survey responses, reports of interviews: having *several* sources of data allows them to be compared and integrated into a final, composite integrated picture.
- *Reflecting* on what has happened, to evaluate it and learn from it.

The analogy of war can be used to describe the *series of circles* that constitutes action research. The war starts with preliminary reconnaissance, and then a plan for stronger reconnaissance in force. After new information arrives from this, plans for another engagement with the enemy can be developed and implemented. And so on.

In practice, the process begins with a general idea that some kind of improvement or change is desirable. In deciding just where to begin in making improvements, one decides on a field of action (a subject area, or location) – where the battle (not the whole war) should be fought. This decision is based on consideration of where it is possible to have an impact. The general idea prompts a reconnaissance of the situation of the field, by carrying out some fact-finding. Having decided on the field and made a preliminary reconnaissance, the action researcher decides on a general *plan* of action. Breaking the general plan down into achievable steps, the action researcher settles on the first *action* step, a change in strategy which aims not only at improvement, but at greater understanding of what it will/may be possible to achieve later as well. Before taking this first step, the action researcher becomes more circumspect and devises a way of *observing* and monitoring the effects of the first action step, the circumstances in which it occurs, and what the strategy begins to look like in practice. When it is possible to maintain the fact-finding by monitoring the action, the first step is taken. As the step is implemented, new data starts coming in and the circumstances, action and effects can be described, *reflected* upon and evaluated. This evaluation stage provides amounts of fresh reconnaissance that can prepare the way for new planning.

For another example of action research, consider a marketing department that uses rudimentary action research circles at fortnightly department meetings. Each meeting produces some *plans* and reaches agreement about which people should be responsible for specific parts of the plan. These people are listed on an *action* sheet that is attached to the minutes of the meeting; they are responsible for carrying out the plans (or part of them) before the next meeting. The next meeting then *observes* and monitors progress through reports from people, *reflects* on them to try to work out what they have learned, and then decides what *future plans* will be.

This procedure might seem rather straightforward. Indeed, many practitioners, on first hearing about action research, exclaim, *but we already do that*! This point is often true, but in an action research project, the process is very *explicit* and the reflection and evaluation stages in particular are carefully done and not rushed through (as often happens at many departmental meetings). You may have heard the saying, *he has not got five years of experience, he only has one year of experience repeated five times*. This implies that he has not reflected on and learned from his experience in the way that an action researcher would have.

It is this reflection and the *understanding about processes in a work system* that are crucial to action research. In their reflection meetings, action researchers often go through three steps:

- replaying the *experience* to agree on what actually happened;
- attending to *feelings* about the experience, so that negative feelings that might obstruct learning can be worked through together, and positive feelings can be used to enhance learning; and
- re-evaluating the experience so that understanding or *theories* about how to solve a problem can be improved and so be the basis for further planning, acting, monitoring and reflection.

Element 2: improving workgroup processes of action

The second core element of action research is that it is about processes of action which aim to solve a specific problem involving *action* or *practice*; it is learning about doing by doing. Thus action researchers investigate a *real* company problem. The spiral in Figure 11.1 illustrating action, planning, monitoring and reflection is clearly about people *doing* something. That is, in action research, theories are not validated independently and then applied in practice. They are validated *through* practice. Action research is especially appropriate for learning tacit knowledge in addition to articulated knowledge (Polanyi 1962). Tacit knowledge is like the knowledge required to ride a bicycle or to swim – it may be very difficult to explain and the practical acquisition of the knowledge may depend on learning from experience. In contrast, articulated knowledge can easily be written down in books or training manuals and grasped by the reader.

This distinction between tacit and articulated knowledge is important for action research, because action research provides for the first as well as the second, while most marketing management and training programmes emphasize the second only. Similarly, Lewin (1951) emphasized that science consisted of two aspects: *general laws* that did not refer to any one particular situation, and their *application in action* taken to improve a particular situation.

The above distinction is somewhat similar to Revan's (1983) discussion of knowledge. He said there were two types of knowledge: programmed (P) knowledge which traditional schools pass on in the form of lectures, textbooks and videos of content experts; and questioning (Q) knowledge which is gained when a group reflects and questions P knowledge in the light of their own experiences and actions, that is, questioning knowledge is 'an ability to ask fresh and useful questions' (Revans 1983: 41).

Q knowledge is not gained simply through *asking* questions. Indeed, actual questions are best asked in order to gain clarification of P knowledge learning. Q knowledge is better focused on positive critique and reflection through vigorous and penetrative discussion of core aspects of P knowledge inputs. Participants bring their own experiential knowledge to the discussion and it is important that this is utilized positively so as not to stifle discussions through prior prejudices stemming from experiential knowledge. Hence again the importance of questions focusing on clarification of P knowledge rather than questions stemming from experiential knowledge prejudices. Full learning consists of both types of knowledge (that is, P + Q = L) and can be achieved only when groups solve practical problems by *doing* something.

Determining the appropriate balance of P and Q is a challenge. If there is too much P, then a project can become a *top heavy* delivery of content knowledge. If there is too much Q, then the participants may simply *pool their ignorance*. Each action research group has to work out the appropriate balance of P and Q, articulated and tacit knowledge, themselves, as they proceed.

Next, note that action research usually involves a *workgroup* of people who collaboratively try to work things out together. There appear to be two reasons for a group to be involved, rather than an individual. Firstly, if two or more people are involved, biased perceptions of what happened are less likely to occur because the people will have to agree. Secondly, discussions in the group will foster the changes in *attitudes* that a successful project requires. For example, in Lewin's action research during the Second World War, housewives who had *discussed* the advantages of buying and cooking whale meat were more likely to use it than those housewives who had merely listened to a lecture about whale meat's advantages.

Element 3: complex, practical problems about which little is known

Action research need not replace other more conventional research methods. For example, action research would not replace *surveys* in the context of seeking knowledge of voters' intentions or *focus groups* about consumers' attitudes to a new toothbrush.

Action research is most useful when a group of like-minded people can be brought together to solve a problem. Unlike focus groups, which are designed primarily to elicit interactive opinions on a topic, action research's main participants' purpose is to *solve a problem*. Such a problem may belong to an individual in the group or it may belong to the whole group.

Equally action research can be used to deal with problems which may arise as the group meets anyway. That is, an action research group need not be established to solve specific problems in the first place; it may be intended to address regular ongoing issues in the workplace, but its existence will often lead it into solving problems as these become apparent. Such a circumstance can be seen in a rapidly changing dynamic environment.

Element 4: a report

In a good action research project, a report is produced which broadcasts the learning of the group. This report is not in the form of an academic journal article or conference paper, but is a report for other managers. It can be presented in different forms, for example it is often a *narrative* of what happened during the action learning process structured around the spiralling pattern of cycles shown in Figure 11.1. Or it can be a *manual of best procedures* to guide future practitioners who face the same complex problem. The report may often emphasize the *balance* of P and Q knowledge, that is, the articulate and tacit knowledge developed during the action research project.

This narrative or manual format of an action research project report may be somewhat unsuitable on its own as a submission for a university research project, which may need two reports: the normal action research report about how work processes have been improved, and another one which addresses how the project added to a body of academic, pro-grammed or articulated knowledge. More details about how to handle these two types of knowledge are in the chapter about writing a report of qualitative research (Chapter 13). However, it is useful in appreciating the scope of action research to discuss the dual role an action research group can perform.

Duality of Action Research and Action Learning

Action research, if appropriate and desired, can provide a meaningful combination of education and training in addition to serving as a research methodology. In a university context, education and training involving P + Q knowledge can for certain recipients be provided through action learning (see p. 158 for other terms used with similar meaning) which consists of programmes that incorporate both P + Q knowledge formats around a series of problems, either individually or group owned.

We do not discuss the detailed procedures of action learning as a training and development mechanism; it is well documented by its founding father Reg Revans (1982, 1983). The brief discussion in Element 2 above on distinct types of learning stem from Revans' theories. Instead we offer here a brief outline of the action learning process and in particular focus on the duality of action learning and action research. Strictly speaking, they are different in that they have different purposes and methodology, but they are sufficiently compatible to be used as one.

Action learning group *sets* in a business or more specifically marketing context, may consist of entrepreneurs or marketing managers who each have responsibility for decision making within their own enterprises. The entrepreneur/marketing manager may present his/her own enterprise's problems and allow the group to help solve these problems. In such circumstances, each group member would have the opportunity to benefit from the collective wisdom of the group in addressing his/her own unique problems. Equally, the group may collectively address a common problem such as devising a framework for a marketing plan that is compatible with their enterprise's resource constraints. As a learning vehicle, action learning groups are a powerful tool. They will also benefit from skilled P knowledge providers and more importantly from an independent but skilled *catalyst* to ensure a balanced progression of learning and knowledge building during the problem solving processes.

The catalyst may also be the academic researcher engaged in a research project with or without the client group's knowledge. In either case an *action learning programme* can be used as a powerful *action research methodology*. Thus, in tandem with the action learning set, the same group can serve as an action learning group which can be observed according to the descriptions above in Element 1. Figure 11.2 attempts to illustrate the duality and mutuality concept. As an action learning set (AL), the participants focus on meaningful problem solving knowledge building. As

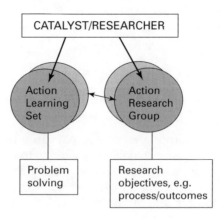

Figure 11.2 *Duality of action learning and action research*

an action research (AR) group they explicitly or implicitly *provide* insights and understanding into the processes and outcomes of this problem solving. This duality is found in the Rapoport (1970) definition given above (p. 159).

Further, in addition to action research providing insights and understanding into the decision making processes, the researcher can assess such processes and how they may be shaped by the degree of ownership of the problem. Let us examine further the researcher's role in action research within a company management context.

Researcher participation in action research

The relationship between an individual researcher and the other members of the action research group also corresponds to the situation in business life where firms contract outside researchers to complement their knowledge basis, or where a team leader has to work with other team members. So what is the purpose of using an action researcher? That is, why should researcher(s) and client(s) interact? A key point is that a researcher and his or her clients differ in knowledge. Clients are the *problem owners*. They have experience-based knowledge from their actual context. The true virtue of the researcher is her/his theory-based knowledge. Such knowledge can be crucial in the precise identification of actual problems, clarifying implicit assumptions, and through interaction and training can achieve change in a client's perspective on the need to undertake actions for improvements (Argyris 1983).

In more detail, there are three levels of researcher participation in an action research project: technical, practical and emancipatory. In the first, *technical* level of participation the action researcher is merely a technical expert, a consultant who tells other people what to do. This is the normal form of a consultant's project; for example, a technical agribusiness consultant is working in a grain development project in a developed country and simply transfers the technology to that country. This is the simplest form of action research and may not even meet the requirements of action research noted above.

The second, *practical* level of participation by a researcher is similar to the starting point of a 'process consultant' (Schein 1990). This is where the researcher has a Socratic role, encouraging participation and reflection about processes so that others can learn about *learning from doing*, and not just learn about doing. The researcher helps the client understand how he or she fits into a system.

The third, *emancipatory* type of researcher participation is the ideal, according to action researchers. Here the researcher becomes a co-researcher *with* the other people, with responsibility for the project shared equally by everyone. In emancipatory action research, the researchers aim to change the whole context of the problem and thus liberate themselves from its causes, including their mental context. This type of participation:

> aims not only at technical and practical improvement [technical] and the participants' better understanding [practical] . . . but also at changing the system itself and/or those conditions which impede desired improvement in the system or organization. It also aims at the participants' empowerment and self confidence. (Zuber-Skerritt 1996: 5)

This third form of participation is indeed an ideal one and can sometimes be likened to *revolutionaries* who change the structure within their whole organization or community (this fits with the philosophy of critical theory defined in the notes to Chapter 1). In other words, the researcher becomes an intellectual who transforms the view that people had of their world and so emancipates them from their mental prison bars. When emancipatory action research was being done in Latin America its aims might have been to lead to revolutions to liberate the poor (Freire 1972). When emancipatory action research is done in education, it can lead to more democratic classrooms. When it is done in business, it may not be so dramatic but it can lead to new ways of thinking that restructure processes and save costs. For example, action researchers from several departments can get together to look at functional interrelationships affecting what was at first thought to be just a marketing problem, as shown in the following example.

A notable case occurred when a firm was asked to examine the traffic department of an international manufacturing company experiencing a large number of late deliveries and customer complaints. It was suggested that the analysis be expanded to include an examination of the inter-relationships and shared responsibilities of *all* related groups that might impact on this problem: traffic, order entry/accounting and international sales. An analysis of the operations of these three areas confirmed that 90 per cent of the activities performed by traffic were duplicated by order entry. This situation had existed for years, because key functional relationships were never examined (Griswold and Prenovitz 1993).

Whether action research is used in business or non-business contexts, it is important that the group selects the problem to be worked on so that the people own the problem and the solution. Sometimes this may be difficult when some members of the group have only peripheral, or no direct involvement with the chosen problem. They may not have the same commitment to the process. Similarly, in a business context the pressures of pragmatic necessity, for example an urgent need for solutions to protect sales and profits, may infringe upon the action research process. However, if the group is established with a clear and cohesive purpose and accept-ance of the commonality of this purpose many such problems will be overcome.

Value of action research

The value of action research lies in its ability to get really close to a business *reality* where a researcher can go beyond just gleaning insights into broad phenomena and can get to the specific aspects of problem solving which are often the basis of business decision making. The reality is strengthened by the inherent dimension of *reflecting* on action and as a result refining and strengthening thought processes and solutions. Action research, with its process of longitudinal research in context, including cycles of observation, interpretation, action and reflection, allows for understanding, construction and testing of explanations, as well as modifications and learning. For the expert researcher, action research also allows for coding and communication of previously uncodified knowledge. Thus there is little doubt that action research has the potential of producing important and useful knowledge of people *in context*.

Furthermore, action research involves multiple research activities, and the action researcher is, in principle, confronted with more challenges than the traditional researcher. In their cycle of planning, acting, monitoring and reflecting, action researchers must be able to:

- make adequate observations (and select and make use of other available data);
- interpret and make sense of the observations, which requires conceptualization and theory (model) building skills;
- plan and execute adequate actions; and
- plan, collect, analyse and interpret data to examine the outcome of the action.

Thus action research presumes important researcher skills in observing and interviewing (and other data collection techniques), adequate theoretical knowledge that allows for observation and interpretation, creativity and ability to construct explanations (theory building), and methodological skills to examine outcomes of proposed action. Of course, action research also requires knowledge of *group* skills for identifying and solving problems (Dick 1991).

An action researcher will accumulate many of these skills by the action of *doing* them, a good illustration in itself of the benefits of action research (and experiential learning) in action.

Summary

In the domain of management, business, commerce and in particular marketing, where there is a strong perception of variance between theory conceptualization at the generalist level, and the pragmatic requirements of practice, action research has the potential to reach across any variance and dichotomy. Indeed, the literature has many examples of action research contributing new insights about management, such as the work of Revans (1982) and Argyris (1983). Action research allows theory to be addressed in *context* and through subsequent 'actions' it allows decisions on problems to be married to articulate (theoretical) frameworks. Most importantly, it enables a 'balance' of theory (P knowledge) and practice (tacit Q knowledge) to be achieved.

For the researcher, action research achieves a deep, rich insight and understanding of complexities within marketing decision making that other non-qualitative methodologies could not hope to achieve. One must recognize that management and, by implication, marketing management decision making is not a highly structured, sequential and ordered concept (as much of the theoretical literature implies) but instead is chaotically complex in its rationality and activity. In this context action research is one qualitative methodology that will help to provide insights and understanding of the chaotic complexity. For qualitative researchers it is a methodology which should be considered with the utmost seriousness. Previous scholars (such as those mentioned above) who have used action research have been viewed as missionaries of the methodology by some; but as action research is increasingly used by many researchers in management and marketing, their groundswell of contributions will provide meaningful illustrations of the value of the method.

Action research provides a framework for marketers and others to work together to improve the way they do things. This chapter has outlined the scope and process of action research and its value as a qualitative methodology.

LEARNING QUESTIONS

What is meant by 'action research'?

What are the elements of action research? What is the purpose of each of these elements?

Describe the researcher's role in action research. How is this different to a researcher's role in an ethnographic study?

What is the value of action research? Consider your answer from the point of view of a marketing manager who needs to develop new managers' skills from an administrative focus to one of decision making in a fast changing context.

References

Argyris, C. (1983) 'Action Science and Intervention', *Journal of Applied Behavioural Science*, 19(2), 115–140.

Argyris, C. and Schon, D. (1974) *Theory in Practice: Increasing Professional Effectiveness*, Jossey-Bass, San Francisco.

Dick, B. (1991) *Helping Groups to be Effective*, Interchange, Brisbane.

Freire, P. (1972) *Pedagogy of the Oppressed*, Penguin, Harmondsworth.

Griswold, H.M. and Prenovitz, S.C. (1993) 'How to Translate Strategy into Operational Results', *Business Forum*, 18(3), 5–9.

Gronhaug, K. and Olson, O. (1999) 'Action Research and Knowledge Creation: Merits and Challenges', *Qualitative Market Research: an International Journal*, 2(1), 6–14.

Lewin, K. (1946) 'Action Research and Minority Problems', *Journal of Social Issues*, 2(4), 34–46.

Lewin, K. (1951) *Field Theory in Social Science*, Harper & Row, New York.

Peters, M. and Robinson, V. (1984) 'The Origin and Status of Adion Research', *Journal of Behavioral Science*, 20(2), 113–124.

Polanyi, M. (1962) *Personal Knowledge: Towards a Post-critical Philosophy*, Routledge and Kegan Paul, London.

Rapoport, R. (1970) 'Three Dilemmas in Action Research', *Human Relations*, 33, 488–543.

Reason, R. (1994) 'Three Approaches to Participative Inquiry', in N.K. Denzin and Y.S. Lincoln (eds), *Handbook of Qualitative Research*, Sage, Thousand Oaks, CA, pp.324–339.

Revans, R.W. (1982) *The Origins and Growth of Action Learning*, Studentlitteratur, Lund.

Revans, R. (1983) 'Action Learning, its Terms and Characters', *Management Development*, 21(1), 39–50.

Schein, E.A. (1990) 'A General Philosophy of Helping: Process Consulting', *Sloan Management Review*, 31(3), 57–64.

Susman, G.I. and Evered, R.D. (1978) 'An Assessment of the Scientific Merit of Adion Research', *Administrative Science Quarterly*, 23(Dec.), 582–603.

Zaltman, G. (1997) 'Rethinking Market Research: Putting People Back In', *Journal of Marketing Research*, 34 (Nov.), 424–437.

Zuber-Skerritt, O. (ed.) (1996) *New Directions in Action Research*, The Falmer Press, London.

Part III   APPLICATIONS AND
           OUTCOMES OF QUALITATIVE
           RESEARCH

---

12   Organizing, Processing and Visualizing Data

In any research study, analysis of empirical data is a large task for the researcher. At start point zero analysing the data appears both enormous and daunting, but approached with the clarity of purpose provided by good organization and construction, it is relatively easy.

The preparation and attention to detail involved in the organization, processing and analysing of data are considered in this chapter. Firstly organizing and preparing for fieldwork is discussed, followed by some consideration of how to go about analysing data. Since we described how to analyse data in each methodology chapter in Part II, we take a somewhat broader approach here that applies to more than just one method. This chapter outlines two stages of data analysis, and considers computer aided analysis programs briefly. Finally we outline the use of graphic *models* as an invaluable aid in both visualizing and analysing qualitative data.

Organizing Fieldwork

Organizing fieldwork entails planning the process of data gathering from the preparation and organization stage to the actual carrying out of fieldwork within a specific timescale.

This chapter discusses some of the practical and operational aspects involved in gathering data and how to anticipate and plan for all eventualities. Before going out into the field it is vital to think ahead in the ways described below. The preparation of a logical plan is essential. Such a plan should allow for problems to arise and be solved on the way and therefore needs time and forethought. It is important to be aware of the time required for each stage of the research, and how to plan and execute each stage of the fieldwork and analysis. As far as possible the researcher should try to identify and clarify each stage of the study at the outset. Nevertheless, although the researcher should aim to have a systematic or relatively structured plan, time and some flexibility must be allowed in order to *loop back* and accommodate change if necessary. It is also always useful to justify each decision made in relation to the overall research plan, aims and objectives.

Understanding and preparing for the different aspects and stages in the process of doing fieldwork, such as the various stages in the data collection, coding and analysis process, helps to avoid reaching a *dead end* later on. It is useful at the outset to consider the stages in each aspect of data collection in terms of understanding the purpose, strengths and weaknesses of each technique; to tentatively consider some alternatives and what to do before embarking on the research fieldwork.

How to embark on a field study

Early preparation for fieldwork will include the following:

- securing co-operation from respondents;
- dealing with refusals to participate and what to do when co-operation is not forthcoming;
- considering the ethics involved;
- planning the implementation of fieldwork.

Let us consider briefly each of these points.

Securing co-operation from respondents

First of all some thought must be given to how to identify respondent(s) and where the location for study will be. Researchers need to think about how to access the people of interest or the locations relevant to the study. If this is a problem then some alternatives need to be considered.

In order to begin communication with potential respondents it is usual to telephone or write to them in advance, explaining the focus, objectives and potential value of the research. The communication should ask for co-operation in a project that has some benefits for the respondent (as well as for the researcher). It should also indicate how much time you need from respondents, and when and where you anticipate carrying out the research. If this step is carried out clearly and ethically then the respondents' words can be treated as *on the record* and *for the record* (Denscombe 1998). At the research interview itself, the researcher should ensure that the informant or respondent understands that the content of and words spoken at the discussion can be used by the researcher at some later date and that the opinions can be taken as a genuine reflection of the person's thoughts. It can be agreed that the respondent's words are not to be attributed to him/her specifically or not to be made publicly available. However unless the respondent specifies to the contrary, the interview talk is on the record or for the record; and therefore taken seriously.

How to deal with refusals

If a researcher fails to gain co-operation from potential research participants then some rethinking is required. If co-operation is not forthcoming this may indicate that information is confidential, valuable to competitors or that potential informants do not see any value in participating in your research. This indicates a need either to think of another approach to gaining the essential information or to rethink the focus and emphasis of the research problem.

Refusals should lead to consideration of different ways to get the essential information. For example:

- Would further secondary data help in guiding the search?
- Are there different sources from which to gather the required information?
- Are there other or different informants and networks of people who could be approached?
- Can information be sought from printed materials?
- Are there different research approaches that would reach appropriate data?

If the answer to all of the above questions is no, then maybe the research problem needs to be given a different focus; in which case existing aims and objectives may need some refinement and adaptation. (This revision stems from the need to ensure that research problems, aims and objectives are researchable; it is an issue which should receive consideration at the outset of a proposed study.)

Ethics in the field

It is important to get respondents' agreement to participate and to recognize their *rights* as research participants. Needless to say, getting a respondent's consent to take part is vital to doing research. Apart from being a prerequisite to access, it is important in context of research ethics to acquire an *informed consent*. That is, interviews should not be achieved through secret recordings of discussions or the use of confidential conversations as research data. The researcher and respondent should be agreed that a research meeting will be used for research purposes and the respondent should understand and explicitly agree to this.

Planning the implementation of fieldwork

Preparation for the physical and mental tasks involved in actually gathering data should focus on the operational aspects and detailed planning involved in the execution of the fieldwork. Thinking of possible outcomes and eventualities helps to achieve a realistic perception of the time required for the research. Practical aspects need to be planned. This includes having the right equipment, such as a tape recorder, camera, video camera, batteries, tapes, notepaper, sufficient copies of the interview, observation and discussion protocols. The numbers of respondents and locations required for the study also need to be decided in advance and these will again depend on the nature and purpose of the research problem, aims and objectives. Some thought must be given to any travel arrangements involved in the research such as the time required for travel, which mode of transport to use, and any maps, directions or confirmation of access required.

Analysis of Data

The next part of this chapter deals with processing and analysing data. All of the research techniques and approaches discussed earlier (in Chapters 6–11) have many variations. They also may have considerable overlap – depending on the context and purpose of use. For example an interview can be highly structured, or it may just be based on one research objective which allows questions to adapt to the overall drift of the interview conversation. Focus group interviews may be based upon a designated topic, or they might focus on how opinions are formulated and changed during the process of a group discussion. In addition they may focus on what people say, what they do not say in a group context, how participants interact, or they may note the body language of the group during discussions on particular topics. Observations can be used at all stages of research, for a variety of purposes. For example, data may be recorded as written notes, photographs, audio and video recordings. Obviously observations can occur while carrying out other research methods such as depth or focus group interviewing. Using more than one technique often adds to the research depth and allows for deeper and contextual *understanding*.

Carrying out data analysis entails a number of key features. First of all the data that has been collected needs to be indexed or labelled, edited and organized. Organization is important at an early stage to allow easy access; the data may be arranged in different ways depending on the purpose and proposed outcome of the study. Often organizing the data chronologically or topically is a useful first step to achieve an overview of the findings. However, the researcher may decide to do a comparative analysis or to use the data for theory building purposes, in which case the data could be organized to contribute to this purpose.

Two stages of analysing data

It is useful to think of the process of analysis having two stages. The first stage is to ensure that all appropriate data has been collected. This entails the tracking down of patterns and consistencies, that is, the *detective work* stage (Mintzberg 1979). The second stage is the consideration of how to integrate all aspects of analysis, that is the creative work or making the *creative leap*. Mintzberg argues that every theory requires a creative leap, however small and states that 'there is no one-to-one correspondence between data and theory' (1979: 584). Furthermore he emphasizes that 'the data do not generate theory – only researchers do that' (ibid.), hence the importance of researchers being creative even in small ways.

Thus the stages of evaluation involve aspects of both *convergence* and *divergence* (these terms are borrowed from Guba 1978). Convergence involves sifting out the aspects of data which fit together and using this *experiential learning* stage to work towards a classification system. Divergence involves developing the categories created in the classification system by building on items of information already known, making connections among different items and proposing and justifying new information that ought to fit. Continuous working back and forth between the data and the classification system to verify the meaningfulness of the categories and the placement of data in categories is required (Guba 1978).

This process ends when 'sources of information have been exhausted, when sets of categories have been saturated so that new sources lead to redundancy, when clear regularities have emerged that feel integrated, and when the analysis begins to "overextend" beyond the boundaries of the issues and concerns guiding the analysis' (Patton 1987: 154). Uncovering patterns, themes and categories is a creative process that requires making carefully considered judgements about what is really significant in the data. The second stage of analysis clearly needs some reflection and intellectual input from the researcher; this should evolve over time from immersion in the data, in-depth consideration of the categories identified in the data and building upon them. At this stage the analysis should link the theory to the data and should be indicative of interrelationships, links, sequentially and general interdependencies of the phenomena within the research context. This is the focus and purpose of developing *criteria for analysis*, as referred to in Chapter 6. That is, criteria for analysis link the raw data with the final conclusion against the background of recognized theories, and focus on the important concepts and issues which explain the interactions and activities of the phenomenon under study (Gilmore 1995).

Use of computer aided packages

One of the drawbacks of qualitative research is the tedious, sometimes monotonous and exceedingly time-consuming analysis and interpretation of vast quantities of *soft*, largely unstructured data. While various manual tools for data analysis have been offered (Miles and Huberman 1994; Strauss and Corbin 1990; Weitzman and Miles 1995), advances in information technology have led to the development of innovative software packages designed to facilitate data analysis. Known by the acronym CAQDAS (Computer Assisted Qualitative Data Analysis Software) a number of programs have been developed over the past 15 years. The software consists of both generic packages, and those specifically developed for the needs of qualitative researchers. The former simply function as data retrieval systems for key words or manage the text base, while the latter are designed to *code and retrieve* data, build theory, or develop conceptual networks. Some programs are only able to perform the first level of analysis, while others are capable of much more (see Catterall and Maclaran 1998; Miles and Huberman 1994; Weitzman and Miles 1995 for a review of different packages).

CAQDAS is designed to do what the researcher might wish to do manually. Therefore, they cover most of the ways in which a researcher would try to analyse data. Weitzman and Miles' (1995) comprehensive guide to programs categorizes them into five basic types that cover most aspects of analysis:

- Text retrievers: these specialize in finding all instances of words, phrases (or other character strings) in one or several data files.
- Text-base managers: these organize, sort and make sub-sets of text systematically with text search and retrieve facilities.
- Code and retrieve programs: these assist with dividing text into segments by theme or category and assigning codes to these. All text segments with the same code attached can be retrieved for examination.
- Conceptual network builders: these systematically build networks and allow the testing of sophisticated semantic relationships between codes.

Overall, software packages are particularly useful where there is a large quantity of data requiring coding, annotation, linking, search and retrieval, development of data displays, and so on. However, there are also a variety of practical issues to be considered before making the decision to use software in qualitative data analysis.

Firstly, to run in an effective and efficient manner, certain packages need careful pre-coding of the data in order to identify and recognize key words, phrases and passages. Where there is a large amount of data, this can be an extremely time-consuming process.

Secondly, the researcher needs to have an intimate personal knowledge of the data, so that appropriate trigger codes and responses can be inserted at the outset of data interpretation. Such knowledge can best come from personal involvement in the entire process, from data collection through to analysis. If there are multiple researchers located in different locations (for example, international collaborative studies), it may be unrealistic to expect the entire research team to have *intimate personal knowledge* of all the data (including how the qualitative data has been interpreted and transformed). The question therefore arises as to whether the software in fact aids data analysis or simply adds another step to the process.

Today many people use computer software for analysis. Some use it as a first stage of data analysis, others use it as a device for complete analysis. However, in our experience computer software is useful for a first stage of analysis only, where data will be further analysed *manually* to achieve more in-depth interpretive input which takes account of contextual issues. Also the technique of using *criteria for analysis* (as described earlier and illustrated in Chapter 6) is very valuable for further analysis and interpretation. Of course, given the speed of technologic change, perhaps developments will enable more comprehensive use of computer aided packages.

Overall, it is likely that computer aided analysis is at best a useful and sometimes additional *first cut* evaluation of the data. While it allows the researcher to organize the data, confirm broad assumptions, and identify emerging patterns, it will not generate richness of interpretive under-standing. This can only come from intimate appreciation of the inherent nuances of meaning.

The Value of Models

This part of the chapter outlines the concept of pictorial models as a means of conceptualizing, describing and explaining an aspect of research. Because of the *creative* and conceptual nature of model construction, they are particularly appropriate within the qualitative research domain. We attempt to reinforce the *naturalness*, *appropriateness* and value of models; to describe a variety of model types, all of which can be seen in their various guises within marketing theory.

Human 'cultural/mystical' origins

As human beings, our societies and worlds are steeped in ancient traditions stemming from our mythologies, practice and customs, handed down by a variety of means over large time spans. An historian of human cultures in many places throughout the world can trace similarities between the mythologies and foundations of different cultures. Ancient cultures stemming from Native Americans, Ancient Greeks, European Celts and Australian Aboriginals, for example, all have their own mythical stories and characters; it is not difficult to trace some similarities in these.

In this context we could argue that ancient cultures all have a sense of *positional* belonging within a context of a wider world of being and belief. It was important within these ancient beliefs that people were aware of their *place* within the grander mystical scheme of things. Often this position would be perceived as part of a *journey* that had a known beginning and end; it would also depict significant *steps* or events along the journey. In human terms this might be seen in the human life cycle, from birth, through childhood, to adulthood, to death and *moving on*. Similarly, our ancient cultures would record significant cycles and circles depicting our stages in the journey. Much awareness of our environment would be placed in contrasts of extremes, thus we would have beliefs and values relating to day and night; light and dark; calm and storm; joy and sorrow; and so on. We would position these extremes as belonging to each other and relating to others, and we would seek to define *balances* of connection and relationship. So, light is what it is only in relation to dark. Similarly, we would connect all dimensions as part of a complete or holistic interaction of togetherness.

The point of this is to say that much of what we are in our everyday society is influenced (mostly implicitly and subconsciously), by our ancient past. For example our celebrations of the various seasons, or significant events such as Hallowe'en and solstices all have their origins in our ancient past. Much of these are accepted as natural or normal occurrences in our everyday lives; it is this natural positioning that we can draw on in describing aspects of our research. We can *draw* models of our research that borrow from much of our ancient cultures: models of positioning such as circles, spirals, sequence, matrix that illustrate comparison and balance and so on. Let us consider some of these model descriptions, illustrate how they are used throughout marketing theory and emphasize how they can be used in describing research phenomena.

Contrasts, balance/relationship models

Research and marketing use such models extensively. Many data gathering methodologies seek preferential opinions on extremes from good to bad; all to none; strongly agree to strongly disagree. For example the Likert-style schematic scales, all depict the element of *contrast*.

Contrasts can also be depicted in the balance and relationship of phenomena. For example, in services marketing we often relate tangibility and intangibility to each other. In doing this we can perceive a balance between the two by placing them on a continuum, as in Figure 12.1.

Within such a continuum we can *position* in balance an aspect of marketing which has dimensions of tangibility and intangibility.

Tangible

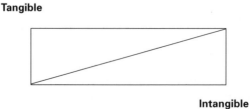

Intangible

Figure 12.1 *Continuum models*

Our own continua models outlined in earlier chapters are a further illustration of contrast and balance between dimensions of research philosophy and position. Continua serve not only to enable a positioning stance to be illustrated and determined, they also serve to define the contrasts of the dimensions placed at their extremes. So in such a simple theorem, it is possible to define two aspects in themselves; further define them by contrast with each other; and to create *positional* definitions along a continuum between them (as we have done in the continua used in this text). These continua can be used to good effect in outlining, defining and describing the parameters of a qualitative research project or domain in marketing.

Sequential models

Sequential models depict the sense of *journey* from a known start point to an equally known conclusion. The journey between the two is depicted by steps which are mostly sequential in that one step must occur before the next. Sometimes, simultaneous steps can occur which may allow an alternative course towards the same destination. Figure 12.2 gives an illustration of three alternatives of such a model.

Such sequential models are numerous in marketing theory, for example:

- in marketing planning, where sequential steps of: Audit–SWOT (Assessment of strengths, weaknesses, opportunities and threats)–Plan–Monitor, are depicted;
- in new product development, where each stage of product development is represented from an initial idea or concept to product commercialization;
- in distribution channels, where we can see producer–intermediary–retailer–end user, in a variety of sequential steps.

In research situations sequential models are equally numerous; many research designs depict research progression sequentially. They are

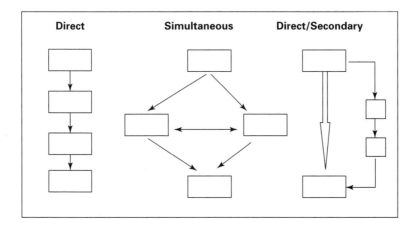

Figure 12.2 *Sequential flow models*

sometimes derived from cause and effect scenarios. Such sequential models can also depict the *funnelling* or narrow sequence of working from broad horizons to a specific situation target.

Life cycle models

Life cycle models are used extensively in a wide range of social science circumstances, and especially in marketing. All marketing scholars have learned the concept of the product life cycle and how different strategies are required for different stages of the life cycle. Such models are designed to illustrate the birth, growth, maturity and decline of a phenomenon (the product). The *cycle* is usually depicted in relation to time and another aspect, such as revenue, profit or complexity. A typical life cycle model will look something like Figure 12.3.

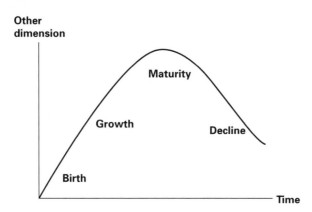

Figure 12.3 *Life cycle models*

In research, life cycle models are particularly useful in illustrating the longitudinal progression of the *life* of an object or happening.

Circular models

Circular models depict sequences of events that are recurring. They may depict sequential steps within a marketing sequence, for example in a service quality improvement context or in consumer purchasing models that focus on repeat purchase patterns. In such circumstances they outline how customers go through events within a continuous circle which they may continue or fall off at any or various points.

In research, circular models illustrate a *closed* circle of research events or stages, which both impact and depend upon each other. A circle model (Figure 12.4) will enable a researcher to illustrate the parameters and confines of a research project or domain.

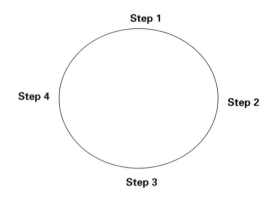

Step 1

Step 4

Step 2

Step 3

Figure 12.4 *A circular model*

Spiral or cycle models

Spiral or cycle models offer a less restrictive flow or progression along a journey than sequential or circular models. Essentially they serve to depict the consequences of some event or occurrence which can then be expected to *spin off* into an environment of change or development. A spiral model best illustrates the progression of events and the deepening insights into such events. Such a spiral may depict, as part of this progression and deepening, stages of change that may or may not be sequential in occurrence.

In the research domain, *hermeneutic* spirals are common in qualitative social science contexts. Whilst they may have elements of cause and effect sequence they do not necessarily need to have. They are particularly useful in depicting longitudinal research progression, where the spiral may also allow additional elements to be introduced at various stages. An illustration of a spiral model is given in Figure 12.5.

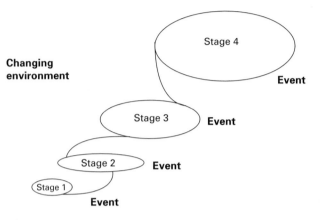

Figure 12.5 *Spiral models*

Interactive or interrelated models

Interactive or interrelated models illustrate how each component relates or connects to another. Such models may have a focal aspect that is the catalyst or link for all the other aspects. Alternatively, they may depict the interconnection of aspects without giving dominance to any one aspect. Figures 12.6(a) and (b) illustrate such models.

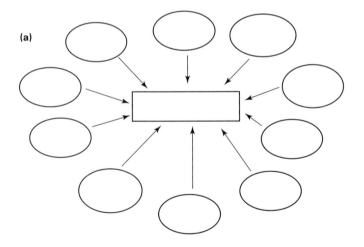

Figure 12.6 *Interactive or interrelated models*

continued

Figure 12.6 *continued*

(b)

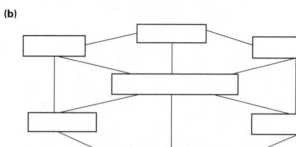

In the marketing literature such models are used to illustrate the components parts within a domain of marketing, for example *marketing mix* models, and even within these, for example, the *communication mix* or *pricing mix* models. There is also a large area of networks and networking which utilizes such models in illustrating and describing a circumstance.

In research, such models can be used extensively in outlining the range of research issues and how they interrelate.

Matrix models

Matrix models allow the illustration of more continuous, detailed or simultaneous interactions and often complex patterns of contrasts, comparisons and positions between two or more aspects. They can be two-dimensional or three-dimensional depending on the number of interactive aspects. Figure 12.7a is an illustration of this.

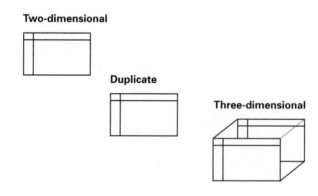

Figure 12.7a *Matrix models*

Matrix models enable the positioning of a circumstance within the contrasting components. Marketing theories in marketing positioning strategies use *positioning maps* extensively to illustrate a positioning theory. Such positioning maps may take various forms. For example, a two-dimensional positioning map depicting two continua as axes is often used (Figure 12.7b).

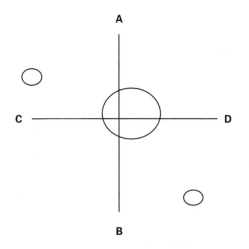

Figure 12.7b *Positioning map models*

In marketing textbooks such a position map is often used where one axis may depict *quality* and another *price*, for example. Similarly, a two by two matrix can be used to illustrate positions between two domains each having two parameters. Figure 12.7c is an illustration of this: for example positioning a product within aspects of market growth and competitor activity, as in the *portfolio matrix* models of the literature.

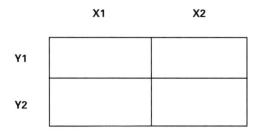

Figure 12.7c *Two by two matrix model*

Matrix models are particularly useful for researchers, because they allow an illustration of the complexity that is inherent in many research projects. In research they can also be used as theory building models, whereby they gradually add new aspects to an already constructed model, for example moving from a two-dimensional to a three-dimensional illustration of research phenomena.

Value of models in research conceptualization and analysis

The value of models in illustrating aspects of research is that not only can we all relate to such constructs (inherent in our ancestral past), but it allows the lateral thinking aspect of our intellect to come to the fore. Such conceptualization is natural not only for the creator to construct, but also for the reader to accept. The visual impact of a pictorial story is powerful, as in the paraphrase, 'a picture is worth a thousand words'. Models allow the researcher to construct a framework that not only enables the description of the research but also ensures that the researcher is confined to and focused on a clear course of action and research. The value of models is easy to see in the academic and textbook literature. Simply observe the number of academic articles that carry illustrative models; also any textbook in marketing would be deficient without colourful and graphic models of illustration.

More specifically in qualitative research, models allow the researcher to conceptualize the research domain. In addressing a research problem a researcher will review the literature to determine the important components and look for gaps in prior studies, in order to relate to his/her specific research context. In so doing the researcher might construct a *theoretical* or *conceptual* model to illustrate what might be the ideal description of a phenomenon. The researcher may then embark upon appropriate empirical research either to validate or to refute the conceptualization. Often in analysing the empirical research findings the researcher can construct a *descriptive* model of 'what actually is happening empirically'. This can then be compared with the conceptual model to explicitly illustrate the appropriate variances determined between *theory and actual practice* within the research context.

Summary

This chapter has described how to organize and prepare for gathering empirical data, taking account of some of the practical issues which need to be planned and considered before going out in the field. It has considered how to analyse data, the use of computer software packages and also how to do more in-depth interpretive analysis using specific criteria. The final section of the chapter outlined and illustrated the use of a variety of models for conceptualizing, describing and analysing the key themes of a research study.

LEARNING QUESTIONS

What are the first stages in preparing for fieldwork? Why do these deserve careful consideration and planning?

Describe two approaches to analysing data. Outline the different stages of each approach.

What is the purpose and value of using models in research conceptualization and analysis?

References

Catterall, M. and Maclaran, P. (1998) 'Using Computer Software for the Analysis of Qualitative Market Research Data', *Journal of the Market Research Society*, 40(3), 207–222.

Denscombe, M. (1998) *The Good Research Guide: For Small-Scale Social Research Projects*, Open University Press, Buckingham.

Gilmore, A. (1995) 'Quality in Marketing in a Services Context'. Unpublished PhD. thesis, University of Ulster.

Guba, E.G. (1978) *Toward a Methodology of Naturalistic Inquiry in Educational Evaluation*, Center for the Study of Evaluation, University of California, Los Angeles.

Miles, M.B. and Huberman, A.M. (1994) *Qualitative Data Analysis: An Expanded Sourcebook*, 2nd edn. Sage, Thousand Oaks, CA.

Mintzberg, H. (1979) 'An Emerging Strategy of "Direct" Research', *Administrative Science Quarterly*, 24(4), 582–589.

Patton, M.Q. (1987) *How to Use Qualitative Methods in Evaluation*, Sage, Newbury Park, CA.

Strauss, A. and Corbin, J. (1990) *Basics of Qualitative Research: Grounded Theory Procedures and Techniques*, Sage, Newbury Park, CA.

Weitzman, E. and Miles, M. (1995) *Computer Programs for Qualitative Data Analysis: An Expanded Sourcebook*, 2nd edn. Sage, Thousand Oaks, CA.

13 Writing Qualitative Research Reports

Matthew browsed through the interview and observation data he had collected. He was happy: 'Oh! This project has been fun. Now I can tackle the writing up stage. I have some fascinating stories to tell.' Sorry, Matthew, your fun is going to be short-lived. You have made some serious mistakes. Your mistakes include leaving the report writing to a final *writing up* stage, and thinking that a qualitative research report is just a story that everyone will want to read.

This chapter aims to prevent us making mistakes like Matthew's. We will firstly cover some general writing skills such as identifying who our audience is, and then we will consider skills more specific to qualitative research like the balance between describing cases and cross-case analysis. Finally the characteristics of an exemplary research report will be covered.

The Writing Process

Three stages of the writing process

If any of the three stages of writing are missed, the process will become unstuck and the final report will take a long time to write, or will never be finished. The three stages are:

1 *Pre-writing* – this is where the audience is identified, the consequent overall research problem or objective of the report is sorted out, and the outline or *table of contents* is roughly drawn up. This part of the report writing process takes a long time and must be gone through carefully if the report is to be finished on time.
2 *Composing* – this is where first draft ideas for any section of the outline are written on to paper in a quick, freewheeling or free-writing way without any editorial concerns like checking the dates of references or whether a sentence has a full stop. Get the first draft of a section down!
3 *Rewriting* – after the first draft is written, it is rewritten because new ideas will have surfaced ('how can I know what I think until I have seen

what I have written?') and so there are at least three or four more *re-drafts* of a section, that improve on earlier drafts. Lindsay (1995) describes the different focus of each re-draft:

- second draft: check for coherence, that is, the parts of the draft flow appropriately from one part to the next part (the cut and paste facility of a word processor is ideal for this);
- third draft: focus on editorial concerns like the length of sentences, and active or passive voice; and
- fourth draft: finally check for referencing, table and figure numbers and mechanical tasks.

Thus there are three drafts *after* the first one, to make a total of four drafts, and it is important not to try to reduce the number of drafts or to do something in one of the drafts that should be done in another. Lindsay (1995) summarizes the aims of the four drafts:

1 first draft – getting started,
2 second draft – getting it together,
3 third draft – readability, and
4 fourth draft – final editing.

Having friends and colleagues check the drafts and give friendly constructive criticism during the second and third drafts is very helpful. In brief, writing is not primarily writing – it is mainly rewriting, time and again: 'usually, to get it right, you have to get it wrong first' (Day 1996: 5).

In summary, the first draft is not the first part of the complete writing process, for *pre*-writing is the first stage (especially its research problem and outline parts); and several other drafts follow the first. A major implication of the existence of these three stages is that the writing process must begin very early in the project. That is, pre-writing and even some composition begins before data is collected – 'You cannot begin writing early enough . . .' 'It might mean writing a first draft before venturing into the field' (Wollcott 1990: 20). Also, writing a draft abstract of the report could help to construct the outline or table of contents developed in the first stage. An abstract should be about 150 to 200 words long, and succinctly say: what the research was about, why it was done, what was found and how it was found, and what the results mean in terms of theory and practice (Day 1996).

A second implication is that when an outline or table of contents is done in the pre-writing stage, then separate sections can be written separately – start with whatever section is the easiest to write. For example, some of the methodology section might be written *before* the literature review section is written, even though it may follow the literature review section in the final report.

Know your audience and write to their needs

The first part of the pre-writing stage is identifying your audience so that you can write to meet their needs. 'The objective is to create a mental picture of real people just like you, trying to do their jobs in the best and least difficult way possible' (Day 1996: 58). Reports of qualitative research are not self-indulgent ego trips for the writer – they are *communications with an audience* that is looking for benefits for themselves. The audience for qualitative research is usually:

- postgraduate research thesis examiners and reviewers of scholarly journals;
- practitioners who are usually like those investigated in the research, but in different settings, and
- government or other policy makers.

There are other audiences, like students who read textbooks and the general public who read magazines or popular books, but let us concentrate on the three audiences above for the moment. Consider each of their different needs in turn, because their needs will determine the structure of the report.

Postgraduate research thesis *examiners* and journal *reviewers* primarily want to know that the relevant theory was covered and the theoretical contributions of the research are evident (Golden-Biddle and Locke 1997), and that the details of processes of the methodology were mastered and carefully done. That is, they want details of how the data was collected and analysed, and they want the results linked back to the previous literature.

In contrast, *practitioners* are more interested in the findings than they are in how the data was collected and analysed. Furthermore, they are more interested in the implications for management action that arise from the findings than they are in the findings themselves – and so should be explicitly warned against generalizing from the research findings excessively. Thus, in a report for practitioners, details of the research design can be placed in appendices and the findings can be summarized in short quotations, and in figures and tables if that is possible.

Finally, government and other *policy makers* are somewhat like practitioners who are more interested in the implications of the findings for them than in the findings *per se*, and are more interested in those findings than in the methodology used to generate them.

In brief, the audience and their needs should determine how your report is structured, and we will return to this point later. But while we are thinking explicitly about the audience, let us consider the issues of style and tone. Style refers to the types of words and sentences used, and tone refers to the writer's attitude to the subject matter. Consider style first.

Style

You are not writing a letter to a friend, so your style should not be colloquial or conversational. Rather, your style should be more formal and succinct (that is, be parsimoniously complete) because you have a word limit and your audience is judging the quality and implications of what you have done rather than your friendliness. The report should therefore be professional, accurate and clear. To see how this style is achieved, find and read another thesis or article that has been accepted by your particular audience and gauge the style of writing required. Does it use the active voice rather than the passive voice? How long are the sentences and paragraphs? Does it use 'I' and 'you' or is it written in the third person?

In all reports, the style must guide the reader along a smooth, easily followed path towards the conclusions that have excited the writer (based on Perry 1998). This *easily followed communication* can be achieved by using several principles.

- Firstly, have sections and subsections starting as often as every second or third page, each with a descriptive heading in bold.
- Secondly, start each section or subsection with a phrase or sentence linking it with what has gone before, for example, a sentence might start with 'Given the situation described in section 2.3.4' or 'Turning from international issues to domestic concerns . . .' The important issue here is that the reader is led on from old ideas which he or she has already digested, to new ideas – we all need 'an opportunity to get "comfortable" with old material before new material is thrown at us' (Lindsay 1995: 56).
- Thirdly, briefly describe the argument or point to be made in the section at its beginning; for example, 'Seven deficiencies in models found in the literature will be identified.'
- Fourthly, make each step in the argument easy to identify with a key term in italics or the judicious use of argument linkers like *firstly, secondly*, or *moreover, in addition*, and *in contrast*.
- Finally, end each section with a summary to establish what it has achieved; this summary sentence or paragraph could be flagged by usually beginning it with 'In conclusion . . .' or 'In brief . . .'. Following these five principles will make arguments easy to follow and so guide the reader towards agreeing with a writer's views.

Other style rules are that the word 'etc.' is too imprecise to be used in most scholarly writing, and that the use of adjectives and adverbs should be kept to a minimum to avoid the impression of being flowery. Furthermore, words such as *this, these, those* and *it* should not be left dangling – they should always refer to an object; for example, 'This rule should be followed' is preferred to 'This should be followed'.

Definite and indefinite articles should be avoided where possible, especially in headings; for example, 'Supervision of doctoral students' is more taut and less presumptuous than 'The supervision of doctoral students'. Paragraphs should be short; as a rule of thumb, about three paragraphs should start on each typed page.

The concept of a 'chunk' can help summarize some of the discussion above. The whole report is one big chunk of an idea – the solution to the research problem set out on the first or second page. But each part of the report should be a chunky part of the whole report, with links to other parts. For a start, each *chapter* should have its own role within the report. For example, Chapter 2 may outline, describe and discuss the literature surrounding the identification and refinement of research issues about which data collection and processing is described in Chapter 3. Each chapter has *section* and subsection chunks, perhaps with a numbering system that reflects their interrelationships (such as 3.2, 3.2.1 and 3.2.2). Then each subsection has chunks of paragraphs within it, sometimes indicated with run-in headings.

Next there are individual *paragraphs*. These are almost always longer than one sentence and take up a third of a page or so. Each paragraph usually has a *link* word or phrase at the start such as 'Next' or 'Furthermore' or 'following on from the argument/discussion above. . .'. These link words or phrases at the start of a paragraph lead the reader from already digested ideas into a new idea. Each paragraph deals with one idea that is introduced and summarized in a theme sentence near the start, as the start of a paragraph is a 'hot spot' that the reader will normally concentrate upon (Lindsay 1995). (For example, the theme sentence at the start of this paragraph shows that the paragraph will be about paragraphs and what is in them.) Finally, each *sentence* has one small idea, with the most important aspect of the sentence presented at its start; do not waste the hot spot at the start of a sentence on a relatively unimportant phrase like 'As shown in Table 6'. Place such phrases at the end of a sentence, after a comma. Sentences may have a link word at the start such as 'However' to guide the reader from the known content of the previous sentence into the new material in the sentence. If there is no link word or phrase, the reader will assume the new sentence leads *directly* from the previous sentence and this assumption may not always be correct. In brief, the thesis should be a string of clear chunks of ideas.

Tone

Tone refers to the stance towards the reader and the subject matter. It is here that qualitative researchers like Matthew confront a dilemma. Qualitative researchers can easily *fall in love* with their data: after all, they are often virtual participants in important parts of people's lives. It is only natural that they want to allow the reader to share their interest and excitement by using a tone of close commitment to the subject matter, even a confessional tone. They want the reader 'to be a co-analyst, experiencing the original setting vicariously, looking at the evidence, weighing the writer's interpretations and perspective – and noting how they changed along the way' (Miles and Huberman 1994: 299).

However, this approach confuses research methodology and the report about the research, and so ignores the needs of the audience. The methodology does not have to have the same philosophy as the report. The *methodology* links researcher and subject in the generation of research data while the *report* links researcher and reader in the generation of benefits for the reader. A qualitative research report has to show that the researcher got close to the phenomenon in a way that was useful. Thus most of a report for an audience of examiners and reviewers normally has the more distant, matter-of-fact tone that examiners and reviewers expect, except in the methodology part where the writer is more confessional to convince the audience that he or she carried out normal, *interpretivist* qualitative research and captured the perspectives of subjects. For example, personal pronouns like 'I' are infrequent in most of the report but can be used in the methodology part because the researcher was directly involved in what went on and unavoidably used his or her own values to make many decisions and interact with the subjects in the field.

In contrast to the blend of distant and subjective writing in a report for examiners and reviewers, a report for policy makers might be more confessional throughout, to draw readers into the frame of mind required for changing their policies.

In brief, writers should use a style and tone to meet their readers' needs, not their own.

Structure of Reports

Structure of reports for examiners and reviewers

Having covered some general aspects of the writing process, we can now approach the details of a report structure. For a start, we will concentrate on reports for audiences of examiners and reviewers. For these audiences, the generic or most usual structure of a thesis and a journal article about *quantitative* research consists of five parts (based on Perry 1997, 1998 and Day 1996). These do not necessarily have to be presented in the order shown but should appear somewhere in the report.

Part I

This part addresses the question, 'What is the report about?'

1.1 research problem(s) that will be solved in the report (presented on the first page of an article);

1.2   delimitations of scope: that is the confines and context of the topic and research; delimitations are within the control of the researcher while limitations in part 5.6 below are not.

Part 2

Background/literature review: this is the background of the research problem (as tributaries are the background of a river); it develops the research issues addressed in part 4 below in the context of data collection and analysis.

Part 3

Methods of data collection: this section describes and justifies the methodology chosen in the context of the specific research problem, how, where, when, from whom data was collected.

Part 4

Analysis of data, with analysis and interpretations of those patterns in separate sections.

Part 5

This part addresses the question 'Why does it matter?' It includes:

5.1   summary of the conclusions derived from analysing the data;
5.2   how those conclusions relate to the research problem's body of knowledge discussed in part 2;
5.3   implications for other bodies of knowledge;
5.4   implications for managers and other practitioners;
5.5   implications for public and organizational policies;
5.6   limitations of the study arising from limitations of the methodology (these limitations are additional to the delimitations of scope in 1.2 above);
5.7   implications for further research (mostly arising from extensions to the delimitations and limitations in 1.2 and 5.6 above).

Qualitative researchers sometimes find this structure a strait-jacket or difficult to fit into because they had little or no theory (with its associated research issues) before they started their data collection, or they mix together the data and their interpretations of it. Moreover, they have to present the data *within its context* and so the data description sections of their reports are longer than the equivalent section of quantitative research reports. All this means that reports of qualitative research are usually longer than other reports and have far more diverse structures than the listing of the five parts above would suggest.

Nevertheless, the additional length and diversity of a qualitative report does *not* mean that anything goes. The report must still meet the audience's needs, which are to check the contributions to existing theory and to check methodological appropriateness and thoroughness. So there are five *principles* of qualitative research report writing that should be followed to varying extents depending on the audience:

1 Links to the literature should be explicit, even if they are only incorporated into a project at the very end, as they are in a grounded theory study for example.
2 The methodology should be described somewhere.
3 An appropriate blend of description and interpretation should be provided.
4 Issues of reliability, transparency, insights and understanding should be addressed.
5 How ethical issues were addressed should be reported.

Principle One

There should be some discussion of how the research's findings extend the body of knowledge, perhaps along the lines of part 5 above. This discussion will include some synthesis of the research with others, so as to generalize the findings to other situations and to other theories. This element of a report is most important for examiners and reviewers; for example, reviewers of journal articles usually concentrate on how the data illustrates theory or points of view about issues that the journal's readers are interested in, rather than in the data *per se*. In effect, a report is a way of entering a 'conversation' with an audience (Huff 1999: 4). The audience's concerns and conventions must be observed or the audience will simply not listen to us when we try to converse with them – examiners will fail a thesis or reviewers will reject an article submitted to a journal. One researcher had collected data about the use of humour in a hospital but to get her report published she had to recast the report into one that added to the theory of emotionality within client–provider relationships and that treated the humour in a serious fashion. In brief, writing a report 'necessarily incorporates the understanding that the meanings we choose to develop and articulate in our work must be directed toward and lay claim to a specific, and preferably, mainstream, audience' of researchers in a particular academic discipline (Golden-Biddle and Locke 1997: 10).

Principle Two

Somewhere in the report there should be a *description of what was done*, including how and why it was done (which will be based on a demonstrated awareness of the literature on the methodology). This description should also explain the usually idiosyncratic parts of the methodology, for instance, how the respondent and content analysis codes were selected. In brief, some elements of part 3 above should be somewhere in the report.

Principle Three

There should be an appropriate blend of data *description and interpretation* (corresponding loosely to parts 2, 4 and 5 above). That is, a report will have parts of *both* of these intermingled; or they are two ends of a continuum that can be described in several ways (see Table 13.1, adapted from Miles and Huberman 1994):

Table 13.1

Description	Interpretation
Data	Theory
Case analysis or within-case analysis	Cross-case analysis
Case-oriented	Variable-oriented
Context	Category
Analytic	Synthetic
Emic	Etic

The *description* parts of a report will include relevant stories and quotations plus the contextual aspects of the data, for example the time of the interviews, where they were held, and some details of the people who were involved. This data is presented to help the reader follow the interpretation parts of the report and believe in the interpretations. That is, the description is *direct* evidence that the researcher did indeed collect raw, qualitative data and that it is the basis of the interpretation that is also included in the report.

By the way, writing this description is the first part of *preparing* for the report because the interpretation part will be based on this description. Not all of this description will be incorporated into the final report, of course. Less than 10 per cent of the data may actually be used, but all the data such as transcripts and documents should be kept in the research database for later retrieval if required. The parts of the description that are used in the report should illustrate the theoretical points raised in the interpretation. They should interest the reader and they should be striking examples of these points. These "condensed examples" [in the description] should not only illustrate the theoretical points but 'also embody vividness that brings the points alive in a way that evokes the human interest of readers' (Golden-Biddle and Locke 1997: 68).

In turn, the interpretation aspects of a report will include the patterns that were similar across many respondents, for example, the common meanings of what respondents said. Judgement will decide what proportions of each of description and interpretation will be in a report. Patton (1990: 376) is precise in his judgement. He suggests that the focus of the project helps determine the balance between description of each individual element or case and interpretation across all the elements or cases. If the focus is on the individual elements of a project, then description should predominate. For example, if the focus was on marketing managers, then each case about an individual manager should be carefully described. But if the focus was on marketing management within an industry, then cross-case interpretation would predominate.

More general advice about the mix of description and interpretation is that 50–70 per cent should be descriptions of events, anecdotes and episodes, and 30–50 per cent should be interpretation (Miles and Huberman 1994: 302, citing Lofland 1974). These percentages of description and the interpretation in a report of qualitative research should *blend* together, that is, they should 'interpenetrate' (Atkinson 1991: 169) because separating the two will make it hard for the reader to grasp the connections. For example, a writer had constructed a 'matrix' that cross-categorized some interview data (Miles and Huberman 1994: 240) about the use of ships by international marketers and called it Table 4.3. Then he discerned patterns in attitudes to shipping in the data. In his report, he mixed the two of them in the example shown below; the example contains some interpretation about why respondents did not think shipping was important, and some description in the form of two quotations from interviewees disguised as A2 and B1:

> Most respondents thought shipping was not important because schedules were reliable (row 2 of table 4.3). 'Thank goodness the unions are tame' (A2). 'No worries – we have good port agents and shipping lines' (B1).

Incidentally, do not change the words, style or grammar of a quotation because a quotation should reflect the respondent's perceptions and not the researcher's interpretation of what the respondent meant; for example, the slang term 'no worries' was left in the quotation above.

Principle Four

The fourth principle is to include a discussion of quality, or reliability. This discussion should be based on the logic of the paradigm involved and should not be based on the inappropriate logic of paradigms like positivism. In interpretivism (such as ethnographic and action research reports), this discussion would probably be based on the logic of 'trustworthiness'. The most significant factor of qualitative research is to demonstrate *transparency* of findings so that they can be trusted.

Principle Five

Finally, how *ethical* concerns were met could be discussed in the report. These concerns include the requirement that informed consent was obtained from participants and whether the respondents are disguised adequately in the discussion. In an ideal world, the respondents should not be disguised so that the reader can bring everything else they know about the respondent's situation to their reading and so understand the context even more. Also, a report is easier to write if newspaper articles or other sources of information can be brought into the report without disguise and details of the respondent do not have to be 'smoothed out' or 'rounded up or down' to maintain their disguise. In a real world, however, most respondents prefer to be disguised even if they do not insist on it. We have found that most respondents will be more open if they are assured at the start of the interview that the research report will disguise them to ensure their anonymity.

An example of a qualitative research report

Consider how these five principles can be applied in the structure of a report aimed at examiners and reviewers (based on Perry and Zuber-Skerritt 1994). In the description below, we take a pragmatic approach to report-writing and try to separate the philosophy of report-writing from the philosophy of doing qualitative research. Thus we accept that an audience may feel more comfortable with the five-part linear structure above and so we try to fit into that strait-jacket or, to mix metaphors, try to 'shoe-horn' the research report into that structure.

The example below is a report about an action research project. The philosophy and processes of action research are far broader and more complex than those implicit in most reports. In particular, the action research project is relatively unfocused, emphasizes practice and has outcomes of reflections that include practical and experiential (group and personal) knowledge as well as the propositional knowledge found in textbooks and articles. Moreover, this knowledge is built up gradually during the project and not in the one stage that is implicit in the five parts above. In contrast to action research's emphasis on a group's experiential knowledge about their own work processes, a report emphasizes an individual researcher's additions to propositional knowledge published in the literature of a discipline. In brief, in the action research project, action research may be an *ideology*, but in a report it is merely a *methodology*.

Writing a report about an action research project without acknowledging these differences between the report and the project is difficult, but let us attempt it in an example that follows the structure above. The example is a rather extreme one, for action research is distinctively non-linear and we will force it into the rather linear, generic structure of a five-part report. That linear structure will highlight the methodological expertise and theoretical contributions that most examiners and reviewers are interested in.

For a start, the overall 'research problem' in *part 1* of the report could be different to the overall 'thematic concern' (Kemmis and McTaggart 1988: 9) of the action research study. The research problem necessarily refers to practices of a workgroup and is written in terms of the literature of a discipline, but the thematic concern is less restricted. For example, a research problem could be 'How can the senior management team at an open-cut mine integrate marketing, operations and financial subsystems in the planning of inventories of mined coal?' The thematic concern of the senior management group could be 'How can our inventory management procedures be improved?' Although the action research study will probably require a multidisciplinary solution to its thematic concern, it is advised that the report should concentrate on the one or two disciplines that the audience is most interested in, to solve its research problem and to facilitate its examination (Golden-Biddle and Locke 1997).

Part 2 of the report would review relevant literature (even though it may not have been read until just before the report was finalized). The review would have relatively 'fuzzy' research issues at its end, that is, it would refer to some unresearched areas of propositional knowledge which appear to be the focus of the data collected from the action research project. However, to be true to the spirit of action research, these research issues should not have been finalized *before* the action research study began – unlike research using some quantitative methodologies when the hypotheses should be crystallized before the data collection begins. That is, these research issues did not focus the data collection and analysis parts of the action research project, but they will probably focus the data analysis part of the *report*. Furthermore, part 2 could outline the boundaries of practical and experiential knowledge (that is, knowledge which was not in the literature) which existed at the start of the action research study. Alternatively, this discussion of practical and experiential knowledge might be restricted to an appendix, if likely examiners are not expected to be familiar with action research methodology.

Part 3 could be used to describe the action research study – not to allow replication of the experiment because that will be impossible, but to demonstrate the researcher's competence in the action research methodology. The part could have sections or refer to appendices which contain the following details of the context of the action research study (Kemmis and McTaggart 1988):

- the names and backgrounds of group members;
- the group's thematic concern;
- details of the multiple sources of data, for example dates of meetings and their attendees and matters discussed, reports and letters;
- the distinctions between the stages of the project through its one or more cycles of plan–act–observe–reflect;
- the group's published report of the study – which is written before the report is completed and for a different audience from the report: this

could be a short narrative or a management report and might be
included as an appendix if it was short enough;
- evidence that the group has reflected on *processes* as well as *content*,
which might be recorded in the group's published report noted above
but does not have to be; and the nature of the action research, that is,
technical, practical or emancipatory (as discussed in the action research
part).

As noted above, an appendix might also reflect on the practical and
experiential knowledge gained in the action research project, but it would
be more usual to include that reflection in the body of the report.

Part 4 could be used to categorize the data collected in the action
research study. This part *organizes* the data from the action research
project into *patterns*. Part 4 begins the researcher's own preliminary
reflection on the project and could be divided into sections according to
the propositions of propositional knowledge, and into sections for
practical and experiential (personal) knowledge if they are to be included
in parts of the report rather than in appendices. So the part should be
written with the ideas to be developed in part 5, in the writer's mind. There
have to be many quotations and stories in this part mingled with the
interpretations of patterns in the data, to allow the reader to be a *co-
analyst* with the writer.

Finally, *part 5* makes conclusions about the research study, linking the
findings of part 4 to the boundaries of the body (or bodies) of knowledge
outlined in part 2. This part is not in normal action research study
reports but is essential in an academic report. A section in part 5 entitled
'Reflections on methodology' should be included in a report that refers to
the value and scope of action research in the study. Then a section about
possible future research will conclude the report.

Qualitative researchers should guard against a report that mirrors their
research philosophy and processes and thus, because of an open
interpretivist mindset, might lead to a report which is inconclusive and
perhaps unrelated to the propositional knowledge published in the
literature of their discipline. That is, the *unstructured* report of qualitative
research could be confusing and unsatisfying to its audience of examiners
and reviewers. Knowledgeable and careful use of the five-part structure
for a report may allay that concern.

Structure of reports for practitioners or policy makers

The structure of a report for an audience of practitioners or policy makers
is different from that for examiners and reviewers because the former seek
approximate truth rather than the *complete* truth. So there are two major
ways that reports for practitioners or policy makers differ from the reports
described above:

- the focus is on implications for *action* rather than contributions to theory; and *methodological* details are far less important.

Let us consider each of these in turn.

Extrapolation to their own management situation

A report for practitioners or policy makers should be closely focused on the audience's concerns about the management implications of the research rather than the theoretical conclusions. It does not contain any details that might have been fascinating for the researcher but are not related to the specific goal of the report. Thus a report about empirical research into the marketing management of technical colleges, for instance, could be arranged around the 4 Ps of marketing because that is how the public sector practitioners had been taught to think about marketing; even if the researcher shared Gronroos' (1994) distaste for the 4 Ps and had developed his or her own perspective on the data that supported Gronroos. The structure should reflect the audience's way of thinking. If you want to change their way of thinking, you can only do that by being read in the first place. Moreover, there need be only a handful of references at the most, because the practitioners will relate the findings back to their own *experience* or colleagues' experiences rather than to what they have read. This emphasis on experience occurs because managers make decisions about *individual* occurrences of social phenomena within their own context, and so they always have to extrapolate any conclusions about another context or any generalizations about many contexts, to their own. This extrapolation to their own context is their major concern.

One implication of this concern is that the structure of a report for practitioners or policy makers has more interpretation than description. As noted, the headings are usually topics to which the reader can relate, and on which the interpretation will focus. For example, the headings could be the four parts of the marketing mix even though the integration of that mix may be more important than any of the four parts. Nevertheless, there should be enough description to convince the reader that the findings have enough authenticity to be worth extrapolating to his or her own situation. But no more description than that is required.

Methodology for practitioners and policy makers

Examiners and reviewers worry about methodology because they want to know that the methodological road a researcher has followed will lead to true or reliable findings. In contrast, practitioners and policy makers will mix a report's findings with other sources of information to produce *utility* in the form of extrapolated ideas for their own situation (Patton 1990: 483–484). So although the methodology cannot be hidden from these readers, its details can be glossed over or perhaps placed in appendices.

Incidentally, the executive summary of a report for practitioners or policy makers is extremely important because quite often that will be the only part of the report that is read. It is a two- or three-page *political* document that is focused on the core issues and argues the case for the specific and detailed implications for management action. These aims of the executive summary may be supported by presentations to the practitioners, and by articles written about the research for industry or trade journals.

Summary

Writing a report is an integral part of most qualitative research projects, and its objective is to disseminate the findings to an audience. This chapter emphasized the importance of thinking about the audience when pre-writing, writing and revising the report. Writers should use a style and tone to meet their readers' needs, not their own. Although the report may not closely follow the rather rigid five-part structure of a report of research, it does follow five principles: links to the literature should be explicit; the methodology should be described somewhere; an appropriate blend of description and interpretation should be provided; issues of validity, reliability, trustworthiness, transparency and ethical concerns should be addressed.

LEARNING QUESTIONS

Describe the importance of writing a report for a specific audience.
   What is involved in pre-writing, writing and revising?
   What are the five principles of qualitative research report writing?

References

Atkinson, P. (1991) 'Supervising the Text', *Qualitative Studies in Education*, 4(2), 161–174.
Day, A. (1996) *How to Get Research Published in Journals*, Gower, Aldershot.
Golden-Biddle, K. and Locke, K.D. (1997) *Composing Qualitative Research*, Sage, Thousand Oaks, CA.
Gronroos, C. (1994) 'From Marketing Mix to Relationship Marketing: toward a Paradigm Shift in Marketing', *Asia-Australia Marketing Journal*, 2(1), 9–30.
Huff, A.S. (1999) *Writing for Scholarly Publication*, Sage, Thousand Oaks, CA.
Kemmis, S. and McTaggart, R. (eds) (1988) *The Action Research Reader*, Deakin University, Geelong.
Lindsay, D. (1995) *A Guide to Scientific Writing*, Longman, Melbourne.

Lofland, J. (1974) 'Styles of Reporting Qualitative Field Research', *American Sociologist*, 9, 101–111.

Miles, M.B. and Huberman, A.M. (1994) *Qualitative Data Analysis*, Sage, Thousand Oaks, CA.

Patton, M.Q. (1990) *Qualitative Evaluation and Research Methods*, Sage, Newbury Park, CA.

Perry, C. (1997) 'How Can I Write a Journal Article in Two Days? A Book Review of Day, A. 1997, *How to Get Research Published in Journals*', *European Journal of Marketing*, 31(11/12), 896–901.

Perry, C. (1998) 'A Structured Approach for Presenting Theses', *Australasian Marketing Journal*, 6(1), 63–85.

Perry, C. and Zuber-Skerritt, O. (1994) 'Doctorates by Action Research for Senior Practicing Managers', *Management Learning*, 25(2), 341–364.

Wollcott, B. (1990) *Writing up Qualitative Research*, Sage, Newbury Park, CA.

14   Integrative Multiple Mixes of Methodologies

The advantages of using multiple mixes of qualitative methods for research in marketing are discussed in this chapter. In particular, the use of an *integrative* qualitative research methodology is described in relation to a study concerning quality in marketing in a service context. The development of an integrative qualitative research methodology is built upon the very practical need for researchers to develop the *best* possible methodologies for their own specific research problem or issues. The notion of such a methodology is combined with the idea of a *stream of research* or research which builds upon earlier studies and explicitly allows the research to evolve and develop through distinctive stages over a given time period. (This chapter is drawn primarily from Gilmore and Carson 1996.)

Qualitative research methods are well suited to the characteristics of marketing. Given that marketing involves an act, a process and a performance, many significant aspects of marketing occur through human interactions. It has been recognized that some aspects of marketing, such as services, are difficult to study using traditional research methodologies (Bitner et al. 1985; Shostack 1977) as they exist only while being rendered and are living processes that cannot be disassembled (Shostack and Kingman-Brundage 1991).

The predominant characteristics of marketing that impact upon the nature of research methodologies used are based on the definition of marketing management as an integration of performances and processes. As such, marketing management exists in a dynamic change circumstance involving interactions of people and will depend on aspects of accessibility and timing in decision making.

The inherent requirement for this interaction during marketing management decision making can create many varying and volatile situations. There is potential for ambiguity, misunderstanding and differing perceptions. The importance of the time dimension in relation to sound marketing decisions and the process and period of time taken for these decisions may require a longitudinal, continuous study in a research project focusing on aspects of marketing.

The adaptability and flexibility of qualitative research methods and techniques throughout the entire research process have many advantages.

For example, at an early exploratory stage of research, qualitative methods allow the researcher to become familiar with the area(s) of interest, explore the field and consider the dimensions involved because of their open-ended, non-pre-ordained nature. This aids early researcher understanding of the topic. During the development of the research design, the adaptability of qualitative methods allows for a relatively flexible plan of action to be followed, evolving with the experiential learning and development of the researcher as new themes, ideas and topics of interest emerge. This contributes to the development and understanding of a topic, allowing the researcher to begin to see connections and the influences upon the phenomenon or topic of interest. Furthermore, researcher immersion in the phenomenon throughout the study aids understanding of the whole context where the phenomenon takes place. Therefore researcher involvement in the analysis and interpretation is built upon the development of experiential understanding throughout the research process over the time of study. The entire qualitative research process should provide an open, flexible, and illuminating way to study the complexity of marketing situations. In this way qualitative methods are well suited to gathering data on dynamic, experiential processes and the interactive nature of marketing phenomena, where it is important to allow for the experience and involvement of the researcher in a fast-changing and fluid environment.

Suitability of Qualitative Methods for Marketing

Taking account of the marketing characteristics and qualitative research characteristics it is possible to determine the features that emphasize the suitability of qualitative methods for research in marketing. Figure 14.1

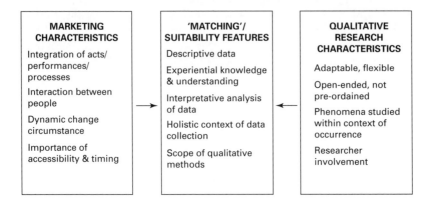

Figure 14.1 *Suitability of qualitative research methods for marketing (adapted from Gilmore and Carson 1996)*

illustrates the *key matching features*, which are considered to be the use of *descriptive data*, the inclusion of the *experiential knowledge and understanding of the researcher*, the emphasis on the *interpretive analysis of data*, the *holistic context of data collection* and analysis and *scope of qualitative methods*. These are discussed below.

Descriptive data

Qualitative data consists of detailed descriptions of events, situations and interactions between people and things, providing depth and detail (Patton 1980). Such data is symbolic, contextually embedded, cryptic and reflexive. They allow phenomena to be studied in detail and depth, so contributing to meaningful interpretation and response (Patton 1980). In addition the longitudinal aspect of many qualitative studies permits data to be gathered over a period of time and thus allows the researcher time to develop experiential understanding of the phenomena. This presents the opportunity to generate 'thick description' (Geertz 1973) and explanation of phenomena, actions, processes and experiences within a *holistic* context. That is, describing the context in which behaviours take place, incorporating cultural meaning into the written text, and 'thick interpretation' (Geertz 1973), providing the reader with 'a road map' to help him or her understand the complex nature of the field. A qualitative report will describe things that really happen in marketing organizations and contexts, as researchers experience them.

Experiential knowledge and understanding of the researcher

One of the chief advantages of qualitative research for marketing contexts is that it permits research to evolve, develop and build upon earlier understanding. It allows researchers to 'directly experience the world of informants and all of its variations. Living through the "highs" and "lows" of informants' lives allows the researcher to know the phenomenon under investigation in a way that few other methodologies permit' (Hill 1993: 260).

Van Maanen illustrates this advantage further when he compares qualitative and quantitative methods:

> Qualitative investigators tend to describe the unfolding of the process rather than the social structures that are often the focus of quantitative researchers. Qualitative researchers in contrast to their quantitative colleagues claim forcefully to know relatively little about what a given piece of observed behaviour means until they have developed a description of the context in which the behaviour takes place and attempted to see that behaviour from the position of its originator. (1979: 520)

Thus qualitative methods take account of what is learnt throughout the research *process* as well as research outcomes and results. We have mentioned some aspects of researcher immersion in qualitative research (Chapter 5) and the role of the researcher in Chapter 1. However, it is important to emphasize that, in doing qualitative research the researcher develops expertise through experience. More, the researcher accumulates knowledge, not only of the topic which in itself is valuable, but also in the research methodology. This experiential knowledge is more than just experience of the research method employed, something which any researcher, qualitative or otherwise, would gain from applying any methodology in a study. It is experiential knowledge that allows the researcher to understand the integral nuances *behind* the explicit or stated perspectives of a study. It is this intimacy with the detail that fuels experiential knowledge and understanding. Equally, recognition of the researcher's experiential knowledge and understanding is also crucial to the development and interpretation of qualitative data. The experiential nature of qualitative research combined with the experiential learning of the researcher allows deeper understanding throughout the research to evolve, building on earlier work and contributing to the interpretive process.

Interpretive analysis of data

The emphasis on interpretation as integral to qualitative methodologies is particularly suitable in the context of marketing phenomena where most marketing involves actions or performance. O'Shaughnessy (1987) writes about 'interpretive understanding of action' where phenomena are considered within the specific context, taking account of the subject's view and understanding, and the meaning of the situation. Furthermore, interpretive analysis can be ongoing throughout the study. This allows data to be initially coded in several ways (according to the research topic), then re-analysed and interpreted as further data is gathered.

The holistic context of data collection

Another characteristic of qualitative research that offers many advantages is the holistic dimension. The object of taking a holistic outlook in any research is to gain a comprehensive and complete picture of the whole context in which the phenomenon of interest occurs. It is an attempt to describe and understand as much as possible. Whilst acknowledging that no study can capture an entire culture or group, the holistic orientation 'forces the fieldworker to see beyond an immediate cultural scene or event in a classroom, hospital room, city street or plush offices' (Fetterman 1989: 29). Each scene exists within a multi-layered and interrelated context and it requires multiple methods to ensure the researcher covers all angles. This orientation helps the researcher discover the interrelationships among the various systems and subsystems in the organization under study, through an emphasis on the *contextualization* of data. Contextualising data involves placing observations, experiences and interpretations into a larger perspective. Using an integrative multiple mix of methodologies as described below contributes to the achievement of a holistic perspective.

Scope of qualitative methods

As we said earlier, qualitative methods are 'an array of interpretive techniques which seek to describe, decode, translate and otherwise come to terms with the meaning, not the frequency' (Van Maanen 1979: 520) of certain more or less naturally occurring phenomena in the social world. They allow flexibility and variety as they are a pot-pourri of interpretive techniques (Hari Das 1983). We have described some of the most commonly used qualitative methods including in-depth interviewing, case studies, focus group discussions, observations, ethnographic studies and grounded theory, and action research and action learning. The use of one or more of these methods or a combination of a number of them will allow data to be gathered on verbal (or *noise*) occurrences, visually recorded occurrences, written reports and documentation. It should also take account of the development of researcher experiential knowledge over the research time period.

Given the advantages of qualitative methods described so far, there are many reasons for borrowing and adapting these methods from their social science background for use in organizational and managerial situations. In particular they can be readily adapted for research into marketing and marketing management decision making in the context of specific organizational and marketing situations. The remainder of this chapter focuses upon the importance and value of *adapting* qualitative methods by using them in an *integrative* way for investigating specific marketing managerial issues. The concept of integrative qualitative research is illustrated in Figure 14.2. The number of methods used can be expanded and adapted as appropriate for the specific research topic. Figure 14.2 simply displays four methods in integration.

The advantages of using qualitative methods in an integrative way for marketing and marketing management decision making is that they will allow the researcher to take account of specific and individual organizational contexts. This is an aspect that many other research methods have neglected. Such studies will not be about testing variables nor about testing techniques but about determining key issues, for example what constitutes marketing activity and how marketing decisions are made in a specific context. The use of a combination of methods for an integrative qualitative research methodology is considered to be a useful development in the study of the complex and interactive process of marketing.

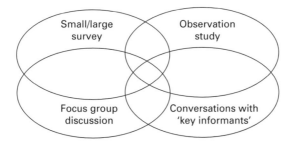

Figure 14.2 *Combination of methods (adapted from Carson and Coviello 1996)*

Integrative Multiple Mixes of Methodologies Studying Aspects of Marketing

So the development of an *integrative* qualitative research methodology has been built upon the very practical need for researchers to develop the best possible methodologies for their own specific research problem or issues. It allows individual studies to be 'carefully designed to build upon what has been learned in previous studies' (Davis et al. 1985: 40). To this end we can borrow from Davis et al. who suggest that a *stream of research* is needed. In this way, different methodological approaches can be tested, avoiding the discontinuity provided by individual, isolated investigations. Such a stream of research could be achieved (for example) by *integrating in a multiple mix*:

1 case studies of successful and unsuccessful firms/marketers; *and*
2 small-scale exploratory or cross-sectoral studies to test different methodologies; *and*
3 large scale survey research to study aspects of marketing on both a cross-sectoral and longitudinal basis; *and*
4 controlled field studies to enable the study of causal relationships.

The cornerstone of the stream of research approach is that it allows the researcher to combine the best and most suitable research methods from the social sciences at specific and appropriate stages of the research. This approach therefore may lead to greater effectiveness than a single research method. At the same time, researchers need to be cognizant of the differences associated with managing comparative interpretation of data, gathered by the different methods, perhaps over time.

A further example of the stream of research in a particular aspect of marketing could be as follows. To integrate the use of :

• small scale exploratory or cross-sector studies, to explore marketing characteristics and identify key conceptual issues, with

- case studies of marketing companies which have the specific characteristics of interest, and
- large scale survey research to study, compare and evaluate aspects of interest on both a cross-sector and a longitudinal basis.

This eliminates many of the deficiencies of a single research method (Carson and Coviello 1996).

In work that was done much earlier, Evans (1971) argues for methodological integration, particularly within the context of organizational research, in order to achieve some confidence in the *representativeness* of a study's findings. He contends that the *generalizability* of findings is enhanced by the co-ordination or integration of findings from studies using different research methods. Evans illustrates this by means of a flow chart outlining the use of a case study, followed by a sample survey, followed by a laboratory experiment and finally a field experiment. This is an example of theory building followed by theory testing. Evans acknowledges that feedback loops are possible (for example, sample survey to case study, laboratory experiment to sample survey and so on) depending upon the purpose of the research.

To some extent this practice has been used in organizational research although it has not been documented as an *integrative* research methodology. Mintzberg (1979) describes his own extensive research on the management of organizations as 'direct research', a term he uses to capture the critical focus of his research in understanding strategy formation in organizations. The development of the 'emerging strategy for direct research', which includes three stages of study as Mintzberg articulates, provides a comprehensive synopsis of the use of a variety of methodological techniques and interpretive methods for a particular research purpose.

The use of qualitative methods in an integrative way can be seen to build on the concept of the stream of research approach as described by Davis et al. (1985) and Mintzberg's three stages. Thus the concept of a stream of research is linked with the development and description of stages of research. This integrative, stage by stage process of data collection and interpretation can aid development of marketing managers' understanding over time by allowing each part or *stage* of the research to build on what had been learned in a previous stage. This will also contribute to the researcher's experiential knowledge and understanding of the phenomena under study, as well as to further development of expertise in data collection methods and interpretation of the data. At the end of each stage specific marketing decisions can be made in relation to the findings of that stage of study.

The use of a variety of qualitative techniques with a combination of interpretive techniques (integrated multiple mixes) will achieve a wider and more in-depth understanding of the complex, often vague marketing processes and outcomes. In addition, they will permit the study of the interactive and performance dimensions of marketing activities studied within their natural setting over a longitudinal time period that incorporates recognition of a *change* environment. An integrative variety of methods can be chosen to suit the purpose of the research, and to build upon and develop understanding as the research time progresses. Clearly the choice of a variety of methods where each one contributes some understanding about specific aspects of marketing management will be important, and should allow the next research stage to build and develop upon previous learning and understanding. The combination of methods used can provide a rich portrait of the phenomena under study. This allows the researcher not only to learn about the inputs and outcomes, but also to gain an understanding of the texture, activities and processes (Belk et al. 1989) occurring in the day to day operations and activities, and of the impact of these occurrences upon managerial activity. In addition the use of multiple mixes of methods may lead to an early configuration of some of the key dimensions involved in marketing phenomena; and encourage rapid progression to further aspects of study (for example, focus on the relevant managerial dimensions impacting upon specific aspects of marketing activity). This also permits further experiential understanding of the worst and best scenarios in relation to the phenomena under study.

A model that may be expanded and reshaped for a variety of different research purposes is shown in Figure 14.3. It illustrates an example of the use of an *integrative multiple mix* of qualitative research methodologies using a longitudinal *stream of research*.

The example shown here shows that at stage 1 a single company can be the focus of an in-depth study using a multiple mix of methods. For example, a small survey, observations, focus group discussions and conversations with staff and supervisors may be used in a service marketing situation. Initially a small survey may be carried out with a sample of users over a relatively short time (for example, a four-week period). The survey may focus on a number of issues in relation to aspects of the marketing delivery, process and activities. The outcomes of the survey may indicate what the majority of customers like and dislike about the marketing process.

In addition to the survey, an observation study may be used in order to delve beneath what customers and staff said they did and their opinions and to gather information about their observed behaviour. This will result in the collection of information which relates to customers' actual responses to marketing activity and the participation and involvement of staff: for example observations to reveal what services people use, how they use them and how staff interact with customers at various stages of the delivery process.

If appropriate, separate staff and customer focus group discussions may also be used. The focus group discussions may be conducted in a non-directive and unstructured fashion to aid in the generation of the

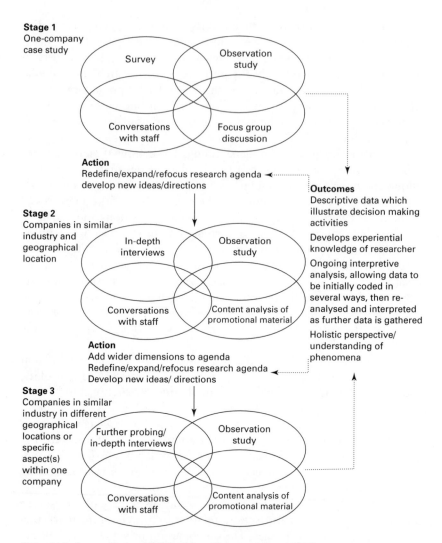

Figure 14.3 *Stream of research (adapted from Gilmore and Carson 1996)*

researcher's experiential understanding and analysis of the activity of the company's staff who deliver marketing. For example, broad, open-ended questions may be used, discussions may focus on the experiences and expectations of customers, and the experiences and opinions of staff. This will provide information about the reasons for opinions, attitudes and perceptions.

In addition conversations may be carried out with frontline staff and supervisors regarding the perception of their roles in the marketing delivery process, for example dealing with customers, handling customers' complaints, and the overall management of customer service throughout the service delivery time. This will build insights and understanding of the feelings of staff delivering the overall marketing activity and indicate how this may impact upon the actual service delivery.

Stage 2 would aim to build upon the descriptive data, experiential knowledge and ongoing interactive analysis of the data gathered during stage 1 by carrying out a study of some similar companies operating within the same industry (for example competitors of the company studied in stage 1). This will develop the researcher's understanding of the phenomena under study, through wider experience of other companies' approaches to carrying out marketing activities. In addition it will provide data on the overall policies and priorities of different companies within the same industry and contribute descriptive data in relation to the different levels of marketing activities and processes. From a research perspective, such *widening* may enable cross-interpretation to be carried out.

A further stage in the research stream, as the model in Figure 14.3 suggests, could add further progression and depth to the study. For example stage 3 could build upon stages 1 and 2 by focusing on companies which operate in the same industry but this time in different geographical locations; or conversely by focusing on a specific aspect or aspects of marketing and researching it or them in more depth within one company. The integrative multiple mix methods could be chosen to suit the specific issues identified in earlier stages of the research and take account of accessibility to these companies.

Summary

The use of an integrative stream of qualitative research methods for investigating complex, indistinct marketing issues has been illustrated here, taking particular account of the processual and interactive nature of marketing management decision making. An integrative stream of research provides a useful and practical application of research methods for specific marketing managerial purposes within an organizational context.

The advantages of carrying out marketing research over the various stages is that it allows for the changing and evolving nature of marketing activity and performance, monitoring the fluctuating aspects of marketing activity and outcomes and the influences on their delivery in the context of a specific organization's environment and relevant competitive activity. The advantage of building the study stage by stage allows for improved researcher experiential understanding and knowledge over time, the ability to look at an increasing depth and/or width of issues and to identify the key components in a given research topic within its context.

In general, whilst we have been extolling the virtues and benefits of each of the qualitative research methodologies discussed in this text, our argument here is that these methods can be *adapted, refined and combined* in a *multiple* variety of ways that enables the construction of a *holistic* research framework. The holistic framework, we argue, will enable a researcher to achieve both deep and comprehensive insights and understanding of marketing phenomena. Also in evidence in this holistic framework is the inherent compatibility of qualitative research methods that can be combined appropriately for any qualitative research study in such a way as to enable greater and more substantial research outcomes.

LEARNING QUESTIONS

In what ways would the experiential knowledge of the researcher progress during a research project and how would this contribute to later data collection and analysis of data?

Describe the value of a *holistic* approach to doing research in a marketing context.

What is meant by integrative multiple mixes of methodologies?

References

Belk, R., Wallendorf, M. and Sherry, J. (1989) 'The Sacred and Profane in Consumer Behaviour: Theodicy on the Odyssey', *Journal of Consumer Research*, 16(1), 1–37.

Bitner, M.J., Nyquist, J. and Booms, B. (1985) 'The Critical Incident as a Technique for Analysing the Service Encounter', in T. Bloch, G. Upah and V. Zeithaml (eds), *Services Marketing in a Changing Environment*, American Marketing Association, Chicago, pp. 48–51.

Carson, D. and Coviello, N. (1996) 'Qualitative Research Issues at the Marketing/Entrepreneurship Interface', *Marketing Intelligence and Planning*, 14(6), 51–58.

Davis, C.D., Hills, G.E. and LaForge, R.W. (1985) 'The Marketing/Small Enterprise Paradox: A Research Agenda', *International Small Business Journal*, 3(3), 31–42.

Evans, W. (1971) 'Introduction: the Organisational Experiment', in W. Evan (ed.), *Organisational Experiments: Laboratory and Field Research*, Harper & Row, New York.

Fetterman, D. (1989) *Ethnography. Step by Step*, Sage, Newbury Park, CA.

Geertz, C. (1973) *The Interpretations of Cultures*, Basic Books, New York.

Gilmore, A. and Carson, D. (1996) '"Intergrative" Qualitative Methods in a Services Context', *Marketing Intelligence and Planning*, 14(6), 21–26.

Hari Das, T. (1983) 'Qualitative Research in Organisational Behaviour', *Journal of Management Studies*, 20(3), 301–314.

Hill, R. (1993) 'Ethnography and Marketing Research: A Postmodern Perspective', *American Marketing Association Conference Proceedings*, Summer, 257–260.

Mintzberg, H. (1979) 'An Emerging Strategy of "Direct" Research', *Administrative Science Quarterly*, 24 (Dec.), 582–589.

O'Shaughnessy, J. (1987) *Explanation in Buyer Behaviour, Central Concepts and Issues*, Columbia University Press, New York.

Patton, M.Q. (1980) *Qualitative Evaluation Methods*, Sage, Beverly Hills, CA.
Shostack, G.L. (1977) 'Breaking Free from Product Marketing', *Journal of Marketing*, 41 (April), 73–80.
Shostack, G.L. and Kingman-Brundage, J. (1991) 'How to Design Service', in C. Congram and M. Freidman (eds), *The AMA Handbook for the Service Industries*, AMACOM, New York, pp. 243–261.
Van Maanen, J. (1979) 'Reclaiming Qualitative Methods for Organisational Research: a Preface', *Administrative Science Quarterly*, 24 (Dec.), 520–526.

15 Qualitative Research: Future Evolution

This book has attempted to describe some core qualitative research methodologies in the context of marketing. Broader contextualization was addressed in Part I, in terms of our research philosophy and position within social science research overall and towards qualitative research in particular. The domains of qualitative social science research and marketing are huge. Both are relatively easily defined and display significant *unity*, but they also have enormous *scope and diversity*.

In writing this book we four authors have implicitly displayed *unity in diversity* in addressing various aspects of our topic: *qualitative marketing research*. For this chapter on future evolution we thought it appropriate each to write a personal perspective, since the future is of course uncertain and often influenced by the individual's personal beliefs and values. You will see in our contributions evidence of both unity and diversity. We see this as a healthy dynamic for commitment to qualitative marketing research; hopefully you will agree.

Qualitative Marketing Research in the Future – David Carson

Any discourse on the future is inherently speculative. Whilst it is possible to extrapolate trends from the past and present, it is easy to enter into realms of fantasy and nonsense. In trying to avoid both of the latter and also drawing from meaningful immediate history, a future perspective of qualitative research methodology is given here under four broad considerations.

- *Growth and expansion* of qualitative research
- *Value* of qualitative research
- *Longitudinal* rigour and validity versus creative conceptualization
- *Technological* developments in qualitative research

Growth and expansion of qualitative research

Research in management/marketing will expand in line with the overall expansion in management/marketing education and training in tertiary level institutions throughout the world. The reasons for this expansion are many and varied; not least is the pace of dynamic change in world economies and with this, similar change in how business is conducted. New ways of doing business, influenced by social, cultural and technological changes, lead to a greater need to understand new phenomena. Whilst there will always be a place for large scale quantitative studies in monitoring aspects of change and customs and practices in management and marketing philosophies and techniques, there will be an even greater need to gain insights into the new social, cultural and technological order. It is in this aspect that the importance of qualitative research will be manifest.

The use of qualitative research methodologies has grown significantly in recent times, particularly so as a *stand alone* methodology in research studies. Whilst broader social science research will continue to use qualitative methodologies in traditional contexts alongside or as an adjunct to other methodologies, increasingly researchers will focus only on qualitative methodologies to address research problems. Such research problems will stem from the dynamic changes mentioned above. It is in the domain of management/marketing, which in itself is a developing stand alone discipline and science, rather than an aspect of the wider social sciences domain, that qualitative research can make a significant contribution.

A focus on *quality*! Often, many social science researchers view qualitative research as *not quantitative*. The term *qualitative* has been allowed to evolve into a generic term signifying a type of research. But qualitative can and should mean quality, quality of approach/method; quality of data; quality of outcomes and insights; quality of understanding. As qualitative research grows in application and its use becomes more sophisticated, its quality will be enhanced and so the value of qualitative research studies will gain greater recognition across a wide domain.

Value of qualitative research

Historically and indeed currently, social science research has been dominated by the importance and concerns of rigour and validity of the methodology. In seeking justification for the *correctness* of the research, researchers have naturally concentrated on ensuring that their research is *sound*, valid and reliable. Further, in many aspects of social science research, for example those concerned with replication studies, or testing methodologies in different contexts, the outcomes of such research studies are simply used to verify the validity and reliability of the methodology.

Most research in management and marketing will adhere to the broader social science research customs and practices, so it is primarily concerned with ensuring that the method is sound when addressing outcomes or research findings. Most researchers go no further than presenting these as being of little or small significance. This is because the methodological requirements can only serve as *possible* insights: methodological rigour requires outcomes to be further *tested* in other contexts different to that of the original study that produced the outcomes. According to this criterion, such outcomes can only ever be of small significance in the wider domain. Such requirements, some might even say *restrictions*, are manifest in any academic journal article which describes research with an empirical dimension. This is compounded in research dissertations, where there is almost an expectation and requirement that outcomes belong only to the study in question and if they are to be related to anything outside this, they require reciprocacy with a wider database or further study.

It appears strange to me that such social science research rigour dominates in an *applied* discipline/domain such as management, and even more so in marketing. Especially so, when considering that the purpose of management/marketing is about *doing* and in doing, performing and achieving. If research does not contribute some significance to this, then what is the purpose of doing research?

Another aspect of research in management/marketing is that there is little connection or overlap between the research domains concerned with management *techniques* and that which is concerned with *behaviours*. This is particularly so in research concerning the *process* of management marketing which invariably should take some cognizance of both. It is this process into which qualitative research can be used to gain most insights and understanding. This is because qualitative research is able to get close to phenomena under investigation and, if combined with a longitudinal element, is able to determine changes and developments in the process. It is the very *closeness* and therefore *quality* of the process that gives the richness and meaning to outcomes. Qualitative research is therefore able to *apply* outcomes in improving management/marketing processes. Rigour will require that this application occurs amongst those firms who contributed to the data.

Our stream of research model in Chapter 14 has as an implicit, that outcomes at each stage are applied and the consequences and impact of these outcomes are further researched in a progression of the process. This is indeed a rich and valuable *application* of research outcomes.

It is interesting to note that the main manifestation of the application of outcomes rests with the management/marketing *gurus* who publish airport-news-stand texts on issues based on their experiential consultancy work with managers/marketers. Their experiential knowledge is different from academic qualitative researchers' only in that it has given less emphasis to rigour and validity.

My argument here is that qualitative research studies should give more emphasis to the application and meaning of findings and outcomes. Qualitative research produces enhanced quality of findings, which deserves application. In our chapter on writing up for various audiences we highlighted that in management-style reports an emphasis should be given to outcomes and implications for the way forward, that is *solutions*. If this is appropriate in applied management circumstances it should also be applicable in more academic circumstances. I am not arguing for a quantum leap in terms of change and philosophy, more a *balance* in recognition of the value of qualitative research outcomes.

Longitudinal rigour and validity verses creative conceptualization

Most social science researchers, trained in the traditional positivist modes of research, will seek to justify qualitative research in terms of its rigour and validity. Such criteria are drawn from the traditional frameworks used in the wider social science research domain.

Increasingly, many enlightened qualitative researchers have little concern for rigour and validity tests in qualitative research studies. It is more important to demonstrate meaningful *transparency* in the research process and as long as this can be achieved the insights and understanding gained are meaningful.

However, rigour and validity can be achieved without interfering with qualitative research data gathering and interpretation. Through longitudinal study they can be achieved in two ways:

1 By longitudinal *reciprocation* of a research methodology using many matched sources, for example a qualitative study of how small business owner-managers take marketing decisions. Usually such research would glean data from a few sources but by compiling a large database of small firms (conforming to some common selection criteria), validity and reliability and therefore rigour will be achieved because aspects of generalizability can be introduced.

2 A more meaningful approach to achieving rigour and validity is where a research focus is on one *topic* over time. So, for example, in seeking to understand how and why small firm owner-managers do marketing, a researcher can engage in a variety of qualitative research studies, using *multiple mixes* of qualitative research methodologies. The accumulation of knowledge, insights and understanding, all contribute to experiential knowledge of the topic. The researcher becomes an expert on the single topic, for example how and why small firm owner-managers do marketing. Because this expertise is accumulated over time, it is, in my view, of far greater value than rigour and validity can provide in a single study.

A key aspect of the second longitudinal description is that usually the researcher gains new insights at each specific study. The synergy inherent in such an approach allows the researcher to create meaningful conceptualizations of the phenomena. The combination of 1 and 2 allows the researcher to adapt, refine and evolve such conceptualizations towards new theories in support of the phenomena. Such conceptualization and theory building is unlikely to derive from single studies constrained by rigour and validity.

Technological developments in qualitative research

Most qualitative researchers today use some kind of IT/electronic analysis program to aid the organization and analysis of empirical data. Such programs satisfy many researchers in the range and quality of their organization and analysis. However, my view is that current programs cannot get close enough to the nuances inherent in the data and therefore the interpretation is always limited directly in relation to the way the researcher has coded the data and whether this coding achieves in-depth penetration of the data.

In future, we can expect data analysis programs to become significantly more sophisticated in their ability to organize, analyse and most significantly, *interpret* findings. We can expect them to be capable of doing all the valuations currently carried out manually by researchers. Programs in the future will no doubt take cognizance of: the individual researcher's perspectives; the specific research topic; perhaps build a memory on prior learning and data inputs from previous studies; interpretation of respondents' views and comments in line with the known research problem and objectives; and will probably give an *interactive* interpretation of different respondents' views within a study or between different studies. What a utopia to look forward to!

Qualitative research in future may be able to combine these four points whereby technology will contribute to longitudinal conceptualization and to rigour and validity. Both will enhance the value and quality of qualitative research and all will contribute to its growth and development as a mainstream research approach in management and marketing where meaningful insights and understanding are required in future applications of decision making.

Qualitative Marketing Research in the Future
– Audrey Gilmore

My thoughts on the future evolution of qualitative research are based on my current perception that qualitative methods are more widely used in marketing contexts today than in the past; peppered with some *wishful thinking* that they will be used much more extensively and creatively in the future.

The use of variety

I would like to see more variety in the qualitative methods used for research studies in marketing; and indeed the use of a wider variety of qualitative methods in combination with quantitative methods for specific research problems. As we have tried to outline in Chapter 14, qualitative methods could be used in a more integrative way both in terms of one-off or cross-sectional studies and in longitudinal studies: that is, a greater number of methods used in tandem or as a *package* of research methods, and less focus on choosing one method as a *stand alone* approach for a complete study. This would allow a wider and/or more in-depth perspective to be taken in relation to a research problem.

Matching research design with aims and objectives

I would like to see a more customized approach to research design in order to suit individual research problems, questions, aims and objectives. Many studies still use 'off the peg' methodologies without adaptation to the specific needs of the research objectives. Every research problem is unique and therefore should be approached in a way that takes account of the unique features and priorities of the research. Combining qualitative research methods, using different methods in different contexts and stages according to the specific purpose of any research study should contribute to this.

Transparency in the presentation of research findings

Qualitative research methods will be much more acceptable to reviewers and other *gatekeepers* if there is more transparency in the presentation of research analysis. In recent years there has been much more evidence of this and I think this trend will continue. However, the responsibility for this lies with the qualitative researcher. It will involve not only stating clearly the reason for the chosen methodology in the context of the research problem, aims and objectives, but will also require some new or creative thought in how best to gather and analyse the data. Given that many industries and individuals are *over-researched* or weary of contributing to research there are times when it may be important to think of different ways of collecting data at different times and locations. Different approaches and methods of data analysis also could be developed. For example, the use of computer aided packages is growing and these are becoming more sophisticated. It looks as if these will continue to develop, be more complex and adaptable in the future. Qualitative researchers themselves should aim to develop appropriate and unique analysis criteria for their studies. The advantage of this is that it emphasizes and contributes to the richness of the study. It does this by *forcing* the researcher to spell out his or her thought processes in terms of making links in the data and allows the reader to see how outcomes were reached and the thinking behind each step and any resultant new theory development.

More creativity in data analysis

Building on the last comment, I think that it is vital to encourage more creativity in data analysis. In particular I would like to see more evidence of *breaking the mould* approaches. Instead of relying on adopting and/or adapting techniques used for analysing quantitative data, qualitative data needs to be evaluated in a way that takes account of its characteristics, such as richness, detail, contextual relevance and influences. The reliance on using positivist criteria to judge the quality of qualitative research has hampered the development and potential of qualitative research in marketing. This has been prevalent in order to get qualitative research through a positivist review process. However, it indicates a weakness or flaw if qualitative researchers cannot devise equally acceptable means of analysis.

To some extent we have tried to develop this idea over the past few years in terms of creating *criteria for analysis* specifically tailored to each individual research project. Nonetheless I believe there is much room for development in this area. Qualitative researchers must focus on the quality of their research findings and make more *creative leaps* in the analysis of findings and the development of theory. It is only when we recognize the value of qualitative research and evaluate its characteristics, purpose and strengths instead of judging it using the frameworks and measurements for quantitative research that we can truly appreciate its importance and value in use. This is especially relevant in the context of fast environmental and technological change.

Doing *good* qualitative research and analysis takes patience and practice. The context of business, marketing and management often is not conducive to these virtues. But researchers need time to practise qualitative research methods, to reflect on the process and outcomes; that is time to develop *experiential learning*. Once such skills have been developed they cannot be lost. People with real experience in the field and in carrying out analysis are the best qualified to *teach* or, more appropriately, *coach* the new generation of qualitative researchers to develop skills in this type of research.

Finally I think that the future of qualitative research lies in who uses it and how it will be used and adapted for different contexts. Because of its flexibility there is much scope for developing qualitative techniques for specific marketing contexts and environments. Researchers with experiential knowledge of these specific contexts will undoubtedly adopt, adapt and refine qualitative methods for their own specific use and contribute to the wider development and value of interpretive research.

Qualitative Marketing Research in the Future – Chad Perry

Professor John Smith was phoning his PhD student after presenting a paper about the student's research to a special qualitative research session at the Academy of Marketing annual conference south of London. The student, Ms Sandra Jones, was the owner–manager of a small management consultancy and had not been able to attend the conference because of work commitments, and so she was grateful that her supervisor had presented the paper. She left a meeting to take the phone call at work and asked how the paper had been received. Professor Smith replied in a straightforward way, 'OK. You know how these conferences are.'

'Well, no, I don't know how they are,' she said. 'I haven't been to one yet. So how many people were at the session?'

He replied, 'Sorry. Of course you wouldn't know yet. Well, qualitative research was a special session and so there were not many people there because qualitative research is not mainstream. Almost all the people there were academic staff or research students and they seemed a bit surprised that our paper was about how managers handled networks between organizations, rather than about how marketing managers operated within an organization or about customers.'

Ms Jones prompted: 'Didn't they like that?'

'That wasn't the problem – it was just that they seemed *surprised* that we were investigating that topic,' Professor Smith replied.

'Well, it is vitally important to me as a manager. Did they have any constructive comments to make to help me improve my thesis?'

Professor Smith thought for a while. 'No, they didn't have anything worthwhile to pass on actually, either constructive or destructive. One person came up to me afterwards and said he was pleasantly surprised we had spent so much effort on issues of validity and reliability.'

'Oh,' said Ms Jones. 'But we knew that was important, didn't we? So what are you so subdued about? What did you expect at the conference?'

Professor Smith replied, 'I didn't expect anything different, really, I suppose. But I hope things will be different in about ten years' time and I'll tell you how, if you have the time. Do you have the time for me to tell you, now?'

She did have the time and so Professor Smith told her about five ways that he was hoping marketing conferences would be different in the future. Firstly, he was hoping that qualitative methods would be *sharing the mainstream* with quantitative methods. There was a 50/50 split between the two in market research companies and he hoped that a more even use would appear within a marketing academia that was supposed to be training students for work outside as well as inside academia. So he was pleased that several universities were starting to place equal emphasis on both types of research methods in their programmes. The journal *Qualitative Market Research: an International Journal* had recently begun and had growing subscriptions. This shift in emphasis should result in qualitative methods papers being more common at conferences and in journals in the future. Then there would be no need for conference special sessions on qualitative methods.

He hoped that this increasing emphasis on qualitative methods would see a corresponding standardization in the procedures followed in research projects. For example, at present there did not even seem to be consensus about whether a tape recorder should be used during interviews. Indeed, at present, data collection and analysis took far longer in a qualitative research project than in a survey project, for instance, because procedures for a survey's questionnaire mailouts and for SPSS runs to analyse the collected data were straightforward and established. If more and more qualitative research was done, *more efficient procedures* for data collection and analysis, and for their reporting, might be developed and disseminated. For example, the number of participants required in various types of projects would be agreed upon by thesis examiners and article reviewers, and procedures for data analysis would be simplified. Ms Jones interrupted him with a 'Hear, hear!' but her supervisor kept on talking.

The third difference he was hoping to see was a recognition of how *realism* research was different from other interpretive, qualitative paradigms such as constructivism. Constructivism considered participants' perceptions as the *end* point of research, rather than as realism's *starting* points for understanding an external reality that was hard to describe. Of course, constructivism is a fine paradigm to use when trying to understand how consumers perceived a product, for example, because those perceptions were the main reason why purchases were made. Indeed, constructivism appeared to be the paradigm behind several postmodern attacks on conventional market research (for example, Brownlie et al. 1999). But in research about issues such as how and why managers could handle their real-world problems, the perceptions of people were merely *windows* on to a more important and complex reality. Without an acknowledgement of the existence of a realism scientific paradigm for researching this kind of phenomenon, marketing was closing itself from being able to effectively research a large part of the phenomena it simply had to study to being a relevant social science.

This acknowledgment of realism led into the fourth difference Professor Smith was hoping to see: *more managers* at future conferences. Managers had to operate in a context that made relationships between variables very hard to predict. For example, whether advertising had its planned results depended on hard-to-predict, competitive forces. Qualitative research within the realism paradigm would provide understanding and meaning that managers would be able to use to handle their complex, interrelated world within its various contexts. Indeed, more qualitative, theory building research would place firmer foundations under other, subsequent theory testing research. In any case, the current emphasis on positivist, stimulus–response research about the 4Ps used upon customers was clearly not relevant to managers. If it was, there would not be the current decline in marketing positions in US corporations and marketing majors in leading US MBA programmes (Hulbert 1998) and the current dissatisfaction among CEOs with the 'ivory tower' performance of their marketing managers (Gatenby 1998). That is, the number of jobs for marketing graduates is declining, and there is some evidence that a marketing degree is no more useful for a successful marketing career than a degree with no marketing in it (Lamont and Friedman 1997). In contrast, in the future, perhaps managers might even come to conferences because they could see the relevance of the research to the world in which they worked!

The fifth and final difference in those conferences that Professor Smith hoped to see was more emphasis on *validity and reliability* in qualitative research. Because interpretive paradigms were different from the positivism paradigm, criteria to judge validity and reliability in qualitative research had to be different from those used in quantitative research but were just as important. Already, Lincoln and Guba (1985) had provided a framework that could be followed to ensure validity and reliability in constructivist research and Healy and Perry (2000) had developed an equivalent framework for realism research. He hoped that more emphasis was placed on the use of these frameworks in the future.

If all these hopes were fulfilled, Professor Smith thought that qualitative research would become a strong *complement* to quantitative research rather than a strong *competitor*. Qualitative research would provide mechanisms for theory building to be done before quantitative theory testing was rushed into a research project. Moreover, the use of qualitative methods would broaden the range of phenomena that marketing could effectively and efficiently address, including marketing management phenomena and the phenomena involved in making a *whole* organization more customer-oriented. With these developments, marketing education and research would become more relevant to real-world careers of managers within and without the marketing function.

Professor Smith stopped talking. There was silence for a short while. Finally he said, 'Sandra, what do you think of all these future differences from today's presentation?' She replied, 'Now I see why you were so subdued today. But I hope your dreams for the future come true.'

Qualitative Marketing Research in the Future
– Kjell Gronhaug

From the proceeding chapters it is evident that qualitative research is in no way something new. Social anthropologists, for example, have been doing observations for more than a hundred years to gain insights into foreign cultures. There are at least two reasons why the early anthropologists made use of (participant) observations. In the beginning they primarily studied cultures unknown to us. When entering the field they did not know the language. Also, detailed and longitudinal observations allow for detailed insights probably not possible in other ways. Of course, over time when acquiring knowledge of the language the anthropologists gradually started interacting with members of the foreign culture. But many aspects of communication are not verbal. Thus observations (in addition to personal interactions) allow for information and insights that cannot be gained solely by *asking questions*.

In a similar way in-depth interviewing (see Chapter 6) has been applied by clinical psychologists and psychiatrists to gain insights into and understanding of the personal problems of their clients (patients), as perceived by the clients themselves. By doing this – and this insight is shared with and accepted by the client – ways of coping with such personal problems are discussed, and gradually accepted.

Early use of the other research methodologies dealt with in Part II of this book can also be traced, primarily in disciplines outside marketing. Even if it was not fully *accepted*, early use of qualitative research is also found in marketing. One example is the use of focus group interviewing mentioned in Chapter 8. Another is the famous *shopping list* study conducted by Mason Haire (1950). When the study was conducted, he was confronted with the following problem. Why do consumers not accept the new product of instant coffee? The producer (Maxwell House) did not have the slightest idea. Mason Haire distributed two versions of an identical shopping list, except for one item: coffee. In one, regular coffee was listed, in the other one instant coffee was listed. The respondents – all women – were asked to characterize the person behind the shopping list. Some striking findings emerged. Women (housewives) who did not have employment outside the home tended to characterize the shopper as *lazy, does not know how to do her housework* and so on. Women working outside the home – in minority at that time – characterized the person behind the shopping as *smart* and *modern*. These findings revealed that the new product met resistance because it was believed to threaten traditional Western housewife values at that time. When the problem was identified, successful marketing strategies were designed and implemented. Even though it can be difficult to define qualitative research it is evident from the above examples (as well as the preceding chapters) that it is valuable when the purpose is to gain understanding, often to acquire an insider's view in order to understand and thus to answer *how* and *why* questions.

In marketing there are many *how* and *why* questions, and very frequently there is a need to acquire the insider's view, whether it is the consumers, distributors or managers. There is no reason to believe that the need for such insights will decline in the years to come, rather the contrary. In the following section I first point to developments that will probably result in increased need for qualitative research. Next, we focus on some future developments in qualitative marketing research.

Developments favouring qualitative research

In Chapter 1 basic ideas about ontology and epistemology were discussed, that is, perspectives on *reality* and how knowledge about that reality may be acquired. It was emphasized that multiple perspectives on reality exist, and that there should be some correspondence between ontology and the way we conduct research. In qualitative research we are interested in getting the insider's view, that is, we want to know how the actors conceive their world, which is their reality, or the world in which they operate. Such insights are of prime importance for understanding why they act (or do not act) as they do. Answers to such *why* questions are also of key importance for improving marketing actions and other business activities. Such *why* questions are almost infinite. A common observation is that many firms pursue highly different marketing strategies even though they are of the same size, and possess approximately the same resources. Why? Another example: some managers in an industry seemingly believe that and behave as if, the firm's performance is solely dependent on their performance, while others leave very much of the work and responsibilities to their collaborators. Why such differences in behaviour, and how can such differences influence the performance of the firms?

We strongly believe that there is a need for understanding – and thus the ability to answer *how* and *why* questions will increase in the years to come. Reasons underlying this belief are as follows:

1 Rapid changes: our surrounding world is not static, it changes. However, it does not change at the same rate. Through the history of humanity, the speed of change has varied over time. Now the rate of change is faster than ever. This imposes uncertainty. Questions like 'What is happening?' 'Why does it happen?' 'How will it affect us?' arise, all of which require understanding to be answered (and in due time to be dealt with).

2 In such periods of rapid change managers need understanding of markets, technologies and so on if they are to act. From a management point of view apparently simple questions like 'Who are our competitors?' and 'What is the nature of the competition?' become complex. Such simple questions in real life are substantially more complex than usually understood. For one thing managers, and then firms, need such knowledge to operate and compete effectively. Managers (like other

individuals) are constrained by cognitive limitation (or what Simon (1957) termed 'bounded rationality'), that is, they have limited capacity to notice and interpret data, as well as limited capacity to store, retrieve and make use of this data. Even though managers try to behave in a *rational*, that is, goal-directed, way, they may fail. An interesting example is reported in the classic *Harvard Business Review* article by Levitt (1960), 'Marketing Myopia', demonstrating that whole industries faded away because firms and their managers defined competition and competitors too narrowly, overlooking substitutes to their offerings. This raises questions like: 'How do managers make sense of their surrounding environment?' and 'How do they define competitors and competition?' Our insights regarding such questions are still very modest, but highly relevant and important.

3 Business firms are market dependent, they are dependent on their customers. For some time we have witnessed a rapid move towards mass customization. In order to keep customers firms must satisfy them. Customers are not always capable of expressing what they need and want. So to keep customers in increasingly competitive markets, deep insights into (the individual) customer's feelings, needs and expectations become an even more important focus for in-depth interpretive marketing research.

4 Rapid changes may also cause established explanations (theories) to no longer hold true. New ones are called for. This situation relates to discovery and *theory construction*. For example advertising has for long been a seemingly well-understood phenomenon, and a subject taught in any business school. A key aspect of traditional advertising is that it represents mass communication, that is, the sending of standardized messages through the mass media, in most cases with slow and biased feedback from the target group. The new interactive media represents a dramatic change from one-to-many to one-to-one communication, potentially offering fast, accurate and individualized responses. What is advertising, then? How are/will the new media be used in the firm's marketing communication, and how will it impact the advertising industry? Our insights into such questions are less than modest, but we know that the world's largest advertiser, Procter & Gamble has declared that the company will spend more on interactive media than on any other media in the years to come. Again, the need for understanding is overwhelming.

At the outset of this book (see Chapter1) an introduction to philosophy of science issues was offered. Philosophy of science underpins assumptions about reality and how it can be understood. Over the years we have witnessed great interest in various trends and issues under the label *postmodernism*. One key aspect is its emphasis on what makes sense to the individual, what she/he likes or dislikes. Such a perspective also influences thinking and expectations, and knowledge requirements.

The trends and issues discussed above are not meant to be a complete listing of factors that may influence the interest and demand for qualitative marketing research. However they are probably sufficient to support our belief that the interest in, demand for, and use of such research will escalate in the years to come.

Future developments in qualitative marketing research

Like other types of research methodology, qualitative research methodologies are rules and procedures serving a variety of purposes. They provide a logic to answer my problem, and a means of communication on how the research has arrived at this or that conclusion. The latter point is important in scientific principles due to the emphasis on *inter-subjectivity*, that is, other people (e.g. users) should be able (or allowed) to examine the logic behind the presented conclusion. Also – as emphasized above – there is (should be) a relationship between knowledge required, assumptions about *reality*, beliefs about how knowledge can be obtained and the methodology(ies) applied. Research methodologies are not rigid and unchanging. They are improved, and new ones are created.

A key characteristic of the qualitative approach described in Part II of this book, is that they are rather informal. The various procedures are described in fairly general terms. It is my belief that in the years to come the procedures underlying the reported research methodologies (as well as other research methodologies) will become more developed. They are expected to become more *scientific*. By this I mean that theory-based explanations will be developed to support choice among as well as specific applications of the various qualitative approaches. A few examples will illustrate this. Asking questions in surveys was for long considered an *art* more than a science (inspect the influential book by Payne 1951). Extensive work primarily based on insights from cognitive psychology is now resulting in theory-based guidelines for construction of questionnaires. Often relevant theoretical knowledge exists to make more adequate use of existing qualitative approaches. For example, focus group interviewing (see Chapter 8) has become an extremely popular research approach, including among marketers. Existing literature concerning groups, their functioning and so on is extensive. These insights – if correctly applied – can offer guidelines to questions like 'Should focus groups be used?' and, if yes, 'How should the groups be composed?'

Until recently, much analysis of *qualitative data* has been conducted in a rather instinctive way, without theory-based guidelines (with a few exceptions). We now witness the development of more developed and theory-based methods for qualitative data analysis (which for long have been used in quantitative data analysis).

Computer programs are used at an increasing rate in qualitative data analysis. A great variety of programs exist, e.g. ETHNOGRAPH,

NUD*IST, CAQDAS. These are primarily helpful in storing, arranging and retrieving (coded) data (see Chapter 12). Few (if any) procedures will arrive at conclusions similar to regression analysis. I believe that the use of computerized programs in analysis of qualitative data will increase, that the programs will become more user-friendly, and that they will be further developed to really assist researchers in their analyses.

In spite of the increasing popularity and use of qualitative research a common complaint is that it is difficult (and more difficult than for quantitative studies) to evaluate the *quality* of such research. I strongly believe that more explicit guidelines (in addition to the existing ones) will emerge.

Research designs, that is, the overall strategy for answering research problems, once termed a 'master-technique' by Kornhauser and Lazarsfeld (1955) play a major role in research. An interesting observation is that classical and influential studies primarily have become so due to existing and well-framed research problems and well-thought-out research designs, not because of the statistical *message*. In qualitative research, the design question is often given only minor importance (for an excellent exception, see Burgelmann 1983). I believe that research designs will become more explicit in qualitative research in the years to come.

Researchers in marketing and business disciplines subscribing to qualitative research are many and they are increasing in number. Their formal training is often modest, however, in contrast to researchers doing quantitative research. This is probably due to the fact that quantitative research has been more focused and appreciated in business schools. This will change, I believe. To do high quality qualitative research demands – as in other types of research – knowledge and skills. The knowledge and skills requirements are, however, (partly) different from those of quantitative research. Key requirements in qualitative research are, among others, skills in interviewing, observations and theory construction (conceptualizing).

Until recently, most qualitative studies have been based on one research approach (methodology) only. All methods have their inherent strength and weakness. I believe that the use of multiple mixes of methodologies, not only qualitative, but also a mix of qualitative and quantitative approaches will become more common.

Summary

In our four personal contributions to this chapter we have to some degree bared our souls. Some issues for the future are easy to see, for example relating to the development and increased sophistication and application of computer aided technology. Other issues highlight our inherently diverse opinions, especially in relation to our own personal research philosophy and position. Two of us have the view that qualitative research will establish firmer constructs for methodology and validity and thereby mirror the rigour of quantitative methodologies. The other two of us believe that qualitative research will expand into new frameworks and methodologies that may or may not seek to apply positivist rigour, but seek more appropriate criteria. Whichever viewpoint emerges (if either), the true value of this personal reflection and speculation will only become apparent in due time. However, we hope that from this book readers will have gained some meaningful insights and some understanding of qualitative marketing research. Further, we hope the book has stimulated readers into doing good sound qualitative marketing research and so helping to shape the future evolution of the domain. We look forward to reading and studying the outcomes of this research in forthcoming published works.

References

Brownlie, D., Saren, M., Wensley, R. and Whittington, R. (1999) *Rethinking Marketing: Towards Critical Marketing Accountings*, Sage, London.

Burgelmann, R.A. (1983) 'A Process Model of Internal Corporate Venturing in the Diversified Major Firms', *Administrative Science Quarterly*, 28 (June), 233–244.

Gatenby, I. (1998) '1998 CEO Views on Marketing Study'. Paper presented at the Australian Marketing Institute, Queensland Conference, Brisbane.

Haire, M. (1950) 'Projective Techniques in Marketing Research', *Journal of Marketing*, 14 (April), 649–656.

Healy, M. and Perry, C. (2000) 'Comprehensive Criteria to Judge Validity and Reliability of Qualitative Research within the Realism Paradigm', *Qualitative Marketing Research: An International Journal*, 3(3), 118–126.

Hulbert, J.M. (1998) 'Marketing of the Future: Some Additional Thoughts', *Australasian Marketing Journal*, 6(1), 22.

Kornhauser, A. and Lazarsfeld, P.F. (1955) 'The Analysis of Consumer Actions', in P.F. Lazarsfeld and M. Rosenberg (eds), *The Language of Social Research*, The Free Press, Glencoe, IL, pp. 392–411.

Lamont, L.M. and Friedman, K. (1997) 'Meeting the Challenges to Undergraduate Marketing Education', *Journal of Marketing Education*, 19 Fall (Special issue on the future of marketing education), 17–30.

Levitt, T. (1960) 'Marketing Myopia', *Harvard Business Review*, July–August, 27–47.

Lincoln, Y. and Guba, E. (1985) *Naturalistic Inquiry*, Sage, Newbury Park, CA.

Payne, S.L. (1951) *The Art of Asking Questions*, Princeton University Press, Princeton, NJ.

Simon, H.A. (1957) *Administrative Behavior*, 2nd edn, Macmillan, New York.

Index